Soul Economy
and
Waldorf Education

Soul Economy
and
Waldorf Education

Rudolf Steiner

Anthroposophic Press
Spring Valley, New York

Rudolf Steiner Press
London

The lectures and discussions presented here were given in Dornach, Switzerland between December 23, 1921 and January 7, 1922. In the collected edition of Rudolf Steiner's works, the volume containing the German texts is entitled *Die gesunde Entwickelung des Leiblich-Physischen als Grundlage der freien Entfaltung des Seelisch-Geistigen* (Vol. 303 in the Bibliographic Survey). They were translated from the German by Roland Everett.

Distributed in the US by Anthroposophic Press, 258 Hungry Hollow Rd., Spring Valley, NY 10977.
Distributed in the UK by Rudolf Steiner Press, 38 Museum St., London WC 1.

Library of Congress Cataloging in Publication Data

Steiner, Rudolf, 1861–1925.
  Soul economy and Waldorf education.

  Translation of: Die gesunde Entwicklung des
Leiblich-Physischen als Grundlage der freien
Entfaltung des Seelisch-Geistigen.
  "The lectures . . . presented here were given in
Dornach, Switzerland between December 23, 1921
and January 7, 1922"—T.p. verso.
  1. Steiner, Rudolf, 1861–1925—Views on education.
2. Waldorf method of education—Addresses, essays,
lectures. 3. Anthroposophy—Addresses, essays,
lectures. I. Title.
LB775.S7G4713 1986   370'.1   85-11247

ISBN 0-88010-139-3 cloth
     0-88010-135-5 paper

Cover: Graphic form by Rudolf Steiner
Title Lettering: Peter Stebbing

Printed in the United States of America

CONTENTS

FOREWORD

This is one of many courses of lectures given by Rudolf Steiner (1861–1925) in the early years of this century, in the amplification of his *spiritual science* or *anthroposophy*. Some of these courses were given to members of the Anthroposophical Society who had been familiar with the subject for many years. Others were given to the general public. In both cases —and naturally more particularly and esoterically so in the former—they were a deepening and extension of what was contained in his written works.

It is the written works that contain the essentials of his teaching. Among them are some which have come to be known as the "basic books," and without some knowledge of them it is impossible to appreciate what was spoken of in these lecture courses. Those basic books are: *The Philosophy of Freedom* (also published as *The Philosophy of Spiritual Activity*), *Theosophy, An Outline of Occult Science, Knowledge of the Higher Worlds and Its Attainment,* and *Christianity as Mystical Fact* (also published as *Christianity and Occult Mysteries of Antiquity*).

It is essential to make this clear to readers, and even to impress upon them the need to have some familiarity with the basic books before attempting the courses. The reasons should be obvious. First, it would be unfair to the readers themselves to be led into buying a book which they might find mystifying and confusing, if not wholly incomprehensible, later; and secondly, and perhaps more importantly, it would be unfair to the cause of spiritual science if the unadvised reader should be led to forming a premature judgment about what is admittedly recondite, if not at times arcane, through insufficient knowledge of its basic principles.

Any scientific investigation—and anthroposophy is just that, even though its field is the supersensible—presupposes a discipline which demands a thorough grounding in its fundamentals. This was all Rudolf Steiner ever asked for the results of his investigations, which he gave out in these and other lectures. So finally, it would be unfair to his unchallenged reputation as a scholar and philosopher to offer to the public such a book as this without these few introductory remarks.

Alan Howard

LECTURE I

Dornach, 23rd Dec. 1921

First of all I should like to express my great joy at meeting so many of you here in this hall. Anyone whose life is filled with enthusiasm for the movement which is centered here in the Goetheanum, is bound to experience happiness and a deep inner satisfaction at witnessing the intense interest for our theme which your visit has shown. I should therefore like to begin this introductory lecture by welcoming you all most warmly. And I wish to extend a special welcome to Mrs. Mackenzie,* whose initiative and efforts have brought this course about. On behalf of the Anthroposophical Movement I owe her a particular debt of gratitude.

I should like to add that it is not just a single person who is greeting you here, but that it is, above all, this building, the Goetheanum itself, which is receiving you. I can fully understand if some of you feel critical about certain features of this Goetheanum as a building, as a work of art. Any undertaking which makes its appearance in the world in this way must be left open to judgment, and any criticism made in good faith is appreciated, certainly by me. But—whatever your reactions may be to this building—the Goetheanum itself is nevertheless welcoming you. By its forms and artistic composition alone you can see that here the aim was not to erect a building which was to serve specific purposes, such as education, for example. The underlying spirit and style of this building shows that it was conceived and erected out

---

*Millicent Mackenzie was Professor of Education at Cardiff University from 1910 until 1915.

of the spirit of our times in order to serve a movement, destined to play its part in this our present civilization. And as education represents an integral part of human civilization, it is right for it to be nurtured here at this center.

The close relationship between anthroposophical activities and educational problems will occupy us in greater detail within the next few days. Today, however, as part of these introductory remarks, I should like to talk about something which really is part and parcel of any established movement.

In a way you have come here in order to acquaint yourselves with the various activities which are centered here in the Goetheanum in Dornach. And in greeting you as guests most warmly, I feel it right, first of all to introduce you to our movement.

The aims of this Anthroposophical Movement, which has been in existence now for some twenty years, are only gradually beginning to manifest themselves. Only lately has this movement been looked upon by the world in general in ways which are consistent with its original aims. But this movement has gone through different phases and a description of these phases may best serve as a proper introduction.

At first the small circle of its adherents looked upon Anthroposophy as a movement representing a religious world-outlook in quite a narrow sense. This movement tended to attract people who were not particularly interested in its scientific background and who were not motivated to explore its artistic possibilities. Nor were they aware of how its practical activities could affect the entire social life. These first members were mainly people who felt dissatisfied with traditional religious practice. They were the kind of people who were prompted out of their deepest human longings to search for answers to problems inherent in the human soul and spirit, problems which could not be answered for them by the religious movements then existing.

2

For me it often was quite astonishing to witness how what I had to say about the fundamentals of Anthroposophy was not at all understood by these members who nevertheless supported the movement with deep sympathy and great devotion. When content of a more scientific nature was given, these first members extracted from it what spoke to their hearts, what appealed to their immediate feelings and sentiments. And I can truly say that this time was the most peaceful time within the Anthroposophical Movement, although this was not at all what I had been looking for!

Because of this situation it was possible for the Anthroposophical Movement in its first phase to join another movement—albeit only outwardly and mainly from an administrative point of view—which may be known to you as the Theosophical Society. People who, out of the simplicity of their hearts, are searching for knowledge of the eternal within human nature, will find satisfaction equally well in the Theosophical Society as in the Anthroposophical Movement, unless they are able to discern vital and fundamental differences. The Theosophical Society is mainly concerned with a theoretical form of knowledge, embracing cosmology, philosophy and religion, and using the spoken or printed word as its medium. People who are really quite satisfied with their lives in general, but who wish to learn more about spiritual matters than traditional doctrines have to offer, may find equal satisfaction in either of the two movements. And only when it became evident—though this was noticed by only a few members—that the aims of Anthroposophy regarding cosmology, philosophy and religion were not merely theoretical, but that these were meant to enter social life quite directly and practically and in accordance with the demands of the spirit of our times, only then, gradually, did it become obvious for inner reasons that the Anthroposophical Movement could no longer work together with the Theosophical Society. For in our time—and this

3

will be made clearer in the forthcoming lectures—any movement which confines itself to questions of cosmology, philosophy and religion in a more or less theoretical way, is bound to degenerate into quite an intolerable dogmatism. And it was the futility of dogmatic arguments which finally caused the separation of the Anthroposophical Movement from the Theosophical Society.

It is self-evident that any sensible person conversant with western culture could not take seriously what became the crux of these dogmatic quarrels at the time when the Anthroposophical Movement split off from the Theosophical Society. These quarrels were sparked off by the claims that an Indian boy* was the reincarnation of Christ. As such a claim was quite baseless, it was totally unacceptable.

To waste energy and strength on theoretical arguments is not the way of Anthroposophy which aims at entering life quite directly. When, in accordance with the true aims of Anthroposophy, it became essential to work in the artistic, social, scientific and, above all, in the educational sphere, the separation from the Theosophical Society became inevitable. Naturally this did not happen all at once but, fundamentally, everything that occurred in the Anthroposophical Movement after 1912 was a sure sign that this movement had to fight for its independent position in the world in order to penetrate practical life.

In 1907, during a congress at the Theosophical Society in Munich, I realized for the first time that it was not possible for me to work together with this movement. My friends from the German section of the Theosophical Society and I had been given the task of arranging the program for this congress. Apart from the usual kinds of items, we also in-

---

*Rudolf Steiner here refers to claims made by Annie Besant and Leadbeater of the the reappearance of Christ in the person of the Indian boy Krishnamurti who, later on, himself refuted these claims.

cluded a performance of a mystery play by Edouard Schure* entitled "The Sacred Drama of Eleusis." In doing so we decided to create a transition from the theoretical-religious attitude of this movement to a wider outlook which would also encourage artistic activities. From our anthroposophical point of view we had looked upon this performance as an artistic endeavor. However, those personalities within the movement who were trying to satisfy their religious feelings—which, at times, can be very egoistical—used this occasion for only a theoretical interpretation of the play. Questions were asked such as: What is the meaning of this personality in the drama? What does this other personality signify? These people were only happy when they had succeeded in reducing the whole play to a kind of theoretical terminology.

Well, a movement which, because of its one-sided attitude, cannot embrace life in its fulness, is bound to end up as a sectarian movement. Anthroposophy, on the other hand, is not at all inclined towards such sectarianism, because its natural tendency is to bring ideals down to earth and to enter life in practical ways.

These attempts at freeing the Anthroposophical Movement from a sectarian attitude through entering the artistic sphere represent the second phase of its history. Gradually, as the numbers of its members increased, a need was felt for the thought content of philosophy, cosmology and religion to be expressed artistically and this prompted me to write my mystery plays. On no account must these be interpreted theoretically or abstractly, for they are intended to be directly experienced on the stage. In order to bring this about, these plays were performed in ordinary hired theaters in Munich from 1910 to 1913. This, in turn, led to the impulse to build a center for the Anthroposophical Move-

---

*1841-1929.

5

ment. Changing situations made it obvious that Munich was not the right place for such a building, and so we were finally led to the Dornach hill, where the Goetheanum was built as the right and proper center for the Anthroposophical Movement.

These new activities showed that, in keeping with its true spirit, the Anthroposophical Movement is ever ready to pervade all branches of human life. Let us imagine that another movement of a more theoretical-religious character had decided to build itself a center. What would have happened? First its members would have collected funds among sympathizers—a step which, unfortunately, is indispensible—and then they would have chosen an architect to design a building for them, possibly in an antique or renaissance style, in a gothic or baroque or any other traditional style.

However, when the Anthroposophical Movement was in the happy position of being able to build its own home, such a procedure would have been totally unacceptable to me. For anything which forms an organic living whole cannot possibly be put together out of heterogeneous parts. What relationship could any words, spoken out of the spirit of Anthroposophy, have had with the forms surrounding the listener in a building of baroque, antique or renaissance style? A movement expressing itself in theories is only capable of presenting abstract ideas. A living movement, on the other hand, must work into all branches of life through its own characteristic impulses. Therefore the urge for expressing life, soul and spirit in practical deeds, characteristic of Anthroposophy, demanded that the surrounding architectural forms, the glowing colors of the wall paintings, the pillars meeting our gaze, that all these forms and colors should speak the same language as that spoken theoretically in ideas, in abstract thoughts. Any previous living movement which existed in the world in bygone times, was equally

6

comprehensive. The architecture of antiquity was by no means divorced from the culture of its days, but it grew out of the theoretical and practical activities of the times. The same can be said about the renaissance, certainly about the gothic but also about the baroque styles.

In order to avoid a sectarian or theoretical ideology, Anthroposophy had to find its own architectural and artistic style. As mentioned before, one may find this style unsatisfactory or even paradoxical, but the fact is that in accordance with its true nature Anthroposophy simply had to create its own physical enclosure. Let me make a comparison which may appear trivial, but which nevertheless may clarify these thoughts: Think of a walnut and its kernel. It is obvious that both nut and shell have been created by the same forces, for both together make a whole. Had Anthroposophy been housed in an incongruous building, it would have been as if a walnut kernel had been found in the shell of a different plant. Nature produces nut and shell and both speak the same language. Likewise, what was needed here was neither symbolism nor allegory, but anthroposophical impulses had to flow directly into artistic creativity. If thoughts are to be expressed in this building, they must have a fitting shell, both from an artistic and architectural point of view.

This, however, was no easy task, for the tendency towards sectariansim is strong today, even among people who are looking for a widening of religious ideals. But Anthroposophy must not be influenced by people's sympathies or antipathies. It must remain true to its own principles which are closely linked to the needs and yearnings of our times, as will be shown in the next few days.

And so Anthroposophy entered the practical domain, as far as this was possible in those days. At that time I surprised some members with the following statement: "Anthroposophy wants to enter all walks of life. Although conditions do not permit us to do so today, I should simply love to open banks run on anthroposophical lines." This may sound paradoxical, but it was meant to indicate that Anthroposophy is only in its right element if it can fertilize every aspect of life. On no account must it be looked upon merely as a philosophical and religious movement.

We now come to the catastrophic and chaotic times of the World War (I) which produced their own particular needs. In September 1913 we had laid the foundation stone of this building. In 1914, when the war broke out, we were building the foundations of the Goetheanum. Here I only wish to say that at the time when Europe was torn asunder by opposing nationalistic aspirations, here in Dornach we succeeded in keeping a place open where people from all nations could meet and work together peacefully, united by a common spirit. This was a source of deep inner satisfaction. —Those war years could be considered as the second phase in the development of our movement.

Despite the efforts made to continue anthroposophical work during the war, the outer activities of the Anthroposophical Movement were largely paralyzed. But one could experience how, gradually, among peoples everywhere, an inner need was felt for spiritual sustenance which, in my opinion, could be given through Anthroposophy. When, after 1918, the war had come to an end, at least outwardly, the interest in a spiritual renewal such as Anthroposophy wished to provide, grew enormously. Between autumn 1918 and spring 1919 a number of friends, many from Stuttgart, came to see me in Dornach. They were deeply concerned about the social conditions of the time and they wanted the Anthroposophical Movement to take an active part in trying to deal with the social and economic upheavals. This led to the third phase of our movement.

It happened that Southern Germany, and Württemberg in particular, was the place which was open to such anthroposophical activities and one had to work wherever this was possible. These activities, however, were colored a little by the problems of that particular region, problems which were the result of the prevailing social chaos. An indescribable misery had spread over the whole of Middle Europe at that time. Yet, seen in a wider context, the suffering from material needs was small compared with what was happening in the soul sphere of the population. One could feel how mankind had to face the most fundamental questions of human existence. Questions once raised by *Rousseau*, which led to outer consequences in the French Revolution, did not touch the most elementary human yearnings and needs to the same extent as the ones which presented themselves in 1919 in the very realms in which we wished to work.

Everything connected with the social organism, as it had developed over the past centuries out of its constituent tribes and peoples, was being questioned. This situation prompted me to address a short proclamation, dealing with the threefold social order, to the German people and to the civilized world in general, and also to publish my book *Toward Social Renewal.* Many other activities connected with the social question took place, at first in South Germany, and they were the outcome of this general situation with its prevailing mood. At that time it was essential, though immensely difficult, to touch the most fundamental aspirations of the human soul. Despite their physical and mental agony people were called upon to search, quite abstractly, for great and sublime truths, but because of the general upheaval they were incapable of doing so. Many a listener at my addresses said to me afterwards, "All this may be quite right and even beautiful, but it concerns the future of man. We who have faced death so often during the last years have given up worrying about the future, we have to live from day to day. And why should we show any more interest in the future now than when we had to face the guns

9

every day?'' Such a typical comment characterizes the apathy, prevalent at that time, towards the most important and fundamental questions of human development.

In this situation there grew in the hearts of my friends an awareness of a specific need within the body social. It was the realization that perhaps the only effective way of working towards a better future lay in our directing our efforts towards the young, towards their education. Our friend *Emil Molt* who at that time was in charge of the Waldorf-Astoria Cigarette Factory in Stuttgart, offered his services for such an enterprise by founding the Waldorf School for the children of his workers, and I was asked to take a leading part in the running of the school.

During pre-war times one could observe all kinds of educational experiments being carried out in various special schools. But in our case there was no question of founding yet another country boarding school, nor of implementing a particular brand of educational principles. Our aim was to attempt to heal social ills and to serve the needs of mankind in general. You will learn more about the fundamentals of Waldorf Education during the coming lectures. Here I merely wish to point out that—as also in every other field—Anthroposophy sees its tasks in involving itself in the realities of a given situation. It was not for us to open a boarding school somewhere in a beautiful stretch of open countryside, where we would be free to do as we pleased. We had to fit into definite given conditions. We were asked to teach children of a small town, that is to say we had to open a school in a small town, where even our highest aspirations had to be founded entirely on pragmatic and sound educational principles. We were not free to choose a particular locality nor to select our pupils according to ability or class, but we accepted given conditions with the aim of basing our work on spiritual knowledge. In this way—as a natural consequence of anthroposophical striving—Waldorf Education came into existence.

The Waldorf School in Stuttgart soon ceased to be what it was in the beginning, namely a school for the children of workers employed in the Waldorf-Astoria Cigarette Factory. It soon attracted pupils from various social backgrounds and today parents wish to send their children from all over the place. From its initial number of one hundred and forty pupils it has now grown to over six hundred pupils and applications for further places are coming in all the time. A few days ago we had to lay the foundation stone for a highly necessary extension to our school buildings and we hope that despite all the difficulties which one has to face when engaged in this kind of work, we shall be able to expand our school further in the near future.

However, I wish to emphasize that the characteristic feature of this school lies in its educational principles, based on the knowledge of man, and in its ability to adapt these to outer given realities. If one is able to choose pupils according to ability or social standing, or if one can choose one's locality, it is comparatively easy to carry out imaginary or perhaps even real educational reforms. But to found and develop a school on educational principles which are closely connected with the most fundamental human impulses while, at the same time, keeping in close touch with the demands of practical life, is no easy task.

In this way, during its third phase, our Anthroposophical Movement has spread into the social sphere and this aspect will naturally occupy us in greater depth during the coming days. But you must realize that what has been happening in the Waldorf School up till now represents only a beginning of the endeavors to bring our fundamental aims right down into the practicalities of life.

Concerning other anthroposophical activities which have

11

been developed later on, I should like to mention that a large number of scientifically trained people came together because they hoped and believed that the Anthroposophical Movement also could fertilize the scientific branches of life. Medical men met here because they were dissatisfied with the ways of natural science which only accept outer observation and experimentation. They were convinced that such a limited attitude could never lead to a full understanding of the human organism, both in its healthy and ill conditions. Doctors came who were deeply concerned about the unnecessary limitations set by modern medical science, such as the deep chasm dividing medical practice into pathology and therapy. (These two branches coexist today almost as if they were separate sciences.) In its search for knowledge Anthroposophy not only uses methods of outer experimentation, that is the observation of outer phenomena synthesized by the intellect, but—looking upon man as a being of body, soul and spirit—it employs also other means which I shall characterize in the coming days. Instead of dealing with abstract thought content, it is in touch with the living spirit. And because of this, Anthroposophy was able to meet the aspirations of persons who were urgently seeking to bring new life into medicine. As a consequence of this, I was asked to give two courses here in Dornach to university-trained specialists in medicine and to practicing doctors in order to outline the contribution Anthroposophy could make in the field of pathology and therapy. Both here in Dornach and nearby in Arlesheim, as also in Stuttgart, medical-therapeutic institutions have sprung up which are working with their own medicaments and which are trying to utilize what Anthroposophy can offer towards healing, towards dealing with sickness and health. Specialists in other sciences have also come to look for new impulses arising out of Anthroposophy and so courses were given in physics and astronomy. In this way anthroposophical spirit knowledge was called upon to bring practical help to the various branches of scientific endeavor.

A characteristic feature of this third phase of the Anthroposophical Movement lies in the fact that gradually—despite a certain amount of remaining opposition—people have come to recognize that Spiritual Science, as practiced here, can meet every demand for an exact scientific basis of working and that Anthroposophy, as represented here, can work with equal discipline and in harmony with any other scientific enterprise. In time people will appreciate more and more what has been the potential of the Anthroposophical Movement all along during these last twenty years.

Another example showing how the most varied fields of human striving can be fructified through Anthroposophy is the creation of a new art of movement which we call eurythmy. This art uses the human being as it means of expression, as its instrument, and in this way it aims at achieving its specific results. And so we try to let anthroposophical life—but *not* anthroposophical theories—flow into all kinds of other activities, such as the art of recitation and declamation, of which more details will be given in the next few days.

This last phase with its educational, medical and artistic impulses is the most characteristic one of the Anthroposophical Movement. Anthroposophy has many supporters as well as many enemies, even bitter enemies. But it has now entered upon the very stage of activities for which it has been waiting. And so it was a satisfying experience during my stay in Kristiania* from 23rd November to 4th December this year to speak about anthroposophical life to educators and government economists, as well as to Norwegian students and to various other circles. All of these were willing to accept—not theories or religious sectarian ideas—but

---

*Oslo

what is waiting to reveal itself directly out of the spirit of our times in answer to the great needs of humanity.

So much about the three phases of the Anthroposophical Movement. As an introduction to our course I merely wished to acquaint you with this movement, to mention its name to you, as it were. Tomorrow, then, we shall begin with our actual theme. However, I want you to know that it is this Anthroposophical Movement with its deep educational interests which is happy to welcome you all here in the Goetheanum.

LECTURE II

Dornach, 24th December 1921

The art of education, about which a great deal will be spoken during this course of lectures, is entirely based on a knowledge of man. A deeply founded knowledge of man, however, can only be attained if it is based upon a knowledge of the entire universe, because man with all his inherent abilities and powers is rooted in the universe. Therefore a real knowledge of man can only spring from a knowledge of the world in its entirety. Conversely one can say that the attitude and the ideas regarding education characteristic of any age also reflect the general world outlook of that particular age. In order to make a correct assessment of contemporary views on education, we therefore must examine these against the background of the general world conception of our present time. In this context it is helpful to look at the ideas expressed by a personality who is a typical representative of the present-day world view as it gradually developed during the last few centuries. There is no doubt that since that time mankind has been looking with great pride upon the achievements brought about through intellectuality,* and this is still largely true today.

Fundamentally speaking, educated people of today have become very intellectualized, even if they will not admit to

---

*Rudolf Steiner here used the German word, "Intellektualismus," translated as "intellectuality." With this word he tried to indicate the parasitic nature of the kind of intellect which proliferates into "intellectuality." A distinction must be made between the words: intelligence, intellect and intellectuality. (Translator's note)

15

it. Everything in the world is judged through the instrument of the intellect. When we think of names which we associate with the first awakening of modern thinking, we are led to the founders of modern philosophy and of present-day attitudes to life. And these personalities have based all their work on their firm belief in man's intellectual powers. Names such as *Galileo, Copernicus, Giordano Bruno* come to mind and they easily make one believe that their mode of thinking is relevant only to scientific matters, but this is not the case.

If one observes without prejudice the outlook on life among the vast majority of people today, one will find a touch of natural-scientific thinking hidden almost everywhere. And in this mode of thinking there lives intellectuality. One may be under the impression that in one's moral concepts or impulses and in one's religious ideas and experiences one is free from such scientific thinking. But one will soon discover that, by being exposed to all that flows through newspapers and popular magazines into the masses, one easily allows oneself to be influenced in one's conceptual life by a natural-scientific undertone.

People who are unaware of the fact that today's citizen sits down at the breakfast table already filled with scientific concepts, that he takes these to bed when he goes to sleep at night, that he uses them in his daily work and that he brings up his children with them, such people simply do not see life as it really is. They live under the illusion of being free from a scientific way of thinking. We even take our scientific concepts to church Services and though we may hear quite traditional views expressed from the pulpit, we nevertheless hear them with ears attuned to natural-scientific ways of thinking. And natural science is fed by intellectuality.

Science quite rightly stresses the fact that all its results are based upon outer observation, upon experimentation and its interpretation. But nevertheless, the instrument of

16

the soul which is used when such experiments are made in chemistry or physics, represents the most intellectual part of the human entity. Therefore the picture of the world which man is making for himself, is nevertheless the result of his intellect.

Educated people of the western world have become quite enraptured by all the progress achieved through intellectuality, especially in our present time. This had led to the opinion that in earlier times mankind was more or less lacking in intelligence. Man of old is supposed to have lived with naive and childish ideas about the world, whereas now we believe we have reached an intelligent comprehension of the world. It is generally felt that the modern view of the world is the only one based on firm ground. People have become afraid of losing themselves in the world of fantasy as soon as they relinquish the same domain of the intellect.

Anyone whose thinking follows along modern lines— lines which have been gradually developing during the last few centuries—is bound to come to the conclusion that a realistic conception of life depends on the use of the intellect.

Now something very remarkable can be observed: What, on the one hand, is considered to be the most valuable asset, the most important feature of our modern civilization, namely this intellectuality, has, on the other hand, become questionable with regard to the upbringing and education of children, especially among people who are seriously concerned with education. Although one can see that mankind has made tremendous strides forward through the development of intellectuality, when looking at contemporary education, one can also find that if children are being educated only intellectually, their inborn capacities and their human potentials become seriously impaired and wither away. In some quarters this realization has brought about a longing to replace intellectuality by something else. One has appealed to children's feelings and instincts. In order to steer away from the intellect, one has appealed to their moral and religious impulses. But how can one really find the right approach? Surely only by a thorough knowledge of man which, in turn, must be the result of a thorough knowledge of the world in its entirety.

As already mentioned, looking at a representative thinker of our times, one can find the present world view reflected in educational trends. And if one considers all relevant features, Herbert Spencer* could be chosen as one such representative thinker.

I do not quote Herbert Spencer because I consider his educational ideas to be particularly valuable for contemporary education. I am well aware of how open these are to all kinds of objections and of how, because of certain amateurish features, they would have to be greatly elaborated. On the other hand, Herbert Spencer, in all his conceptions and ideas, is firmly grounded in the kind of thinking and the general culture as it has developed during the last few centuries. *Emerson* wrote about personalities whom he considered to be representative of the development of mankind, personalities such as *Swedenborg, Goethe* and *Dante.*** But for modern ways of thinking and feeling it is, above all, Herbert Spencer who is a typical representative of our time. Although such a person's way of thinking may be tinged with national traits according to whether he is French, Italian or Russian, Herbert Spencer transcends such national influences. It is not the conclusions reached by him in his many books on most aspects of life which are of importance, but the way in which he reaches them, for his mode of thinking is representative to a high degree of the thinking of all educated people, of people who are influenced by a scien-

---

*Herbert Spencer, 1820–1903. The following remarks relate to his book "Education" (1861).
**Ralph Waldo Emerson, 1803–1882, see "Representative Men."

tific outlook and who endeavor to live in accordance with it.

Intellectualistic natural science is the very matrix of all he has to say. And what are his conclusions? Herbert Spencer, who naturally never loses sight of the theory that man has gradually evolved from lower forms of life and who then compares the human being with the animals, voices the following question: Are we educating our young in accordance with our scientific ways of thinking? And he answers this question in the negative.

In his essay on education he deals with some of the most important questions of the modern science of education, such as: Which kind of knowledge is of the greatest value? He critically surveys intellectual, moral and physical education. But the real core of all his considerations is something which could have been postulated only by a modern thinker, namely: We educate our children so that they learn to put their physical faculties to full use in later life. We educate them in order to fit them into their professional lives. We educate them so that they may become good citizens. According to our conceptions we may educate them to become moral or religious persons. But there is one thing for which we do not educate them at all, namely: to become educators themselves. This, according to Spencer, is what is missing in all our educational endeavors. He maintains that, fundamentally speaking, people are not educated to become educators or parents.

Now, as a genuine natural-scientific thinker he goes on to say: Just as the development of a living creature is complete only when it has acquired the capacity of procreating its own species, so should it be with perfect education: The educated person should be able to educate and guide growing children.—Such a postulate aptly illustrates the way in which a modern person thinks.

Looking at educational practice of today, what are Herbert Spencer's conclusions? Speaking metaphorically,

19

he makes a somewhat drastic but, in my opinion, a very appropriate comparison. First he characterizes the tremendous claims made for education today, including, among others, also those made by Pestalozzi. Then, instead of qualifying these principles as being good or acceptable, he asks how they are implemented in practice and what life is really like in schools. In this context he uses his somewhat drastic picture, saying: Let us imagine that some five to six centuries hence an archeologist, digging up some archives, were to unearth a description of our present educational system. Studying these documents he would hardly be able to believe that these were representative of the general practice of our time. For in them he would find that children were taught grammar in order to live themselves into their language. Yet we know well enough that the kind of grammar children are taught is hardly conducive to their being able to express themselves livingly in later life. Such an imaginary archaeologist would also discover that a large proportion of pupils were being taught Latin and Greek which, in our time, are dead languages. From this he would conclude that the people those documents he was studying had no literature of their own or, if at all, that little benefit would be gained from studying it. In this way Spencer tries to show how inadequately our present curricula prepare pupils for their later lives, despite all the claims made to the contrary. Finally he lets the archeologist conclude that as the unearthed document could not be indicative of the general educational practice of their times, he must have come across a syllabus used in some monastic order! He continues—and this, naturally, represents his opinion—: The fact that adults who have undergone such educational practice are not entirely alienated from society, behaving like monks, is due to the pressures and the cruel demands which life makes upon them. Nevertheless—so judges our imaginary archeologist—when having to face life's challenges, the former pupils respond clumsily because they have been educated as monks who now need to get on in an entirely different milieu.

These views, expressed by a man of the world and not by someone engaged in practical teaching, in their own way characterize contemporary education.

Now it may be asked: What kind of value does a person put upon his life after having been immersed in a natural-scientific, that is, in an intellectualistic attitude to the world?

With the aid of natural laws we are able to comprehend lifeless matter. This leads us to conclude that, following the same methods, we shall also reach an understanding of living organisms. This is not the time to go into the details of such a problem, but one can say that at our present state of civilization we tend to use thoughts which allow us to grasp only what is dead and what, consequently, lies outside the human sphere. Through research in physics and chemistry we construct a whole system of concepts which we then apply to the entire universe, albeit only hypothetically. It is true that today there are already quite a number of people who question the rightness of using laboratory results or information gained through telescope and microscope as a basis for a general picture of the world. However, the natural-scientific explanation of the world was bound to come and with it the ways in which it affects human feelings and emotions. And if one applies concepts which are the result of laboratory or observatory research to explain the origin and the future development of the earth, what happens then? One is driven to imagine the primeval nebulae of the Kant-Laplace theory, or—as views have been modified since their time—something of a similar nature. But this notion of primeval nebulae makes sense only if we apply to it the laws of aeromechanics. These laws, however, contain nothing pertaining to a soul or spiritual character. People

21

who long for such a soul-spiritual element therefore have to imagine all kinds of divine powers as existing side by side with the aeromechanical conception of the universe and then, somehow, these spirit beings have to be skilfully blended into the picture of the nebulae. Man, certainly in his soul and spiritual aspect, is not part of this picture. He has been excluded from such a world conception. People who have grown accustomed to the idea that only intellect-based natural science can give concrete and satisfactory answers, will find themselves in a quandary when looking for some kind of divine participation at the beginning of world existence.

A hypothetical conception of the end of the world is bound to follow the laws of physics. In this context we encounter the so-called second fundamental law of thermodynamics. According to this theory all living forces are mutually transformable. However, if they are transformed into heat or, vice versa, if heat is transformed into them, the outcome is always an excess of heat. The final result for all processes on earth would therefore be a complete transformation of all living forces into heat. This destruction through heat would produce a desert world containing no other forces except differences of temperature. Such a theory conjures up a picture of a gigantic graveyard in which lie buried all man's achievements, all his intellectual, moral and religious ideals and impulses. If we place the human being between a world-beginning from which he has been excluded and a world-end in which again he has no place, all human ideals and achievements become nothing but nebulous illusions. In this way an intellectualistic natural-scientific philosophy reduces the reality of man's existence to a mere illusion. Such an interpretation may be dismissed simply as a hypothesis. Yet, even if people today do not recognize how scientific theories affect their attitudes towards life, the negative consequences are nevertheless a reality. But the majority of people are not prepared to face realities. Neither do such scientific theories remain the prerogative of an educated minority, for they reach the masses through magazines and popular literature often in very subtle ways.

And against the background of such a negative soulmood we try to educate our children! True enough, we also give them religious content but here, above all, we are faced with a cleavage. For if we introduce religious ideas alongside our scientific conception of life which is bound to affect our attitude of soul, we enter the realm of untruth. And untruth extracts its toll not only in ways the intellect can perceive, for it is active through its own inner power. Untruth, even if it remains unrevealed, even if it remains in the realm of the unconscious, nevertheless assumes a destructive power over life.

We enter the realm of untruth if we are not willing to search for clarity regarding our attitudes to life. This clarity will show us that with the prevailing contemporary ideas we can only gain knowledge of a world in which there is no room for man.

Let us examine a scientific discovery which, rightly, fills us with pride: We follow the chain of evolution in the animal world from the simplest and most imperfect forms via the more fully developed animals right up to the coming of man, whom we consider to be the most highly developed being. Does this way of looking at evolution not imply that we consider man to be the most perfect animal? In this way, however, we do not concern ourselves with the true and real nature of man at all. By such a question, even if it remains an unconscious one, man's feeling for his essential humanity is diminished and set aside.

Again I wish to quote Herbert Spencer because his views on contemporary education are so characteristic, especially with regard to latest attempts at reform, at bringing education into line with present-day scientific thinking. These reforms generally are based on conceptions which are quite alien to the human spirit. And again Herbert Spencer is a representative example for what we meet in practical life almost everywhere.

Spencer maintains that we ought to do away with the usual kind of influence exerted by adults over children, by parents or teachers. According to him we have inherited from earlier times the bad habit of becoming angry if a child has done something wrong. We punish the child, we make him aware of our displeasure. With other words, we react in a way which is not directly linked to what the child has done. The child may have left things strewn all over the room and we, the educators, may become angry when seeing it. To put it drastically, we might even hit the child. Now, what is the causal link—and the scientific researcher always looks for causal links—between our hitting the child and his being untidy? There is none at all!

Herbert Spencer therefore suggests that in order to educate rightly, we should become "missionaries of causal processes." For instance, if we see a boy playing with fire by burning little bits of paper in a flame, we should recognize that he does so out of an inborn curiosity. We should not be upset because he might burn himself or possibly even set fire to the whole house, but we ought to realize that he acts out of an instinct of curiosity. We should make it happen—with all due caution, of course—that he burns himself ever so little, for then, only then, will he experience the causal connection. Following such or similar methods we should establish causal links, we should become missionaries of causal processes.

Whenever you meet people who wish to reform education, you will hear the opinion expressed that this principle of causality is the only possible one. Any unbiased person will reply: As long as we consider the intellectualistic

24

natural-scientific approach to be the only right one, this principle of causality also is the only right one. As long as we think along accepted scientific lines, there is no alternative in education.

But where does all this lead to if we follow these methods to their extremes and if we are absolutely truthful? We completely fetter the human being with all his powers of thinking and feeling to the processes of nature. His thoughts and feelings then also become mere processes of nature, bereft of their own identity and mere products of an unconscious and unfree participation. If man is considered to be nothing more than a link in the chain of natural necessity, he cannot free himself from nature's bonds in any way.

This may seem to be the very opposite of what I said a few minutes ago when stating that, if seen as the last link in evolution, man loses his separate identity and is therefore cast out of the world order. But just because his identity remains unknown, he is seen to be nothing but part of nature. Instead of being elevated from the complexities of nature, he is merely added to them. He becomes a being embodying the causal nexus. Such an interpretation casts out the human being and, consequently, education places man into a sphere devoid of humanity; it completely loses sight of man himself. People do not see this situation clearly because they lack the courage to do so. But we have reached a turning point in the evolution of the world and we must summon up the courage to face fundamental facts, for in the end our conceptions will determine the paths of our lives.

We have been opposed by people who in all good faith are convinced that the ordinary scientific explanation of world evolution can be the only right one. They equate the origin of the world with the primeval nebulae which are comprehensible only through the laws of aeromechanics. They equate the end of the world with total heat destruction resulting in the final world grave. Into this framework they place the human being who materializes from somewhere outside the human sphere and who is destined to find that all his moral aspirations, his religious impulses and all his other ideals are nothing but illusions.

A mood of tragedy pervades such people. They are the ones who have to live consciously with what for the majority of mankind lies dormant in the subconscious. And this underlying mood has become the burden of our contemporary civilization. However, out of such a mood we cannot educate because it excludes the kind of knowledge of the world from which knowledge of man can grow. It cannot sustain a knowledge of man in which he can find his true value and his true being, a knowledge of which he is in need if he is to experience himself as a reality in the world. We can educate to satisfy the necessities of outer life, but such an education hinders man from becoming a free individuality. If nevertheless we see children grow up into free personalities, this happens in spite of our education and not because of it.

Today it is not enough merely to think about the world. Today we have to think about the world in such a way that our thinking becomes gradually transformed into a general feeling for the world, because out of such feelings grow impulses for reform, for progress. It is the aim of Anthroposophy to present a knowledge of the world which does not remain in the abstract but which will enliven the entire being of man, thereby becoming the right basis for educational principles and methods.

Today we can already see the consequences of the materialistic world conception as a historical fact: Through his materialistic interpretation of the world man was cast out. And the echo of what has thus lived in the thoughts of educated people for a long time can now be heard in the slogans of millions upon millions of the proletariat. But the civilized world shuts its eyes to the direct connection which exists between its own world conception and the echo coming from the working classes. The mood of tragedy, experienced by discerning people who have come to the conclusion that moral ideas and religious impulses are of an illusory nature and that humanity exists only between the earth's nebulous beginning and its ultimate destruction by heat, this same mood we meet again in the outlook on life of millions of workers. For the only reality in their philosophy consists of economic processes and problems.

According to the proletarian conception of life, the only things that matter are economics, how they have been dealt with in past ages, how labor and production were managed, how buying and selling were organized and how through this process of production the physical needs of the people were satisfied. On the other hand, any moral aspirations, any religious ideas or political ideals are looked upon as ideology of a fundamentally illusory character and are considered as an unrealistic super-structure imposed on the only reality in life, namely the process of material production. In this way, what has been a theoretical and, at best, a semi-religious conviction among some educated circles of society has, in proletarian circles, become the determining factor for all human activities.

This is the situation which man is facing today. Under these conditions he is trying to educate. But to do justice to such a task, he must free himself from any bias and he needs to observe and grasp this present situation.

It is a characteristic feature of intellectuality with its naturalistic world outlook that it alienates man from the realities of life. From this point of view you only need to look at earlier conceptions regarding life. There you will find modes of thinking which could well be linked to life, thoughts which people of past ages would never have looked upon as mere ideologies. These people were rooted in life and because of this they never treated their thinking as if it

27

were some kind of vapor rising up from the earth. Today this latter attitude has already invaded the practical spheres of a large part of the educated world. And people are groaning under the consequences of what has come to pass. Yet mankind is not ready to recognize that what is happening in Russia today and what will spread into many other countries, is the natural consequence of the kind of teaching given at universities and schools. In these institutions one teaches, one educates and while in one part of the earth people lack the courage to recognize the dire consequences of their teaching, in the other part these consequences are ruthlessly pushed through to their extremes. We shall not be able to stop this wheel from running away unless we penetrate to clarity especially in this domain, unless we learn to place the laws of causality into their proper context. Then we shall realize that the human being is placed into a reality which will leave him no room for maneuvering as long as he tries to comprehend the world by means of the intellect only. We shall recognize that intellectuality as an instrument does not possess the power of taking hold of realities.

I once knew a poet* who, already decades ago, tried to picture how the human being would end up if he were to develop more and more in a one-sided intellectualistic way. In the district where he was living, a somewhat drastic idea of men of intellect, of the intellectuals, was prevalent, for such people were called "big-heads" ("grosskopfet"). Metaphorically speaking they were supposed to carry large heads on their shoulders. This poet took up the local expression, arguing that human development was becoming more and more intellect-centered and that, consequently, the human head would grow larger and larger while the remaining parts of the body would gradually degenerate into some kind of rudimentary organs. He foresaw only rudimentary

---

*Hermann Rollett, 1819–1904

arms ending in tiny hands and rudimentary legs with tiny feet dangling from a disproportionately large head, until the moment would come when humans would move by rolling along like spheres! The day would come when one would have to deal with large spheres from which arms and legs were hanging like rudimentary appendages. A very melancholic mood came over him when he tried to foresee the consequences of man's one-sidedly intellectual development.

Looking objectively at the phenomenon of intellectuality one can see that it alienates man from himself, that it removes him from reality. Consequently an intellectual person will accept only the kind of reality which is recognized by the proletariat, the kind which cannot be denied because one hits against it, suffering many a bruise! In keeping with present educational systems, even the avowedly reformed ones, such people believe that one can draw conclusions only within the causal complex. Alternatively, if they have to suffer from deprivation, again they limit their grasp of the situation to the laws of causality. When one is deprived of the necessities of life one can feel, see and experience only too well what is real. But one is no longer able to penetrate into real causes. While thus distancing himself from reality, man becomes less and less differentiated. Metaphorically speaking, he is really turning into such a rolling sphere. It will become necessary for us to gain an insight into how in our universities, colleges and schools we are cultivating the very things which we abhor when meeting them in actual life, as is the case today already to a high degree. People express criticism of what they witness, but little do they realize that they themselves have sown the seeds of what they criticize. The people of the West look at Russia and are appalled at what is going on there, but they do not realize that their western teachers have sown the seeds of these events.

As said already, intellectuality is not the instrument with

which one can reach reality and for this reason one cannot educate by its means. But if this is so, the important question arises: Can we make any positive use of the intellect in education at all? This poignant question challenges us right at the beginning of our lecture cycle. We must use means other than those offered by intellectuality. And the best way of doing this is to look at a particular problem in such a way that it is seen as part of a totality.

In what activities does modern society excel and what has become a favorite pastime? Well—in public meetings! Instead of quietly familiarizing oneself with the real nature of problems, one prefers to attend conferences or meetings to thrash them out there, because intellectuality feels at home in such an environment. Often it is not the real nature of a problem which is discussed—for this, so it seems, has already been dealt with—but discussions are held for their own sake. Such a phenomenon is a typical by-product of intellectuality which leads us away from the realities of a given situation. And so one cannot help feeling that, fundamentally, such meetings or conferences are pervaded by an atmosphere of illusion hovering above the realities of life. While down below, at ground level, all sorts of things are happening, clever discourses are held about them in multifarious public conferences. I am not trying to criticize or to run down efforts made at such meetings. On the contrary, I find that brilliant arguments are often put forth on such occasions. Usually the arguments are so convincingly built up that one cannot help agreeing with two or even three speakers who, in actual fact, represent totally opposing views! From a certain point of view one can agree with everything that is said. Why? Because it is all permeated by intellectuality which is incapable of providing realistic solutions. Therefore contemporary life might just as well be allowed to take its own course without the many meetings called together to deal with its problems. Life could well do without all these conferences and debates, even though one is able to enjoy and admire the ingenuity displayed at such meetings.

During the last fity to sixty years it was possible to follow most impressive theoretical arguments in the most varied fields of life. At the same time, when quietly observing life without prejudice, one could also notice that daily affairs moved in the opposite direction from that indicated by these often brilliant discussions. To give an actual example: When, some time ago, in various countries questions regarding the gold standard were discussed, most ingenious speeches were made recommending its usage. One can really say—I do not at all feel cynical about it but am sincerely earnest—that in various parliaments, chambers of commerce, etc., most erudite speeches were made about the positive results the gold standard would bring. Discriminating and intelligent experts, also those of real practical experience, proved that if we accepted the gold standard, we should also have free trade, that the latter was the consequence of the former. But low and behold! In most countries which adopted the gold standard, quite unbearable customs tariffs were introduced, which means that instead of allowing trade to flow freely, it was shackled. The opposite of what intellect-bred cleverness had predicted was the answer that life was giving! One must be clear about the fact that intellectuality is something quite alien to reality, that it makes the human being into a "big-head." Hence it can never be the basis of a science of teaching, for it leads away from the understanding of man. Since teaching involves a relation between human beings, namely the relation between teacher and pupil, it must be based on human nature. This can only be done out of a real knowledge of human nature. It is the aim of Anthroposophy to give such a knowledge of man.

LECTURE III

Dornach, 25th December 1921

If you study at greater depth what was brought before you yesterday, you will find that the current interpretation of the world cannot lead to an understanding of the human being. And if you go into further detail of what could be but briefly indicated here and relate it to specific problems of life, you will find confirmation of all that has been postulated in yesterday's lecture.

Now, strangely enough, exponents of the modern world view seem quite unaware of the significance of their being unable to reach the specifically human sphere. Nor are they willing to admit that in this respect their interpretation of the universe is incomplete. This fact alone more than justifies all the efforts made by anthroposophical research.

We shall grasp this situation all the more clearly by observing characteristic examples. When quoting Herbert Spencer, it was not my aim to prove anything; I merely wished to illustrate the modern mode of thinking.

Herbert Spencer had already formulated his most important and fundamental ideas before the spreading of Darwinism. This so-called Darwinism aptly demonstrates how scientific-intellectualistic thinking approaches questions and problems which are the outcome of a deep-seated longing in the human soul.

Charles Darwin's book *The Origin of the Species*, published in 1858, certainly represents a landmark in modern spiritual life. His method of observation and the way in which he draws his conclusions are exemplary for a modern conceptual discipline. One can truly say that Charles Darwin observed the data offered to his sense perceptions with utmost exactitude and that he searched for the underlying laws in quite a masterly fashion, taking into consideration everything that such observed phenomena could teach to his powers of comprehension. Never did he allow himself to be deflected, not even to the slightest degree, by his own subjectivity. He developed the habit of learning from the outer world in a way commensurate with the human intellect.

Observing life in this way Darwin was able to trace a link between the simplest, i.e., the least developed organisms, and the highest organism found on earth: man himself. The entire range of living organisms was contemplated by him in a strictly natural-scientific manner. But what he actually observed was external to and not part of the essentially human nature. Neither the real being of man, nor his spiritual aspirations were the object of his enquiry.

However, when Darwin finally had to face an impasse, he reacted in a characteristic manner. For, after having formulated his excellent conclusions, he now asked himself: Why should it not have pleased the Divine Creator just as much to begin His creation with a small number of comparatively undeveloped and primitive organic forms which He gradually allowed to develop further, as to miraculously conjure forth fully developed forms right at the beginning of the world?

But what does such a reaction signify? It shows that a personality who has made the intellectualistic-naturalistic outlook his own, applies it as far as a certain inner sensing will allow him to go, and that then he is prepared to accept newly found boundaries without pondering too much whether possibilities exist of transcending them. In actual fact, he is even ready to fall back on traditional religious conceptions. Also in his subsequent book *The Descent of Man* Darwin did not fundamentally modify his views.

Apart from being a characteristic example of the times.

Darwin's attitude also reveals certain national features, characteristic of Anglo-American attitudes and differing from those of Middle Europe. For if one looks at modern life with open eyes, one can learn a great deal about such national characteristics.

In Germany Darwinism was received at first with open enthusiasm which, however, spread into two opposite directions. There was, first of all, *Ernst Haeckel** who with youthful ardor took up Darwin's methods of observation, valid only in non-human domains. But, according to his Germanic disposition, he was not prepared to accept given boundaries with Darwin's natural grace. Haeckel did not capitulate to traditional religious conceptions, speaking of an Almighty who had created some imperfect archetypes. Using Darwin's excellent methods—relevant only for the non-human realm—as a basis for a new religion, Ernst Haeckel included both God and man in his considerations, thus deliberately crossing the boundary hitherto accepted by Darwin.

Du Bois-Reymond** took up Darwinism in another way. According to his views the naturalistic-intellectualistic mode of thought can only be applied to the non-human realm. He therefore remained within its limits. But he did not stop there, unquestioning and guided by his feelings, but made this stopping point itself into a theory. Just there, where Darwin's observations tail off into the undefined, Du Bois-Reymond postulated an alternative, stating: Either there are limits or there are no limits. And he found two such limits: One, when we turn our gaze outward into the world, we are confronted with matter. The second limit is when we turn

---

*Ernst Haeckel, 1834–1919. See "Riddles of the World. Studies of Monistic Philosophy," Bonn 1899.
**Emil Du Bois-Reymond, 1818–1896; see "Darwin versus Galiani," Berlin 1876.

our gaze inward to the experiences of our own consciousness and find also these ultimately impenetrable. He therefore concluded that we have no means of reaching the super-sensible, and made this into a theory: One would have to rise to the level of super-naturalism. That is the realm where religion may hold sway, but science has nothing to do with what belongs to this religious sphere. In this way Du Bois-Reymond leaves everyone free to supplement, according to personal needs, all that has been substantiated by natural science with either mystical or traditionally accepted forms of religious beliefs. But he insists that such supernatural beliefs could never be subject to scientific scrutiny.

The characteristic difference between the Middle-European and the Western people lies in that the latter naturally lean towards the practical side of life. Consequently they are quite prepared to allow their thoughts to tail off into what cannot be defined, just as it happens in practial life. Among Middle-Europeans, on the other hand, there is a tendency of putting up with impracticalities, as long as the train of thought remains theoretically consistent, until an "either–or" situation has been reached. And this we can see particularly clearly when fundamental issues regarding ulti-mate questions are at stake.

But there is still a third book written by Darwin which deals with the expression of feeling. (*The Expression of the Emotions in Man and Animals*) To anyone who occupies himself with the problems of the soul, this work appears to be of far greater importance than his *Origin of the Species* and *The Descent of Man.* If one lets this book, so full of fine observations regarding the expression of human emotions, work upon oneself, one can derive great satisfaction from it. For it shows that a person who has disciplined himself to observe in the natural-scientific manner can also achieve faculties which are very well suited for research into the soul and spiritual sphere of man. It goes without saying that

Darwin advanced along this road only as far as his instinct would allow him to go. Nevertheless, the excellence of his observations shows that a training in natural-scientific observation can also lead to an ability of penetrating into the realm of the supersensible. On this fact rests the hope of anthroposophical endeavor, which does not wish to depart by a hair's breadth in any task that it undertakes from the disciplined training of the natural-scientific method of thought. But at the same time Anthroposophy wishes to demonstrate how the natural-scientific mode of working can be developed further, thereby transcending the practical limits established by Darwin, crossed so boldly with Haeckel's naturalism and laid down as a theory by Du Bois-Reymond. It endeavors to show how the supersensible world can be reached so that real knowledge of man can finally be attained.

The first step towards such higher knowledge does not take us directly into the world of education which is to be our central theme during the coming days, but it consists of our trying to build a bridge from ordinary conceptual and emotional life to supersensible cognition. This can be achieved if—using ordinary means of cognition—we learn to apprehend the characteristic nature of the sense-bound interpretation of the world.

In order to do so I should like you to accept two hypotheses: Suppose that, from our childhood days on, the world of matter had been transparent and clear to our understanding. Suppose that the material world surrounding us were not impermeable to our gaze, but that with our ordinary sense-observation and thinking we were able to penetrate and fully grasp its nature. If this were the case, we should be able to comprehend the material aspect of the mineral kingdom. We should also be able to understand the physical aspect of man. The human body would become entirely transparent to our gaze.

However, if such a hypothesis were reality, you would have to eliminate from your mind something without which real life could not exist: You would have to think away all that we mean when we speak of love. For what does love depend upon, be it love for another person or for mankind in general, or for spiritual beings? It depends on our meeting the other person or being with forces which are totally different from those which illuminate our thoughts. If transparent or abstract thoughts were to light up as soon as we met another being, then even the very first seeds of love would immediately be destroyed. We simply would be unable to engender love. You only need to remember how in ordinary life love ceases to be when the light of abstract thought takes over. You only need to remember how right it is to speak of the coldness of abstract thoughts, how all inner warmth ceases when we approach the thinking realm. Warmth, revealing itself through love, could not come into being if we met outer material life only with our intellect. Love would be extinguished from our world.

And now suppose that there were nothing to prevent you from looking into your own inner organization; that, when turning your gaze inwards, you could perceive the forces and the weaving of substances within you with the same clarity with which you can see colors or hear tones in the outer world. If this were to happen, you would have the possibility of continuously experiencing your own inner being. However, in this case, too, you would have to eliminate something from your mind without which the human being could not exist in the world as it is today. For what is it that lights up within when you turn your gaze inward? You behold memory pictures of what you have experienced in the outer world. In actual fact, when looking inward, you do not see your inner being at all. You only see the reflection, the memory pictures, of what you have experienced in the world.

If you consider that, on the one hand, without this faculty of remembering, without memory, personal life would not be possible, and, on the other, that in order to perceive your own inner life you would have to eliminate your memory, you will recognize the necessity of the limit inbuilt into our human organization. The possibility of clearly perceiving the nature of outer matter would presuppose a human being devoid of love. The possibility of perpetually perceiving one's own inner organization would presuppose a human being devoid of the faculty of remembering.

Thus the two hypotheses help us to realize the necessity of the two limits set to human nature in ordinary life and in ordinary consciousness. They exist for the sake of the development of love and because of the need of personal memories for man's inner life. But if there is a path beyond these boundaries into the supersensible world, the obvious question arises: Can we tread this path without on the one hand damaging our personal life and on the other shunning social life with our fellows?

Anthroposophy has the courage to declare that with the usual and established naturalistic approach it is not possible to attain to supersensible knowledge. But at the same time it must raise the question: Are there any means which, when applied with the strict discipline of natural science, will enable us to enter supersensible realms? We cannot accept the statement that the crossing of the threshold into the supernatural world marks the boundary of scientific investigation. It is the aim of Anthroposophy to open up a path into the supersensible by using equally exact means with which hitherto accepted science has succeeded in penetrating into the sense-perceptible world. In this way Anthroposophy is merely continuing to tread the path of modern science. Anthroposophy does not wish to rebel against present achievements, but it endeavors to bring what is needed in our time and what contemporary life cannot provide out of its own resources.

If one looks at Darwin's attitude in the way I have presented it, one might feel prompted to say: Well, if science can deal only with what is sense-perceptible and if therefore one has to fall back on religious beliefs in order to approach what is supersensible, one simply has to accept the situation as being inevitable. Such a response, however, would do nothing to solve the fundamental and urgent human problems of our times.

In this context I should like to speak about two characteristic aspects of present-day life because, apart from supplementing what has been said already, they also throw light on educational questions. They may help to illustrate how modern intellectual thinking, which is striving for absolute lucidity, nevertheless is prone to drift into the dark domains of the unconscious and instinctive.

If you observe man's attitude towards the world in past ages, you will find that in ancient times religion was never looked upon as mere faith—this only happened in later times —but that religions were based on direct experience and on insight into the spiritual worlds. The knowledge thus gained was considered to be as real as are the results of our modern natural-scientific investigations. Only in subsequent ages was knowledge confined to what is sense-perceptible and, consequently, supersensible knowledge was relegated to the religious realm. And so the illusion came about that anything pertaining to metaphysical existence could be only a matter of faith. Yet, as long as religions rested on supersensible knowledge, this knowledge bestowed great power, affecting even the physical nature of man. Our modern civilization is not able to generate this kind of moral strength for the man of today. For when religion has become only a matter of faith, it loses power, it can no longer work right down into man's physical constitution. Though this is instinctively felt nowadays, its importance is not recognized. This instinctive feeling and searching for revitalizing forces has found an outlet which has become a distinctive feature of our civilization and which belongs to all that we call sports.

Religion has lost the power of strengthening man's physical constitution. Therefore an instinctive urge has arisen in people to gain access to such a source of strength by outward, physical means only. As life tends towards polarizations, we find that man instinctively wants to substitute the loss of invigoration, previously drawn from his religious experiences, by cultivating sportsmanship. I have no wish to harangue against sports. Neither do I wish to belittle their positive aspects. In fact I feel confident that these activities eventually will develop in a healthy manner. Nevertheless it must be said that sport will take on an altogether different position in human life from that of today, where it is a substitute for religious experience. Such a statement may well appear paradoxical, but truth, today, is paradoxical because modern civilization has drifted into so many cross-currents.

A second characteristic of our intellectual and naturalistic civilization is that, instead of embracing life in full, it tends to lead to soul-destroying contradictions. A person's thinking is driven along until it becomes entangled in chaotic thought-webs and contradictions, without his or her becoming aware of the confusion wrought. For example, the fact that a young child to a certain extent will go through the various stages mankind has passed through from the days of primitive man up to our present civilization, fills certain naturalistic intellectuals with admiration. They observe the somewhat turned-up nostrils of a young child and the position of the eyes which lie further apart than in later life. They observe the formation of the forehead with its characteristic curvature and also the shape of the mouth. All these features are reminiscent of those found in primitive tribes and so they look upon the young child as being a young savage.

Yet, at the same time, sentiments such as those expressed by *Rousseau*, are trying to rise to the surface, sentiments which are completely at loggerheads with what has just been said. When contemplating educational aims, some people wish to "return to nature," both from a physical and moral aspect. But, being under the influence of an intellectual atmosphere, they soon aim at arranging educational ideas according to the principles of logic, for intellectuality will always lead to logic in the thinking realm. Observing many illogical features in present education, they now wish to base it upon principles of logic which, in their eyes, are entirely compatible with the child's natural development. Logic, however, does not meet the needs of the child at all. One close look at primitive races will make one realize soon enough that members of such tribes hardly apply logical thinking to their ways of living.

And so some reformers are under the illusion that they are returning to nature by introducing a logical attitude in educating the young—who are supposed to be little savages—an attitude which is altogether alien to the child. In this way, adherents of Rousseau's message find themselves caught in a strange contradiction with an intellectualistic attitude. Striving to live in harmony with nature does not fit into an intellectualistic outlook. And as far as the education of the will is concerned, the intellectualistic thinker finds himself completely out of touch with reality. According to his ways of thinking the child should above all be taught what is useful in life. For instance, such people never tire of pointing out the impracticability of our modern mode of dress, which does not satisfy the demands of utility. They advocate that, in order to return to more natural ways, we should concentrate on the utilitarian aspects of life. Especially the education of girls is criticized most sharply by such reformers.

And now they are faced with a paradoxical situation: Did primitive man—whose stage young children are supposed to recapitulate—live a life of utility? Certainly not. According to the findings of archeologists, he neither developed logic in his thinking nor utility in his living. His essential needs were satisfied through the help of his inborn instincts. But what was it that captivated the interest of primitive man? Adornment! He did not wear clothing for practical reasons, but out of a longing for self-adornment. Whatever the members of such tribes chose to wear—or not to wear in order to be able to show the patterns painted on their skin—was not intended to serve useful purposes, but was an expression of their yearning for beauty, as they understood it. Similar traits can also be found in the young child.

If a person interested in education thinks along rational and logical lines and in terms of what is practical and useful in life, and if, on the other hand, he or she feels pulled in the direction of Rousseau's call to return to nature, he will find himself victim of strange contradictions. What he really does is to pass on to the child what appears to him of value to himself as a grown-up. He tries to graft on to the child something which is entirely alien to the child's own nature. Children really do seek—only in different ways from those advocated by Rousseau—for beauty which for them neither expresses the good nor the useful, but which exists for its own sake.

Anyone able to perceive these contradictions and imperfections in modern life, will be ready to look for their causes. And he will recognize more and more how one-sided and limited the generally accepted intellect-based naturalistic mode of thinking is, which does not look upon man in his entirety at all. Usually only man's waking state is taken account of, whereas in reality the hours spent in sleep are just as much part of human life as those of his day consciousness. You may object by saying that natural science has closely examined also the sleeping state of man and indeed there exist many interesting theories about the nature of sleep and of dreams. But all these are premises made by persons in their waking state and not by investigators who were able to penetrate the domains of sleep.

In his waking state man not only has consciousness, he also undergoes inner experiences and he takes an active part in life. During sleep, on the other hand, he loses his ordinary consciousness, and consequently he can examine sleep only from the perspective of the awake person. However, a proper study of such a life phenomenon demands more than an abstract theory. To be able to enter sleep-life in full consciousness is an essential prerequisite for its understanding.

Though experiencing both wonder and astonishment when studying the phenomena of sleep, a serious and unbiased investigator is not likely to advance further along lines which, for example, Greek philosophy considered to be of importance. According to an ancient Greek adage, every philosophy—as a path towards cognition—begins with wonder. But this indicates only the beginning of the search for insight. One must move on. One must progress from wonder to cognition.

However, the first step towards supersensible knowledge must not be made with the expectation of one's being able to enter the spiritual world directly, but rather with the intent of building a bridge from the ordinary sense-perceptible world to supersensible knowledge. One way of achieving this is by applying the same discipline with which we have learned to observe the phenomena of the sense-perceptible world to what comes to us from the realms of sleep and of dreams. Modern man certainly has learned to observe accurately, but in this case it is not just a matter of observing accurately. In order to gain insight one has to be able to direct one's observations to specific areas.

I should like to give you an example of how this can be done when studying the phenomena of dreams which infiltrate into our waking life in strange and mysterious ways.

Here and there one still comes across people who have remained aware of the characteristic difference between waking and sleeping, but their awareness has become only a dim and vague feeling. Nevertheless such people are aware that an awake person is an altogether different kind of creature from the one who is asleep. Therefore when they are told that sleep is a waste of time and that a sleeper is an idle and lazy fellow, these simple minds will answer, "As long as we sleep, we are free from sin." In this way they wish to express that man, whom they consider to be a sinful creature as long as he is awake, is innocent while he sleeps. A good instinctive wisdom is hidden in this somewhat naive attitude. But in order to reach clarity, one needs to train one's own observation. I wish to give you an example: Surely there are some among you here—perhaps all of you—who have had dreams which are reminiscent of what might have happened to you in daily life. For example, you may have dreamed that you were taken to a river and that somehow you had to get across. So you found yourself searching for a boat which, after a great deal of trouble, you managed to secure. Now you had to make great efforts to row across. In your dream you may have felt the physical exertion of plying the oars, until at last you managed to get across—just as it might have happened in waking life. There are many such kinds of dreams. Their contents are definite reminiscences of our physical and sense-perceptible lives. But there are also other kinds of dreams which do not echo our waking life. For instance, someone again may dream that he or she has to cross a river. Wondering how this urge could possibly be fulfilled, the dreamer suddenly is able to spread his wings and—Heigh presto!—he simply flies across to land safely on the opposite bank. Such a dream certainly is not a reminiscence of what happens in waking life because, to my knowledge, this is hardly the way ordinary mortals transport themselves across a river in real life. Here we have something which simply does not exist in physical life.

And now, if we accurately observe the relationship between sleeping and waking life, we shall discover something really interesting: We shall find that the kind of dreams in which we experience the toil and exhaustion of waking life, dreams which reflect our waking life, make us wake up tired. On waking, our limbs feel heavy and tiredness seems to drag on throughout the course of the day. With other words, if strains and pains of a life of drudgery reappear in our dreams, we wake up weakened rather than refreshed. But now observe the effects of the other kind of dream: If you have managed to fly, weightlessly and with hearty enthusiasm, with wings which you do not possess in ordinary life, once you have flown across your river, you wake up bright and breezy and your limbs feel light. We need to observe these differing effects of dreams on the waking life with the same accuracy with which we make our observations in mathematics or in physics. We know quite well that we should not get far in these two subjects without it. Yet dreams are not generally made the object of exact observations and, consequently, no satisfactory results are achieved in this field. And such a situation hardly encourages people to strive for greater powers of insight into these somewhat obscure spheres of life.

It is not just a case of putting forward some isolated glimpses of something which apparently confirms previous indications. The more one ponders about the relevant facts, the more such reciprocal links between sleeping and waking life become evident. For instance, there are dreams in which you may see some very tasty dishes which you then enjoy with a hearty appetite. You will find that usually, after having thus eaten in your dreams, you wake up without much appetite. You may even not eat during the following day, as if there were something wrong with your digestion. On the other hand, if in your dream you had the experience of speaking to an angel, and if you entered fully into a dialogue with him, you will awake with a keen edge to your appetite, which may persist during the whole of the day. Needless to say, partaking of food in one's dream represents a memory picture from waking life, for in the spiritual world one neither eats nor drinks. This, surely, you will accept without further proof! Therefore, enjoying food during a dream is a reminiscence of physical life, whereas speaking to an angel—an event which is unlikely to happen to people nowadays—is something which cannot be looked upon as an echo of daily life.

Such an observation alone could show even an abstract thinker that something quite unknown happens to us in sleep, something which nevertheless plays into our daily lives. It is wrong to surmise that it is not possible to gain exact and clear conceptions in this realm. For is it not a clearly defined discovery that dreams echoing earthly reality—the kind so popular among naturalistic poets ever eager to imitate earthly life and never ready to enter the supersensible realms—that such dreams have an unhealthy effect upon our waking lives? If ordinary life impressions reappear in dreams, these dreams have an injurious effect upon our health. On the other hand, if unrealistic dream pictures appear—the kind which would be so scornfully dismissed as mystical rubbish by an intellectualistic philistine—these will make us feel bright and fresh upon awakening in the morning. It is certainly possible to observe the strange interplay and the reciprocal effects between dreaming and sleeping.

And so we can say: Something which is independent of man's physical condition must be happening to him during sleep, the effects of which we can observe in his physical organism. Dreams cause astonishment and wonder to ordinary consciousness because they elude us in our waking state. The more you try to collect such examples, the more you will find a real connection between man's sleeping and waking state.

You only need to look closely at dreams to find their characteristic difference from what we experience in waking life. When awake, we are able to link, or to separate, mental images at will. This we cannot do when dreaming. The dream pictures are woven as objective appearances which lie beyond the influence of our will. In dream the activities of the soul become passive, benumbed and paralyzed.

If we study dreams from yet another aspect, we shall find that they can reveal to us other secret sides of human existence. Observe, for instance, your judgment of people with whom you may have a certain relationship in life. You may find that you do not allow your full inner feelings of sympathy or antipathy to rise to the level of consciousness and that your judgment of such people is colored by varying facts, such as their titles or their positions in social life, etc. However, when you dream about such a personality, something quite unexpected may happen: You may find yourself giving him a thorough hiding! Such behavior, so completely at odds with your attitude in waking life, allows you a glimpse into the more hidden regions of your sympathies and antipathies, some of which you would never dare to admit even to yourself while awake, but which the dream conjures up in your soul. Subconsious images are placed before the dreaming soul. These are comparatively easy to observe. But if you were to investigate at depth certain inexplicable moods of a person, moods of ill-temper or of euphoria which cannot be attributed to outer circumstances, you would find that they, too, were caused by dreams, completely forgotten by the people concerned. What is experienced in sleep and

47

what may become revealed through dreams, works into the unconscious and may lead to apparently inexplicable moods. Unless we consider this other side of life, this hidden domain of man's sleep life, by making exact investigations, we cannot understand human life in its totality.

However, all these reciprocal effects happen without man's participation. Yet it is possible to lift what is thus happening unconsciously and involuntarily to a state of clear consciousness, which is equal to that of a person engaged in mathematics or other scientific investigations. When achieving this, one's powers of observation are enhanced beyond the indeterminate relationship between waking and sleeping to the fully conscious states of Imagination, Inspiration and Intuition.

Only through these three capacities is it possible to attain to a true knowledge of man. What life vaguely hints at through the phenomenon of sleep can be developed in full consciousness by applying methods given by Anthroposophy, which strive towards a real knowledge of the world and of man.

LECTURE IV
Dornach, 26th December, 1921

In trying to comprehend the world through a natural-scientific interpretation of its phenomena—both from a cognitional and a practical point of view—people generally take into account conditions only as they meet them at the present time. Such a statement may appear incorrect to anyone who merely looks at the surface of things. However, as we proceed with our deliberations, it will become evident that this indeed is the case. We have grown accustomed to investigate the physical organism of man with the accepted methods of biology, physics and anatomy, but—though this may appear incorrect at first—in the results thus obtained we are dealing only with what the present moment of time reveals to us. For example, we observe the lungs of a child, of an adult and of an old person in their successive stages from the beginning to the end of life and we draw certain conclusions. But in this way we do not really penetrate the element of time at all, for we are limiting ourselves to observations in space. These, in turn, we invest with qualities of time. We are doing the same thing, to use a simile, when we read the time by looking at a clock. We note its hands, say in the morning, and their spatial positions indicate the time to us. We may look at the clock again at midday and conclude the passage of time from the spatial changes of its hands. We take our bearing as to the course of time from the movements of the hands from point to point in space. This has become our habitual way of judging time in everyday life. But in this way we cannot experience the true nature of time. And yet, only by penetrating the element of time with the same awareness with which we experience space, can we rightly judge human life between birth and death. I should like to illustrate these theoretical remarks by examples which will show the importance of living oneself into the dimension of time, especially if one wishes to practice the art of education.

Take, for example, a child who is full of reverence towards grown-up people. Anyone with a healthy instinct would consider such an attitude in a child as something wholesome, especially if such reverence is justified, as indeed it should be in the case of an adult. However, people usually think no further. They merely attribute such a feeling of reverence towards adults to certain characteristics of childhood and leave it at that. But one will never be able to recognize the importance of such reverence unless one includes the entire course of a human life in one's considerations.

As one grows older, one may have the opportunity of observing old people. One may discover that some of them have the gift of bringing soul comfort to others who are in need of it. Often it is not the content of what such old people have to say which acts like balm on a suffering soul, but merely the tone of their voice or the way in which they speak. If now you trace back such an old person's life to his or her childhood days, you will find that as a child he or she was full of such reverence and respect for the adult. Naturally, this attitude of reverence will disappear in later life, but only on the surface. Deeper down, it will gradually become transformed, only to reemerge later as the gift of bringing solace and elevation to suffering and troubled minds.

One could also put it in this way: If a young child has learned to pray, if it has learned to develop an inner mood of prayer, this mood will enter the subconscious, there to undergo a metamorphosis into the capacity of blessing in ripe old age. When we meet old people whose mere presence radiates blessing upon those around them, you will find that in their childhood they had experienced and developed such an inner mood of prayer. Such a transformation can only be discovered if one has learned to experience time as concretely as we are accustomed to experience space. We must learn to recognize the time element with the same awareness with which we experience space. Time must not be experienced in spatial terms only, as is the case when we look at a clock face.

What I have been trying to illustrate with this example regarding the moral aspects of life needs to become very much part and parcel of our concept of man, certainly if a real art of education is to be developed. I should like to elaborate this point in greater detail:

If we compare the human being with the animal, we find that from the moment of birth animals, especially the higher species, are equipped with all the faculties necessary for their living. A chick leaving its shell does not need to learn to walk, for it is already adapted to its surroundings. Each animal's organs are firmly adapted to the specific needs of its species. This, however, is not at all the case with the human being who comes into this world as a completely helpless creature. Only gradually can he develop the capacities and skills necessary for his life. And this is due to the fact that the most important period in his earthly life lies between the end of childhood and the coming of old age. This middle period, this time of maturity, is the most important feature of human life on earth. During that time man adapts his organization to outer life by acquiring specific aptitudes and skills. He develops a reciprocal relationship to the outer world, based on the range of his own experiences. This middle period during which the human organs remain capable of evolving and adapting, is completely missing in the life of the animal. The animal is born into life in a state which, fundamentally, is comparable with that of the aged person whose organic forms have become rigid. If you wish to understand the animal's relationship to its surroundings, you must look upon it in terms of the human stage of old age.

Now the question may arise: Does the animal show characteristics of old age also with regard to its soul properties? This is not the case because in the animal there also exists the opposite pole which counteracts this falling into "crabbed age," and that is its capacity of reproduction. The ability of procreation—be it in the human or animal kingdom—always engenders forces of rejuvenation. While on the one hand the animal falls prey to the influences of aging too rapidly, on the other it is saved from premature aging through inflowing forces of reproduction, until it reaches sexual maturity.

If you are able to observe an animal or an animal species without preconception, you will come to the conclusion that at the time when the animal is capable of procreation, it has already reached the stage which is equivalent to that of old age in man. The characteristic difference in the case of the human being consists in the fact that both old age and childhood, during which the reproductive system in the latter is slowly maturing, are placed at either end of the human middle period and that during this middle period the flexibility of the human organism remains intact, thus enabling man to relate and adapt himself individually to outer conditions. By such an arrangement the human being will be a child at the right time, leaving childhood at the appropriate age to enter the period of maturity. He will leave the age of maturity when the time comes for him to enter old age.

If you look at human life from this time aspect, you can also understand certain abnormalities. You may come across individualities who—if I may put it this way—prematurely slip into old age. I am not so much thinking of obvious features generally associated with old age, such as grey hair or baldness. Even a "bald-head" may have remained a childish person! I am thinking of more subtle symptoms, detectable only upon more intimate observations. One could call such features signs of a senile soul life, manifesting in a person already at a stage when he or she should still be living in the middle period of flexibility and adaptability.

But the opposite may also happen. A person may be unable to leave the stage of childhood at the right time, carrying infantile features over into middle life. Then strange things may happen in the life of such a person, the symptoms of which we can only touch upon today. If we include the time element in our picture of man, we shall be able to diagnose various aberrations of human behavior.

We know that as we approach old age, our head organization in particular loses inner mobility. Consequently all the capacities which we have acquired during life attain more of a soul and spiritual quality. But this is only possible at the expense of the head organization taking on certain animal-like properties. From a physical point of view an old person undergoes conditions akin to those of a newborn animal. To a certain extent he or she becomes "animalized." In this way—provided their education was right—old people gain something which they may preserve for the rest of their lives. Their spiritual and soul experiences of the outer world no longer enter fully into their organization. The cranium has become to ossified and fixed. The aged person therefore depends more on soul and spiritual links with the surrounding world. He or she is no longer able to transform to the same extent outer happenings into inward qualities. Thereby a kind of animalization of the upper regions is taking place.

Now it is possible for such an animalization in the head organization to take place prematurely, that is, already during the middle period of life. But because a human being will remain human despite such a tendency towards animalization, we do not come across any outer symptoms, but we must become aware of certain changes within the realm of the soul. If the relationship to the outer world, characteristic of an aged person, establishes itself prematurely—and this can happen already during childhood—such a person's experiences will be drawn too much into the physical system, for, naturally, the general flexibility of the remaining human organization, typical of the younger age, still retains the upper hand. In this case such a person will experience inwardly, but too early, what normally would result from a relationship to the outer world appropriate to old age. Communications between inner and outer world would be linked too much to the physical organization, thus bringing about properties of soul more akin to the animal world than would be the case in normal human beings.

One could say—if one wished to express it in this way—that the animal has the advantage of a certain instinct over man. It is an instinct which links it more directly and more intimately to its surroundings than is the case in the normal human being. It is no mere myth, but absolutely accords with the peculiarities of animal life, that certain animals leave localities which are in danger of impending natural catastrophes. Regarding the self-preservation of life, animals are gifted with certain prophetic instincts. It is also correct to state that the animal experiences far more intensely the changing seasons than man does. It is able to sense the approach of the time when it has to migrate to other regions, for it has such an intimate and instinctive relationship to its surroundings. If one could look into an animal's soul life, one would find there—albeit entirely unconsciously—an instinctive wisdom of life, manifesting in the animal's entirely living within the manifold processes and forces of nature.

Now, if a person falls victim to encroaching age too early, such an animal-like instinctive experience of the surroundings begins to develop, naturally in sublimated form because in a human being everything is lifted into the

54

human sphere. And what today is known as lower forms of clairvoyance, as telepathy, telekinesis and so forth—often described correctly and often quite wrongly—these faculties which occur abnormally in human life, are nothing but the result of such premature aging playing into the middle period of life. If the process of aging occurs at the right time, one will experience it in a healthy manner, whereas if it already makes its appearance in one's twenties, one becomes a clairvoyant of a low order. Symptoms of a premature aging represent an abnormality in life which does not reveal itself outwardly but in a more hidden manner. If these forms of lower clairvoyance were to be studied from the aspect of man's premature aging, a far deeper insight into these phenomena could be achieved. This, however, is only possible if one observes life in a more realistic way. It is not good enough merely to investigate what one can see before one's eyes at the present moment of time. One must learn to recognize in these symptoms indications of a time shift from later to earlier stages of life.

We shall see in the next few days how healing processes can come about through an exact insight into human nature. It is indeed possible that a kind of animalization of man could be manifested not in an outwardly visible aging process, but rather in that a close and instinctive relationship with the environment can encroach upon the lower regions of man, otherwise characteristic of the animal.

The resulting phenomena of telepathy, telekinesis and so on, do not lose in interest by being recognized for what they really are, namely, not manifestations of the spiritual world, but the intrusion of a later stage of life upon an earlier. By developing a time consciousness, one is able to fathom the very depths of human nature. To live in the dimension of time is to survey the course of time until one is able to see into both past and future from the present moment of time.

You will yourself feel how actually our present day

observation, even though it may appear outwardly otherwise, is very remote from this more inward means of observation, which is more concurrent with time and its course. Insufficient interpretations of what meets us in life result from present day observation. Contemporary scientific explanations and their effects upon life are full of such insufficient interpretations.

Looking at the course of human life, we find that the reverse case of what has here been described is also possible: Childishness is carried over into the age of maturity. It is characteristic of the child that it not only experiences the external world less consciously than grown-up people, but also that its experiences are much more intimately bound up with metabolic changes. If a child sees colors, their impressions strongly affect its metabolic processes. The child takes in outer sense impressions right down into its metabolism. It is no mere metaphor to speak of a child digesting its sense impressions, for its digestion responds to all its outer experiences. An aged person develops certain animal characteristics within the physical. But the child's entire life is filled with a sensitivity towards the vegetative organic processes which also affect the child's life of soul. Unless we are aware of this fact, we shall not be able to understand the child's nature.

In later years man leaves the digestive, metabolic processes more to themselves. He experiences the external world more independently of them. He does not allow his soul and spiritual reactions to the outer world to affect his metabolism to the extent that a child does. His response to his surroundings is not accompanied by the same lively activity of glandular secretion as in the case of the child.

The child takes in all outer impressions as if they were edible substances, but the adult leaves his digestion to itself and this fact alone makes him into an adult under normal circumstances. But there are cases where the vegetative-organic forces which work in a legitimate way during childhood, still continue to work in an adult, affecting also his psyche. Then other abnormal symptoms are liable to occur. An example will make this clear: Suppose, for instance, someone develops a love for a dog which makes a deep impression on his nature. If he or she is one who has carried childishness over into later life, this tenderness will work right into the metabolism. Organic processes corresponding to his feelings of affection will be set up. In such a case digestive processes take place not only after the intake of food or as a result of normal physical activities, but certain areas within the digestive system will develop a habit of secreting and regenerating substances in response to the strong emotions evoked by the love for such an animal. The dog will become indispensible to the well-being of such a person's vegetative system. What happens if the dog dies? The connection in outer life is broken off. The organic processes go on by force of inertia, but they are no longer satisfied. The person's feelings miss something they had got used to and in an inward trouble ensues. The strangest disturbances may occur. A friend may advise the buying of a new dog and so restore the previous dog owner to health, for now the inner organic processes can find satisfaction again through external experiences. We shall see later that there are better ways of curing such an abnormality, but anyone may reasonably try to solve the problem in this way.

There are of course many other examples to be found, less drastic than such a deep affection for a dog. If an adult has not outgrown certain forces of childhood destined to absorb external impressions within the digestive system, and if he or she no longer can satisfy this abnormal habit, certain cravings within the vegetative organism will result. But there are also other things which may have been loved and then lost and which cannot be replaced. Then the individual concerned remains dissatisfied, morose and hypochondriacal.

One must try to find the true causes of apparently inexplicable symptoms arising from the depths of the unconscious.

There are people who can sense what needs to be done to alleviate the suffering caused by unsatisfied emotions which affect inner organic processes. They manage to coax out and to bring to consciousness what the patient desires to call to mind and in this way they are able to help a great deal.

Due to the present state of our civilization there are many people who have not progressed from childhood to adulthood in the normal way and, consequently, the ensuing symptoms, both light and serious, have been noticed far and wide. While in ordinary life this naturally led to conversations among helpful and interested people, the situation has stimulated—and in many respects quite rightly so—scientific-psychological research. A new scientific terminology sprang up. The patient's psyche was examined through investigation into dreams or by free or involuntary giving-of-oneself-away. In this way unfulfilled urges were raised from the subconscious into consciousness. This new branch of science was called psychology or psychoanalysis, the science of probing into the hidden regions of the soul. However, we are not dealing with "hidden regions of the soul," but with the remains of vegetative organic processes which have been left behind and which crave satisfaction. When such thwarted desires have been diagnosed, one can help the patients to readapt themselves. And herein lies what is valuable in psychoanalysis.

When judging such matters, Anthroposophy finds itself in a difficult position. It has no wish to quarrel with the findings of natural science. On the contrary, Anthroposophy is very ready to recognize and to accept anything which remains within its proper and justifiable realm. In this way, Anthroposophy also accepts psychoanalysis within its proper bounds. But Anthroposophy endeavors to see all problems and questions within the widest context, encompassing the entire universe and the entire being of man. It feels compelled to widen the arbitrary restrictions laid down by natural science, which often carries out its investigations in quite an unprofessional and dilettantish way—even today. Anthroposophy has no wish and no intention to quarrel. It only puts into a wider perspective what is declared in a one-sided manner. Yet such a way of working is distasteful and unacceptable to anyone who prefers to wear blinders and, consequently, furious attacks are being made upon Anthroposophy. Anthroposophy has to defend itself against a one-sided attitude, but it will never be aggressive. This has to be said regarding present-day currents of thought, such as we find in psychoanalysis.

It is important that we distinguish between two polarized situations:

Either a person draws the last period of life too much into middle age and, consequently, abnormal relationships with the external world develop, manifesting as lower forms of clairvoyance, such as telepathy. In this case such a person extends his horizon beyond the normal human scope in an animal-like fashion.

Or, a person may move in the opposite direction by pushing into later periods of life what rightly belongs only to childhood. In consequence he becomes enmeshed too strongly with his physical organism with the result that organic surges swamp his psyche, causing disturbances and inner abnormalities. Such a person suffers from a too close relationship with his own organic system. This latter relationship has been diagnosed by psychoanalysis which, however, ought to direct its attention to human organology in order to grasp the roots of the problem.

If we wish to reach a comprehensive knowledge of man, it is absolutely necessary to include in our considerations the entire course of human life between birth and death. It is essential to focus one's attention upon the effects of the passing of time and inwardly to live with them and to experience them. Anthroposophy which pursues knowledge of man in his totality by penetrating into the supersensible through its own specific methods, therefore fully takes into account the time element which, in the present stage of our civilization, is generally completely ignored. Imagination, inspiration and intuition, which are the specific methods of anthroposophical endeavor, must be built upon an experience of the element of time.

Imagination, inspiration and intuition, the ways leading to supersensible cognition, should not be looked upon as faculties lying outside ordinary human life, but rather as a continuation, an extension of ordinary human capacities. Anthroposophy dismisses the prejudice which holds that only through some special grace can we attain this kind of cognition, but it maintains that man is able to become conscious of certain faculties lying deep within him and to have the power to train them.

The usual kind of knowledge gained through contemporary scientific training and in ordinary practical life certainly must be transcended.

What happens when we try to comprehend the world around us—not as scientifically-trained specialists but as ordinary people? We are surrounded by colors, sounds, by varying degrees of warmth, and so on, all of which I should like to call the tapestry of the sense world. We surrender ourselves to these sense impressions and weave them together without thoughts. If you think about the nature of memories rising up in your soul, you will find that they are the result of sense impressions woven into our thoughts. Our whole life depends on our imparting this texture of sense impressions and thoughts to our life of soul.

But what is it that really happens? Look at the diagram. Let the line a to b represent the tapestry of the sense world which surrounds us, consisting of colors, sounds, smells, etc. We give ourselves up to our observation, to this tapestry of the senses, and weave its impressions together with our thinking—here indicated by the wavy line.

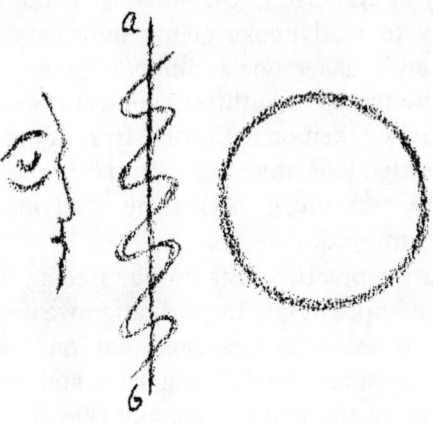

When living in his senses, man unites all his experiences with his thoughts. He interprets the sense stimuli through his thinking. But when thus projecting his thoughts into his surroundings, this tapestry becomes for him a barrier, a metaphorical canvas upon which he draws and paints all his thoughts, but which he is unable to penetrate. He cannot break through this incorporeal wall with his present-day ordinary consciousness. As they are being stopped by this canvas, his thoughts inscribe themselves upon it.

The only possibility of penetrating this wall is gained by raising one's consciousness to the state of Imagination through systematic and regular meditation exercises. It is equally possible to undergo an inner training in meditation as a method of research in an outwardly directed study of chemistry or astronomy. If you read my book *Knowledge of the Higher Worlds and Its Attainment* and the second part of *Occult Science*, you can convince yourselves that, if one

61

wishes to reach the final goal, the methods employed for such meditative exercises are by no means simple and less time-consuming than those needed to acquire knowledge of astronomy or chemistry. On the other hand, it is comparatively easy to read books giving information about such exercises and, using one's common sense, to be able to examine the truths of anthroposophical research. These do not have to be taken on authority. Even if one is not able to make investigations into the spiritual world oneself, it is possible to test given results by studying the specific methods employed.

Meditative practice rests on our freeing ourselves from outer sense impressions. In meditation we do not surrender ourselves to sense impressions, but only to the life of thoughts. However, by dwelling again and again in meditation on a given thought or mental image—one that is easily and fully comprehensible—we gradually bring our life of thought to such a strength and inner substance that we are able to move in it with the same certainty as in our sense impressions. You will all have experienced the difference between the striking effects of outer sense impressions and the rather limp and pale world of our thoughts during ordinary consciousness. Sense impressions are intensive and alive. We give ourselves up to them. Thoughts, on the other hand, turn pale, they become abstract and cold. But the very core of meditating consists in our becoming able, through regular practice, to imbue our thoughts with the same intensity and liveliness with which we normally experience our sense life. If we succeed in grasping a meditation content with the same inward intensity with which we usually grasp the stimulus of a color, then we have brought to life, in the right way, the underlying thoughts of a meditation. But all this has to happen with the same inner freedom as the normal weaving of thoughts or as ordinary sense perceptions. Just as we do not allow ourselves to be taken over by nebulous moods or mystical dreaming, or become fatuous visionaries when observing the external world, so must we not lose firm ground when meditating in the right way. The same sane mood with which we perceive the world around us must hold sway also when we meditate.

This attitude of taking outer sense perceptions as an example for one's conduct when meditating is characteristic of the anthroposophical method. There are plenty of nebulous mystics who look down upon sense perception as something inferior which ought to be left behind. They proclaim that the meditant should reach a state of mystic dreaming. The result, naturally, is a state of semi-sleep, but not of real meditating. Anthroposophy pursues the opposite aim. It considers the quality, intensity and liveliness of sense perception as an example to be followed until the meditant inwardly moves with the same freedom with which he encounters sense perceptions. He need have no fears of ending up as a dry philistine. The content which he objectively experiences in his meditative practice will save him from that. When meditating, there is no need for him to enter trance-like, nebulous states because of the inner content which he experiences while thus freeing himself from workaday life.

Through rightful meditation one can achieve the ability of moving freely in one's life of thinking. This, in turn, redeems the thoughts from their previous abstract character. They become image-like. And this happens in full waking consciousness, just as any healthy thinking does. It is essential never to lose full consciousness and this is what distinguishes meditating from any hallucinatory state. Anyone given up to hallucinations, any futile enthusiast or visionary, relinquishes his sound common sense, whereas anyone wanting to follow the methods here advocated, must ensure that sound common sense accompanies him in all his weaving of thought pictures. And what is the result? Though fully awake, he will experience the pictorial quality of the dream

63

world. The significant difference between Imagination and dream pictures lies in that we are completely passive when receiving the latter. If they rise from the subconscious to enter our waking state, we can observe them only after they have happened. When practicing Imagination, on the other hand, we ourselves are the initiators. We create images which are no mere fancy, but which differ in their intensity and strength from the fanciful as much as the dream pictures do. The main point is that it is we ourselves who initiate the images and this frees us from the illusion that they are a manifestation of the external world. Anyone given up to hallucinations always believes that what comes to him represents reality because he is aware of not having been the creator of what he sees. In this lies the cause of the deception. Whoever practices Imagination through meditating cannot possibly be under the impression that the images he creates represent outer reality. The first step towards supersensible cognition depends on one's freeing oneself from the illusion that the images one has created—images which are of the same intensity as those of the dream world —are real. This, however, is self-evident because the meditant is fully aware of having initiated them in complete freedom. Only a madman would mistake them for outer reality.

Now, the next step in meditation consists of acquiring the ability of letting these images vanish without a trace. This is not as easy as one might expect because, unless the meditant has created them in full freedom, such images become quite fascinating, fixing themselves on the mind like parasites. One has to gain the strength to let such pictures disappear at will. This second step is of equal importance to the first. Just as in ordinary life we need to be able to forget, as otherwise we would always have to walk about with the sum-total of all our memories, so the total extinction of all these images is as important as their creation in the first place.

When one has thoroughly practiced these exercises, one has done something to one's soul life which could be compared with the strengthening of a muscle through repeated bending and stretching. By learning to weave and form images, and then again to obliterate them—and all this out of an entirely free will activity—one has performed an important training of the soul. One has developed the faculty of consciously forming images which under normal circumstances only appear in dreams, that is, during a condition which escapes our ordinary consciousness and which is confined to the time between falling asleep and waking. But now this condition has been induced both consciously and in full freedom. Training in Imagination is to train the will, consciously to create images as well as consciously to remove them from the mind. And through this activity we acquire yet another faculty.

Everyone has this faculty involuntarily, not during sleep, but at the moment of waking and of falling asleep. It is possible that what was experienced between these two moments comes over to us as remnants of dreams, often felt to come from the beyond. Naturally, it is equally possible that what we meet on waking up so surprises us that all memories of dreams sink below the threshold of consciousness. In general one can say that, because dream imaginations are experienced involuntarily, something chaotic, something erratic which normally lies beyond our consciousness, finds its way to us. If, while fully awake, one develops the ability of creating and of obliterating Imaginations, one can reach a condition of emptied consciousness. This is like a new awakening and then, from beyond the tapestry of the sense world, spiritual entities pass through the tapestry to reach us on paths smoothed by the meditation content. (See the red circle in the diagram) While thus persevering in emptied consciousness, we push through the senses' barrier and images, Inspiration-born, come to us

65

from beyond the sense world. We enter the world which lies beyond the sense world. Through Imagination we prepare ourselves for Inspiration which consists in our being able to experience consciously something which happens unconsciously at the moment of waking. Just as at the moment of waking something from beyond our waking soul life enters our consciousness, so something lying beyond the consciousness of the sense world enters us if, through Imagination, we have trained our soul life in the way described.

In this way we experience the spiritual world lying beyond the world of the senses. Faculties of supersensible cognition are an extension of those naturally given to man in his ordinary life. It is one of the main tasks of Anthroposophy to train and to foster the development of these higher faculties. The grasping of the time element in the course of human life is fundamental to any such higher development.

If you look up the preparatory exercises for Imagination, Inspiration and Intuition, as given in my book *Knowledge of the Higher Worlds and Its Attainment* or in my *Occult Science*, you will find that all that is stated there aims at one thing, namely at the development of the ability to experience the course of time. The human being goes through the various stages of experience in the world first as a child, then as a mature person and finally as an old person—or he may suffer from an abnormal overlap of one stage into the other. It is not Imagination in itself, but the meditative preparation towards it, which should give man the possibility of developing his full potential and of learning how to give himself to the world out of the fulness of his life. To this end harmony must be brought about between the specific contributions to the world of childhood, middle age and of old age. These must flow together harmoniously into a world outlook capable of reaching the spiritual world. Man in his wholeness, which includes also the domain of time, must be actively engaged in his work in the world. In order to achieve a world outlook which reaches beyond the barriers of the sense world, the human being must preserve the freshness of experience which is proper to youth; the clarity of thought and the freedom of judgment proper to middle age; and the power of loving devotion to life which can reach its perfection in old age. All these qualities are a necessary preparation for the right development of Imagination, Inspiration and Intuition.

LECTURE V

Dornach, 27th December 1921

As described in the previous lecture, imaginative cognition can be attained by one's lifting into consciousness what is happening subconsciously and involuntarily in dreaming. To put it more precisely: It is not the dreaming itself with its inherent dream content which is lifted into consciousness— for if this were to happen, we should remain in the realm of unreality—but the activity underlying it. For the moment I shall not define what this activity—going on while we are dreaming—entails. It is this activity, lifted into consciousness by controlled will power, which becomes the basis for imaginative cognition. And this conscious activity is of a very different kind from that of dreaming. For in the latter —just because we are not active participants—we are under the impression that our experiences represent reality. However, if we lift our dream-producing activity into consciousness, we realize only too well that we are seeing images of our own making. It is this awareness which saves us from becoming victims of hallucinations instead of working as investigators of Spiritual Science.

This first meditative activity of creating images must now be superseded by a second step which consists in obliterating these images, thus leading to an emptied consciousness. If one has been able, in full consciousness and under full control, to enhance one's soul powers in this way, one has in fact entered the spiritual world. One is then able to engage in an activity which, being of soul and spirit only, is independent of the physical body. One no longer perceives with physical organs. While one's thinking becomes freed from the body, one is able consciously to experience content of a purely spiritual nature.

Yesterday I pointed out that for an anthroposophical investigator, dreamlike experiences are not to be looked upon as a model for spiritual perception. Only fully controlled experiences, similar to those characteristic of our sense perceptions, are valid. Obviously there is no possibility for sense perceptions in supersensible cognition. Nevertheless we can look upon the freedom with which we move when surrounded by our sense perceptions and upon the independence from our personal makeup during the act of perceiving as upon a definite capacity. An example will make my meaning clear:

Let us look at one of our most characteristic and representative sense organs, the human eye. Already by the way in which it rests in its cavity, attached to the remaining organism by quite insubstantial links, we can recognize the relative independence of this organ. Leaving alone for the moment what happens in the act of seeing, we can find another, more external process also taking place. Near the eye are the lachrymal glands which during our waking state continually secret a liquid, mainly composed of salt water. This liquid flushes the eyeball and also the part which is exposed to the outside air when the eye is open. Through this glandular activity the eye is constantly bathed so that any dust particles entering the eye from the outside are washed away through tearducts entering the nose. This process, which forms part of the normal function of our organ of sight, is hidden from ordinary consciousness.

Now this wisely ordained but completely unconscious activity of the lachrymal glands can be accelerated by stimuli of various kinds, by pressure, cold, and so on, or through the exhaustion of the eye and the organism in general. The lachrymal glands then become more active and the cause of their secretion, as well as the secretion of tears itself, begins to enter our consciousness. However, a further increase of this activity may come about in quite a different way; if some sad event makes us weep, tears flow as a result of a purely emotional stress or because our feelings have been deeply moved. Here we see how under normal circumstances the lachrymal liquid is constantly being secreted in complete unconsciousness, and how outer irritants will lead to an increase in consciousness of this activity. But when a person weeps because of some soul distress, this lachrymal activity is lifted into the sphere of consciousness only through soul or moral issues and not through any physical causes.

Such a simple fact can help to illustrate what happens when, through meditation, one is able to lift oneself into a body-free state of consciousness in which one is able to live entirely in soul and spiritual experiences. If you shed tears because you receive a letter which makes you unhappy, you must admit that the cause of your tears has nothing to do with your physical eyes. Nevertheless, it affects your physical eyes. (The fact that the tears are not connected with your actually reading the letter can easily be proved if someone else is reading the letter to you with the same tearful consequences.) Something non-physical has set an organic process in motion.

Now suppose that you have gained such mastery over yourselves that you are able to suffer great sorrow without shedding any tears. (This does not imply that the anguish is less intense than when you weep.) In that case your soul experiences do not directly affect your bodily functions. This example may illustrate how, through self-training, one can achieve a state of soul and spirit which has become emancipated from the physical organism. It may help you to form some conception of how Imagination, Inspiration and Intuition, as methods of Spiritual Science, can open the gates into the supersensible world. If you take the proper steps,

70

you will then be able to describe experiences from beyond the tapestry of the senses, experiences which may be looked upon as an enhanced continuation of what the ordinary person experiences in normal life. This, however, is only possible through the practice of specific exercises of a soul and spiritual nature.

If now, by continued spiritual training, you have reached the stage where you can suppress previous imaginations of your own creating, and if in the ensuing stage of emptied consciousness you nevertheless are able to experience real soul and spiritual content, the first thing which will come to meet you is a tableau-like picture of your earth life, approximately from birth up to the present moment. You will not be able to see your own physical body in that picture, for that vanishes away when you have reached body-free perceiving. But everything you have experienced, everything which belongs to the stream of your memory—which normally remains unconscious and out of which only separate images rise up from time to time—stands there before you to meet your soul. It confronts you as an entity, as a kind of time organism which is full of its own inner movement.

If you look at the physical body as it appears in space, you will find that its various members are dependent on one another, together making up the whole. What happens in the head has a certain relationship with the stomach and vice versa. Everything that happens in an organism is interrelated. The same is also true for an organism existing in time: Later happenings depend on earlier happenings. The past lives in the present. At such a moment you are suddenly confronted by the totality of your life tableau.

If one's ability to suppress, in full consciousness, the tableau of one's memory pictures—that is, if not only one's body but the entire life tableau has vanished away—one reaches the stage in which experiences prior to birth, or rather prior to one's conception, are revealed. The realm of soul and spirit which one inhabited before entering this earthly existence, remains part of one's inner being, also during life on earth. It works and lives in us in a similar way in which hydrogen lives together with oxygen when these two elements form water. But just as one cannot examine hydrogen separately from the oxygen while it forms the compound water, so one cannot examine separately the soul and spiritual part of man while he lives on earth. Just as the oxygen first has to be isolated out of the water before one can examine the remaining hydrogen, so must the soul and spiritual part of man first become isolated. And when this happens we are led, not into the present time, but into our pre-earthly existence. In this way one is really able to perceive what has descended from the spiritual world in order to take on earthly form. The realm in which we lived before entering earthly life becomes revealed to us.

It is quite understandable if some people are not prepared to go to such lengths in order to be able to investigate the eternal part of man. Certainly everybody is free not to follow the paths here indicated. But to believe that it would be possible to examine man's soul and spiritual nature by ordinary methods of cognition would be like naively believing that one could examine hydrogen while it formed part of the compound water, without first isolating it. One has to realize that by means of ordinary consciousness it is not possible to enter the realm of soul and spirit. If one is not prepared to accept the results of spiritual investigation, one will have to remain silent with regard to the supersensible world. In that case one will have to be content with occupying oneself with the material side of existence only. The truth may well be irksome to some, but there are certain facts of life which one simply has to accept.

Continuing this path of spiritual training, we gradually reach inspirational knowledge. We become inspired by something which does not normally enter our consciousness, but which permeates our being as does the oxygen which we take in from the outer air in our breathing. In full consciousness we are being filled with inspirational cognition, filled with the experience of our pre-earthly life, just as in respiration we are filled by material oxygen. We breathe in our soul and spiritual being, rising to the stage of Inspiration. This name has not been chosen arbitrarily, but in keeping with the characteristic nature of this type of cognition.

Inspirational cognition has yet another characteristic feature. You will find more about it in my book *Knowledge of the Higher Worlds and Its Attainment.* In order to develop this higher cognition, one further faculty is necessary, namely that of presence of mind. It is the faculty that enables one to act spontaneously during a given life situation. In order not to miss the right moment, one may have to act without waiting until one has had time to judge the issue properly. One should really use such moments which life offers in order to become practiced in acting swiftly and decisively, in quickly grasping the moment, for whatever comes to us through inspiration, passes as if in a flash. As soon as it makes its appearance, it has already vanished again. One needs to be able to catch such fleeting moments with the utmost attentiveness.

When confronted with the ordinary sense world, it appears to you spread out in space. But if you are confronted by your own life tableau, you behold it as if existing in time. However, during inspirational cognition one is outside the realm of time. One depends on being able to perceive in the flash of a moment. Time has lost its meaning, as soon as one experiences inspirational cognition.

If one lives oneself into this life tableau, one finds there something far more real than the ordinary memory pictures can give us. The latter are neutral and lacking in inner strength. They are there and we are free to take them up, but in themselves they have no strength. What we meet when beholding our life tableau, on the other hand, is full of its own life and strength, containing the very forces which actually form the human being. These are supersensible formative forces which are active, for example, in forming the brain of a young child before its final structure has been accomplished. It is these formative forces which one begins to recognize, for they are contained within this life tableau. One is not grasping something abstract, but a full reality, something which is encompassing the course of time, something that is full of strength. It is the refined non-material body of forces which we have also called the ether body or the body of formative forces. This body only momentarily presents a well-defined appearance in space, for it is in constant motion. If we were to try to paint a picture of it, we should be painting something unreal, because the ether body is in constant flux. Its subsequent stage would be quite different again, just as a former stage was totally different. This etheric body is a time organism through and through and it lies at the basis of the growing processes and those forces active in the human metabolism.

If one has advanced far enough in imaginative cognition, consciously to live in the realm of one's soul and spirit which lies beyond the physical, and if one has progressed far enough to be able to behold one's own life tableau at will, that is, one's etheric body or body of formative forces, then one has truly experienced a complete transformation of one's cognitional life. One finds that what is experienced in this etheric world is both similar, and yet very unlike what happens in the world of artistic activities. In order to experience it, one has to develop a more creative kind of thinking, which is so very different from any abstract naturalistic thinking. Although in certain respects this kind of thinking resembles that of a creative artist, in other ways it is again quite different. For an artist's creations have to reach a certain finality within the realm of fantasy. His or her creativity

remains bound to the physical; it is not freed from corporeality. But the activity practiced in imaginative cognition
is entirely freed from the physical and therefore is capable of
grasping spiritual reality. For instance, when looking at the
Venus of Milo, you will hardly have the feeling that this
statue will begin to move and walk towards you. An artist's
creation does not embody outer realities. If you saw the
devil painted on a canvas, you would hardly feel afraid of his
coming to fetch you! What matters is how the artist, bound
to physical reality, deals with this material reality. But he
does not dive into the reality of soul and spirit. What has
been achieved in imaginative cognition, on the other hand,
is immersed in ultimate reality, in the reality of spiritual
processes.

Now the objection may well be raised that pure cognition should be kept quite separate from the realm of artistic
activities. It is easy to prove by logic that cognizing means
moving from one conception to the next in logical sequence
and that, if one enters the sphere of art, one is in fact trans-
gressing the realm of cognition. One can argue for a long
time about the laws of cognition. But if Nature herself is an
artistic creator, she will never reveal herself to mere logical
thinking. Logic alone will never be able to reach her true
being. Therefore, however much it can be proved by logic
that cognizing must not be confused with being engaged in
artistic activities, one will not be able to enter the reality of
the etheric world without applying an artistic mode of cognizing. What matters is how the world is and not what the
laws of our cognizing ought to be. Even if certain supposi-
tions are logically tenable, they may nonetheless prevent us
from reaching our goal. Therefore it is right to maintain that
an artistic element has to enter our efforts if we wish to raise
our ordinary cognition to the level of imaginative cognition.

When reaching the stage of Inspiration, we can again
compare our experiences with something which they resem-

ble and yet from which they differ greatly, namely experiences of a moral nature and the grasping of moral ideas. Viewed qualitatively, Inspirations are similar to moral ideas. And yet, they are totally different through the fact that any moral ideal which we may have, in itself does not have the power of realizing itself by its own strength. In themselves, our moral ideals are powerless. We must make them effective through our own physical personality. We must put them into the world by means of our physical existence. Otherwise they remain mere thoughts. But this cannot be said of an Inspiration. Though qualitatively similar to moral ideas, to moral impulses, Inspiration shows itself to be a reality, existing in its own right. It is a powerful force which works as do the elemental forces in nature. And so one enters a world which one has to imagine as being similar to that of the world of moral idea, yet one that is a reality through its own primal power.

If, having advanced far enough in reaching the state of Inspiration, one is able to take one's stand in the world of soul and spirit, then something else is still required in order to be able to experience its content. One has to carry something into this realm which does not at all exist in our abstract world of thoughts, namely a complete devotion to one's chosen objective. It is not possible to learn to know a being or a power in the spiritual world, unless one surrenders oneself lovingly and completely to what comes to meet one during the state of Inspiration. At first Inspiration remains only a manifestation of the spiritual world. Its full inner nature reveals itself only if, with loving devotion, one pours oneself out into its own substance. And only after having experienced the reality of soul and spirit in this way, full of life and with heightened consciousness, has one entered the realm of Inspiration.

And this is already intuitive cognition. Shadow forms of Intuition can be found in ordinary life where they exist in religious feelings and in religious moods. However, a religious feeling remains a purely inward experience which does not lift one up into outer spirituality. Intuition, on the other hand, is an experience of an objective spiritual reality. In this way, also Intuition is similar, and yet again quite different from a purely religious experience.

If one wishes to put down these degrees of higher knowledge in a more or less systematic order, one can say: First of all, in ordinary life, we have knowledge of the material world, which we could call naturalistic knowledge. Then we come to knowledge gained through Imagination, which is of an artistic nature. The next step is knowledge attained through Inspiration which, in essence, is a moral one. Finally we reach knowledge through Intuition which is akin to religious experiences, but only in the sense just characterized.

Such supersensible experiences of an artistic, moral and religious kind work upon and transform the whole human being. Even though ordinary consciousness knows nothing of them, they nevertheless form part of the human being. Therefore supersensible cognition as gained through Imagination, Inspiration and Intuition, enables us to know the whole human being. And because these powers, streaming from the spiritual world into earthly existence, work particularly strongly in the child, higher cognition especially enables us to understand the nature of the child. However, it is important to recognize how these supersensible forces are related to physical forces.

This can be illustrated particularly well if we take memory as an example, because active memory definitely depends on the functioning of physical organs. Even quite commonplace experiences can demonstrate how our body has to play its part when we use our powers of memory. For instance, we may wish to memorize the part of a play or a poem, only to find that the lines simply refuse to become imprinted in our mind. Yet, after having slept on them during the night, we may suddenly be able to remember them without much difficulty. This happens because during the night's sleep our body has become regenerated so that on the following morning we are able to use its renewed vitality for the task of remembering our lines.

One can also prove anatomically and physiologically that through paralysis or separation of certain areas within the nervous system, specified areas of memory can be wiped out. In short, one can definitely see that memory is dependent on the functioning of the physical organization and that physical organs are active during the process of remembering. However, this kind of memory activity is completely different from what is experienced in heightened consciousness through Imagination, Inspiration and Intuition. For supersensible experiences of this kind simply must not be involved in any way in the functioning of physical organs. This is the very reason why such experiences cannot be remembered in the ordinary way. They do not impress themselves into ordinary memory.

Anyone engaged in anthroposophical research has to allow ordinary memory to run its course side by side with what he or she experiences supersensibily. Ordinary memory must remain intact. In a way, a student of Anthroposophy has to keep his second personality, representing his ordinary life, always by his side. But he knows full well that there is this other, first personality in him which is engaged in supersensible knowledge and which will not allow itself to become imprinted in the memory. In ordinary life we can retain only a memory picture of a fish we have seen and not the actual fish itself. In supersensible cognition one has direct perceptions—not mental images—and therefore one cannot carry them in one's memory. Consequently one has to return to them time and time again. However, it is possible to remember what one has done in order to gain supersensible cognition and if one repeats these efforts, supersensible beholding will reemerge, albeit only passively, for it cannot live in the memory. It can only be attained through renewed inner activity. The fact that these higher faculties lie beyond the reach of memory is a characteristic feature of supersensible cognition. One can regain it, but only by following a route similar to the one travelled before. One is able to remember the path trodden previously, but not the supersensible experience itself.

It is this fact which distinguishes supersensible experiences from ordinary ones. But one must point out again and again that a healthy memory must go parallel to true supersensible experiences. Anyone losing the stream of common memory while engaged in supersensible experiences would pour his or her subjective personality into them. In this case he or she would not be a student of anthroposophical research but someone living in hallucinations and personal visions. It is important to realize that all forms of hallucinations should be strictly excluded from supersensible cognition and that the latter must be developed side by side with the normal and healthy life of the soul. Anyone remonstrating that Imagination and Inspiration gained through Anthroposophy could equally well be mere hallucinations, does not know the characteristic properties of the anthroposophical path and only talks out of ignorance.

It is essential to recognize this difference between supersensible cognition and memory. Both are realities in human life. Supersensible substance gained through Imagination and Inspiration has its own separate existence of which, through our own efforts, we can be come aware. Memory, on the other hand, is not only the result of our own activity, for here our unconscious also plays its part. What we experience through Imagination remains in the spiritual world. It is as if it came towards the human being and united with him. But memory streams right through him, entering the physical organization, making it participate. It penetrates the physical part of man. Comparing memory with Imagination helps us to appreciate the difference between what is linked to our physical body and what lives in us as a supersensible force, everlastingly, also between birth and death. Because it escapes our ordinary consciousness, it has to be revealed through anthroposophical investigation.

Only by immersing oneself into the relationship between the part of man's being which can be experienced only supersensibly and that of his physical existence, can one learn to know the entire human being. If one lives oneself into what supersensible knowledge reveals, one also learns to know the child, the growing human being, in a way which enables one to develop a true art of education. And the example of the relationship between the supersensible being of man and what is at work in memory can help to shed light on this problem.

Now let us suppose that a teacher were introducing a subject to a class. First he or she would approach it in a more general way and might be under the impression that all was going well. But from a certain moment on he might notice that one of the children in the class was getting paler and paler. Such pallor need not be of an obvious kind and might easily have been passed unnoticed by anyone not trained in exact observation. A proper teacher, however, should always be fully aware of each pupil's condition.

Symptoms which I am about to characterize could have manifold causes. But if a teacher has deepened his knowledge of man through anthroposophical training, he will have awakened and enhanced his ordinary pedagogical instincts to the extent of being able to diagnose and deal also with other causes. A science of education which lays down fixed and abstract rules would have a similar effect upon a practicing teacher as if he were constantly treading upon his own feet while trying to walk. It would rob him of all creative spontaneity. If he were always wondering how to apply rules prescribed by educational science, he would lose all ingenuity, all rightful pedagogical instincts. On the other hand, educational principles based on Anthroposophy have quite the opposite effect. They do not let his inborn pedagogical sense wither away, but they enliven and strengthen his whole personality. This at least is the purpose of practical pedagogy springing from Anthroposophy. Therefore, however varied outer symptoms may be—for life is full of surprises—a teacher whose pedagogical sense has been stimulated and sharpened by Anthroposophy, may suddenly realize when seeing such a paling child, that he has overfed it with memory content. Naturally, there could be many other reasons for such a symptom which a gifted teacher would also be able to discover. I am quoting this example to illustrate one of the fundamental tasks of Anthroposophy, namely to make people aware of the mutual interaction between soul and spirit with what belongs to physical man and to the world of matter. Anthroposophy does not merely aim at revealing spirit knowledge but, above all, it endeavors to open the eyes of people to how the living spirit works and reveals itself in matter. Such knowledge will enable us to deal rightly with the practical problems of life. It will place us strongly into the world in which we have to fulfil our tasks.

If the pallor of a certain child, caused by the overburdening of the pupil's memory, is not recognized in time, a perceptive teacher will notice a further change in the child, this time of a psychological kind: The child will develop an anxiety complex. Such a symptom again may not be at all conspicuous and would be detected only by a teacher who has made intensive observation his second nature. And the final consequence of overtaxing a child's memory could eventually lead to a retardation of his growing forces. Somehow even the physical growth of such a child can become affected.

Here you have an example showing how soul and spirit

interact with what is physical. It can teach us how important it is for the teacher to know how to deal with children's tendencies towards health and sickness. Of course, actual illnesses have to be treated by medical doctors, but the educator is always confronted by inherent trends towards health or sickness in the child. These he should learn to recognize. He should also be aware of how illnesses breaking out in later life often can be traced back to what has happened at school. Knowledge of these facts would make a teacher become far more circumspect in choosing his methods of teaching. In the instance quoted, he certainly would avoid too much stress on the pupil's faculty of remembering. Then he might see a healthier complexion return to the child's face again. He could bring about such a change by showing his pupil something beautiful which would give him pleasure. The next day he might show him again something beautiful or something of a similar kind which is like a variation of the previous object, in this way bypassing mere memory.

Now a teacher may also discover opposite symptoms in a child: At a certain time he may notice a boy or girl whose face appears permanently flushed, even if only very slightly. He may find that this change of color is not at all due to any feelings of shame but that it manifests a shift in the conditions of the health. Again, this symptom may be so slight that it would only be detected by a perceptive teacher. Again this condition could have many other causes which, however, would not escape his notice either. It could well be that the tendency to blush was the result of the teacher not appealing sufficiently to the child's faculty of memory. Realizing this, he would try to rectify this condition by giving the pupil more memorizing to do. If left to itself, such an irregularity could become intensified, spreading to the pupil's psyche where it would manifest in mild but significant outbursts of temper. Such a connection between slack-

82

ness in memorizing and slight, yet unhealthy fits of temper is absolutely possible. More general repercussions of such a condition would be injurious to the pupil's health. The mutual effects between soul and spirit on the one hand and the body on the other, in such a case could lead to disturbances in breathing and to circulatory troubles. In this way, a teacher unaware of such links unwittingly may have implanted in his pupils illnesses which may remain dormant throughout long years of life and which, triggered off by some additional causes, may finally culminate in serious illnesses. It is for this reason that an educator worthy of the title should know of these connections, characteristic of human nature.

As mentioned previously, acute cases of illness have to be dealt with by medical doctors, but during their developmental stages children are always treading paths leading to either health or illness. The art of education demands that teachers should be conversant with them and able to observe them even in their finer manifestations.

In order to illustrate this point even more drastically, I wish to give one more example which, I realize, may well be open to challenge, but life presents us with the most manifold situations. Consequently, the case I am going to describe may also be the result of completely different causes. If one lives with what Anthroposophy can give to teaching, one grows accustomed to looking around for the most varied causes when confronted with a particular problem. But the following links between symptom and cause could certainly be possible.

Let us suppose that a boy or a girl in a class had been following the lessons attentively and to the satisfaction of the teacher. However, one day he or she suddenly appeared somewhat blasé and no longer inclined to pay attention, so that much of the subject matter seemed to pass by unnoticed. Depending on the experience and outlook of the teacher concerned, he might even resort to corporal punishment or other forms of correction in order to bring about greater participation. However, a teacher who is aware of the interplay between spirit and matter manifesting in health and illness, would follow a completely different line. He might say to the girl or the boy, "You must not let your finger and toenails grow too long. You must cut them more often." For what expresses itself outwardly as growth—as seen in the growing of finger and toenails—this, too, is permeated by soul and spirit. And if finger and toenails are allowed to grow too long, these forces of growth become dammed up. Being thus held at bay, they are no longer able to pour themselves into finger and toenails. Such an obstruction to the flow of growing forces—which is removed when the nails are cut—has a similar effect also upon the soul and spiritual counterpart, manifesting in difficulties to concentrate. For the ability to pay attention can be developed only with a free and unlimited flow of life forces which permeate the whole organism. In most cases of this kind a change in the pupil's powers of concentration may well pass unnoticed. I gave this example in order to show that anthroposophical principles and methods of education by no means neglect the physical aspects of life. They do not lead to a nebulous kind of spirituality, but the spirit is fully taken account of, so that life can be understood and treated appropriately.

In this way, an educator who gradually learns to comprehend human nature, may gain insight into how to deal rightly with matters pertaining to his pupils' health or illness.

LECTURE VI

Dornach, 28th Dec. 1921

It was not my intention in yesterday's lecture to single out certain types of illnesses or to specify differing degrees of health, nor is it my aim to do so in today's continuation of our subject. I merely wish to bring to your notice how important it is for the teacher to learn to recognize both healing and harmful influences in the lives of his pupils. A real educator, above all else, must have acquired an insight into the entire human organization. He must not allow abstract educational theories or methods to let him deviate from his natural or, as one could also call it, from his instinctive-intuitive insights. Abstract theories will only hamper him in his efforts. He must be able to look at his children free from any preconceptions.

In Middle Europe the following quotation is frequently heard—I do not know whether it is also known in the West:—* "There is only one health, but there are many, many illnesses." This saying, however, in which so many people believe, does not really stand up to a proper scrutiny, for the human being is so individualized that each person, and also each child, has his own specific state of health, or represents an individual modification of the general idea of health. One might just as well coin the phrase: There are as many differ-

---

*Because of the large numbers of participants at this conference, Rudolf Steiner had to give each lecture twice. He stipulated that the non-German speaking members—many of whom came from England—should attend the repeat lecture which was translated into English by George Kaufman (Adams).

ent kinds of health and illness, as there are people in the world. This fact alone is an indication of how we must always consider the individual nature of each person. But this is only possible if we learn to look upon the human being in his totality. In every person soul and spiritual forces are always interacting with physical forces, just as in water hydrogen and oxygen react upon each other. And in man, as he stands there before us, it is as little possible to observe directly his soul and spiritual being separately from his physical and material existence, as it is to observe hydrogen and oxygen separately in water. In order to recognize the true relationship between the soul-spiritual part of man and his physical nature, one must first get to know them intimately. But this is not possible by the ordinary means of knowledge alone. Nowadays one is accustomed to look upon man from two points of view. The one is reached through the study of physiology and anatomy, where a picture is arrived at which is not based upon the living human being at all, but only upon his corpse, for man's soul and spiritual counterparts are there excluded. The other is that of psychology, the study of man's inner life. But the psychologist can only form abstractions, only thin and cold concepts in these naturalistic and intellectualistic times. The investigator seems to warm up only when he tries to plumb the depths of human emotions and will impulses. These, however, he cannot grasp in their true essence either. In a vague way he can only see in them surging waves welling up from within.

It is quite obvious that by producing only cold, thin and pale conceptions regarding the human psyche, no true sense of reality can be achieved. What I am about to say may well appear paradoxical to present-day attitudes, but it is nevertheless true: People today adopt a materialistic attitude because for them the spirit has become too attenuated, too far distant, and consequently, what they can observe of man's inner life, no longer bears any sense of reality. The very people who live in the most abstract thoughts have become the greatest materialists in our cultural epoch. Our contemporary kind of thinking—and thinking is a spiritual activity—turns people into materialists. On the other hand, people who are relatively untouched by the scientific thinking of today, people whose minds turn more to external material happenings, are the ones who can sense some of the mysteries underlying outer processes. Our scientific thinking of today hardly leaves any room for life's mysteries. Its thoughts are thin, transparent and, above all, horribly clear-cut and consequently not anchored in the realities of life. Material processes in nature, on the other hand, are full of mysteries. These need not be approached with the clarity of intellectual thoughts only, for they also evoke a sense of wonder in us. In this way, our feelings, too, become engaged. Therefore people who have not become influenced by to-day's sterile thoughts, people who have kept aloof from the rigorous discipline of a scientific training, are more open to the mysteries of external material processes. However, there is a certain danger in that their longing to find the spirit in what they thus behold in nature, makes them look upon the spiritual as if it, too, were only matter. They become spiritualists. Modern scientific thinking will not produce spiritualists but materialists. A natural openness towards the material world, on the other hand, will easily produce a spiritualistic attitude, and herein lies a strange paradox typical of our times. However, neither a materialistic thinking nor a spiritualistic outlook on life will produce a true picture of the human being. This can be gained only by discriminating how—in every single organ and in the entire human being—the soul and spiritual element in man interweaves with what is physical and material.

People, today, do talk about soul and spirit. They talk about the physical aspect of man. Then they philosophize about the relationship between the two members. Detailed theories have been put forth by learned people. But these theories, however ingenious they may be, cannot touch reality, simply because reality can be found only if one is able to perceive how the soul and spiritual element and the physical, material element of the entire human being completely interpenetrate each other. If one looks at the results of today's investigations both in physiology and in psychology, one cannot help but find them both nebulous and grey.

Nowadays, when one person looks upon another, he feels that he is confronting a complete unity. This impression is due to the fact that the other person is neatly wrapped up in his skin. One does not generally realize that this apparent oneness is the result of the working together of the most diversifying organs. And if one makes the statement that this unity must not be taken for granted, opponents rise soon enough to accuse one of destroying the concept of the unity of the human being, which they consider to be fundamental. However, their conception of a human oneness remains merely an abstract thought, unless they are able to build it up by harmonizing the manifold members of the human being into one organism.

And when people look inward, they sum up all that lives within them with the little word "I." Eminent people, such as *John Stuart Mill*, had to make strenuous efforts in formulating theories about what is contained within this inner feeling of identity which expresss itself through the word "I." But only pause to consider how nebulous such an idea of a point-like "I" really is. You will soon see that with this concept you are no longer grasping concrete reality. In the German language three letters suffice to form this little word (ich) and in English even fewer. People hardly manage to get beyond the outer meaning of these letters, with the result that today's knowledge of man remains nebulous, no matter whether you look upon his inner life or upon his physical constituents.

It is the ability of seeing the spiritual and physical working together which fructifies one's efforts at comprehending man. There are many people today who experience inner satisfaction at hearing *Goethe's* words: Matter in spirit, spirit in matter. It is good if these words make people happy, for they certainly express a truth. But for anyone who has made a habit of seeing spirit and matter working together everywhere, such words express a mere triviality, for they extol something which is obvious. The fact that so many people receive this somewhat theoretical dictum with such acclaim only goes to show that they no longer experience its underlying reality. Theoretical explanations usually hide the loss of concrete inner experiences. We can find an example of this in history when looking at the theories about the Holy Communion, theories which were widely discussed from the very point of time when people no longer could experience its reality. Usually theories are formulated in order to explain what is no longer experienced in practice.

The attitude of mind expressed so far will be helpful to anyone who wishes to practice education as an art. It will enable him to gain a concrete picture of man's manifold members, instead of his having to work with some vague idea of a human oneness. To him a picture of man as an organic whole will also emerge, but in it he will recognize how the different members are working together in harmony. Such a picture inevitably leads to what I have indicated in my book *Riddles of the Soul*, namely to the discovery of man's three fundamental parts, each different from the others both in functions and in character. Already externally the head organization appears very different from, let us say, the organism of the limbs and metabolic system. I link these two latter systems together because the metabolism shows its real nature when the human being is active in his limbs. In morphological terms one can look upon the digestive system as a kind of continuation—even if only inwardly—of the human being in movement. There exists an intimate kinship between the limb and the digestive systems. For instance, the metabolism is more lively when the limbs are active. This kinship could be demonstrated in detail, here I am merely indicating it. Because of their close affinity, I group these two systems together, although—when each one is looked at individually—they also represent certain polarities.

Now let us look at the human figure, beginning with the head. For the moment we will ignore the hair which, in any case, grows away from the head and which, because it is a dead substance, really remains outside the living head organization. (Human hair is really a most interesting substance, but further details would only lead us away from our main considerations.)

The head is encased by the skull, which is formed most powerfully at the periphery, whereas the soft and living parts are enclosed within. Let us now compare the head with its opposite pole, with the limb system: Here we find the tubular bones enclosing the marrow which is generally not looked upon as being of equal importance for the entire organism as the brain substance which is enclosed by the skull. On the other hand, here the most important parts, the muscles, are found attached from outside and from this point of view we can see a polarity, characteristic of human nature. This polarity consists of the nerves and senses, mainly centered in the head—I say mainly, but not exclusively so—and the metabolism, which is localized in the metabolic and limb system.

Despite this polarity, the human being is of course a unity. At this point we must not be tempted into making schemes, dividing the human being into three parts which we then

90

define as the nerves and senses organization, a second part which will be mentioned shortly and finally the metabolic and limb organization, as if these parts ever could exist separately. It is not like that at all. Metabolic activities as well as muscular activities are constantly going on in the head and yet we can say that the head is the center of the nerves-and-senses organization. Conversely the digestive-limb system is also permeated by forces emanating from the head, but nevertheless we can call it the seat of the metabolic-limb system.

Midway between these two regions we find what one can call the rhythmic system of man which is located in the chest. Here the most fundamental rhythms take place, namely those of breathing and blood circulation. Each follows its own speed: The breathing rhythm, visible in a person's breathing, is slower and that of the blood circulation, which can be felt as the pulse beat, is quicker. This rhythmic organization acts as mediator between the other two poles. It would be tempting to go into further detail, but as we have come together to study the principles and methods of Waldorf Education, I must refrain from doing so. However, if you can look upon the chest organization from the point of view just indicated, you will find in every single one of its parts, be it in the formation of the skeleton or in that of the inner organs, a transition between the head organization and the metabolic and limb system. Such is the picture which emerges if we observe the human being according to his own inner configuration instead of accepting foggy notions about a human unity. But this is not all, for we are also led to an understanding of the various functions taking place in the human being, and here I wish to give you an example. One could quote countless examples, but this one must suffice in order to show how important it is for a real educator to follow the directions here indicated.

Let us imagine that a person suffers from sudden outbursts of temper. Such eruptions may already occur in childhood and then a good teacher must find ways of dealing with them. Anyone following the usual methods of physiology and anatomy might include in his considerations also the psychological effects in such a person. Furthermore he may take into account that when someone is in a state of extreme anger, there is an excess of gall secretion. However, these two aspects, the physical and psychological aspects, are not generally seen as the two sides of the same phenomenon. The soul and spiritual aspect of anger and the physical one of an over-active secretion of bile are not looked upon as a unity. In the case of a normal person the bile is of course a necessary ingredient of the nutritive process. In an angry person this gall activity reaches an imbalance and, if left to himself, such a person will finally suffer from jaundice, as you all know.

If we consider both the soul-spiritual and the physical aspects, we can see how a tendency towards a certain illness may develop, but this alone is not yet enough to judge human nature. For while in the metabolism bile is secreted, in the head organization an accompanying but polar opposite process is taking place. Unless we realize that while bile is secreted, at the same time an opposite process is also taking place in the head organization, we are not observing human nature fully. For in the head a milk-like sap, produced in the remaining parts of the body, is being absorbed. If in an abnormal case too much bile is secreted into the metabolism, the head organization will try to fill itself with too much of this milk-like liquid with the result that when the temper has cooled down, the person concerned feels as if his head were bursting. And while an excess of bile secretion will cause the milky sap to flow into the head, the face of such a person may turn quite blue, once the temper has cooled down.—If we study not only the outer forms of bones and organs, but also the organic processes involved, we certainly can find a polarity between the nerves and senses organization centered in the head and the limb and metabolic system. Between these two lives the rhythmic system with its lung and heart activities, which always regulate and mediate between the two outer poles.

If we keep our images mobile, avoiding a too simplistic approach which pictures the various organs always at rest— possibly in order to make accurate and sharply outlined illustrations of them—we cannot help being captivated by the multifarious relationships and the constant interplay which is taking place within these three members of the human being. If we look at the rhythmical activity of breathing, we can see how in in-breathing the thrust of inhalation is led to the cerebrospinal fluid. While receiving these breathing rhythms, this fluid passes on the vibrations right up to the brain fluid which fills the various cavities of the brain. This "lapping" against the brain, caused by rhythmic breathing, stimulates the human being to become active in his nerves and senses organization. There is a constant passing on of the rhythms resulting from the process of breathing via the vertebral canal into the brain fluid. Thus the stimuli activated by the breathing constantly strive towards the head region.

If we look in a downward direction, we see how rhythmical breathing in a certain way becomes more pointed, more "excited" in the rhythmical beating of the pulse and how the blood circulation affects the metabolism with each outgoing breath, that is, while the brain and cerebrospinal fluid pushes downward. If we look at the process of breathing and blood circulation with living and artistically sensitive insight, we can follow the effects of the pulsing blood both upon the nerves and senses organization and the metabolic-limb system. We see how on the one side the processes of breathing and blood circulation reach up into the brain, that is, into the head region, and on the other, into the diametrically opposite direction, into the metabolic-limb system. If in this way we gradually attain a living picture of man, we can really make progress in our investigations. We can form conceptions which are in full accord with the nature of man's middle system. Such conceptions may not be simple enough to be made into diagrams, but schemes and diagrams in any case are always problematic when it comes to an understanding of the ever-weaving and flowing elements of human nature.

When, in the early days of our anthroposophical endeavors, we were still moving among theosophical circles—permit me to mention this here—we were faced time and time again with all kinds of diagrams, generously equipped with all kinds of data. Everything seemed to fit into elaborate yet neat schematic ladders, high enough for anyone to climb into the highest regions of existence! Some members seemed to look upon such diagrammatic ladders as a kind of spiritual gym-equipment, with the aid of which they hoped to reach olympic heights. Everything was neatly enclosed in boxes. Such things made one's limbs twitch convulsively. They were hardly bearable for anyone who knows that in order to get hold of the ever-mobile nature of the human being supersensibly, one must keep one's ideation flexible and alive. These fixed habits of thinking made one wish to run away. Well, what matters is that in one's quest of real knowledge of man, one must always keep one's thinking and ideation mobile. And then one can advance yet another step.

If now one tries to build up mental images of how this rhythm between breathing and blood circulation becomes modified and metamorphosed in the upper regions, one is led to the following conception which I shall sketch on the blackboard—not as a fixed scheme but merely as an indication. (See reproduction of blackboard drawing)

94

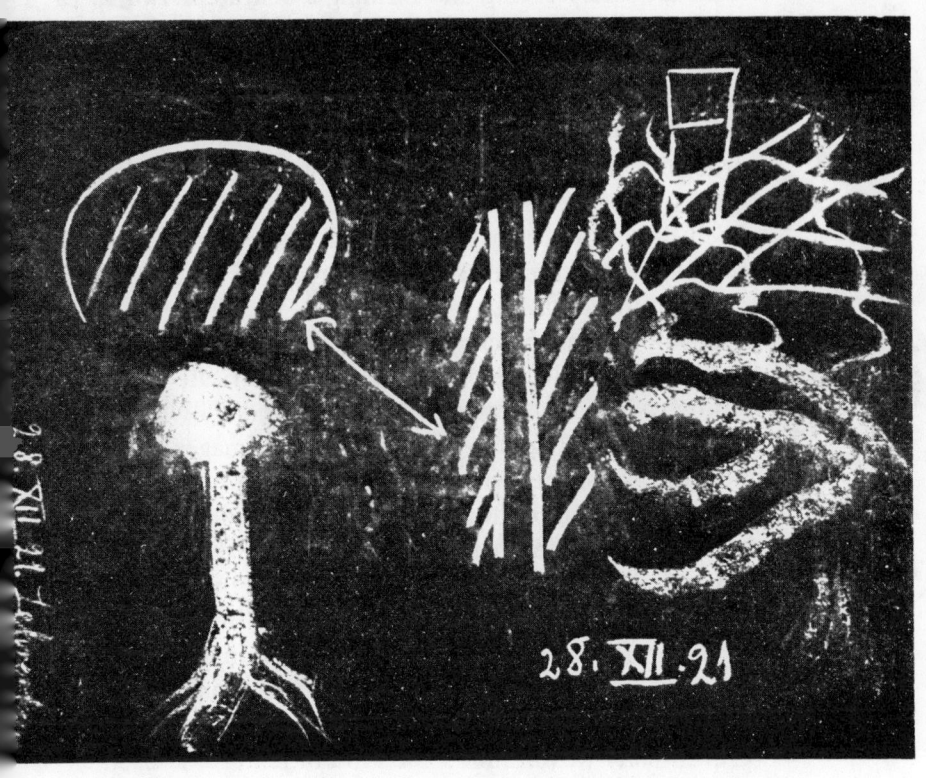

Let this thick line represent the mental image of some kind of rope, which is to help us to picture, in quite a rough-and-ready manner, the processes going on in our breathing and blood circulation. This is one way—so one could say—of getting hold of what exists beyond the material blood in the much finer and imponderable substance of the etheric nerves. If now, using one's mental imagery, one goes further by turning one's gaze from the chest organization upwards, one feels inwardly compelled to "fray out," as it were, one's images, to transform them into fine threads

95

which are interweaving and forming a delicate network. In this way one will succeed in grasping with one's mental imagery, now turned in an upward direction and modified, something which is actually happening outwardly and materially. One finds that one simply has to fray out these thick cords into threads. Imagining this process, one gradually comes to the experience of the white, fibrous brain substance which lies under the grey matter. In one's mental imagery one becomes as mobile as the very processes which are pervading human nature.

If you look at the creation of man with the reverence it deserves, you will not over-simplify his intricate organization by calling it a nature-given unity. And if—when looking at his chest region—you form mental images of coarse and rope-like shapes which become more refined as you approach the region of the head until they fray out into simple threads, you begin to reach actual, material reality. You find your imagination outwardly confirmed by the physical nerve fibers and by the way in which they interweave.

Directing your image-making activity in the opposite direction downwards, you will find it quite impossible to split up or fray out your mental images into fine threads to be eventually woven into some kind of texture, as seen externally in the nervous system. Such threads simply vanish away. You lose all trace of them. Otherwise you would be led astray into forming images which no longer corresponded to exernal reality. For if you follow the way the brain continues downward into the spinal cord through the twelve dorsal vertebrae, through the lumbar and sacral vertebrae, and so on, you find that the nerve substance, which now is white on the outside and grey inside, gradually dissolves away towards the region of the metabolism. Somehow it becomes impossible to imagine the nerves continuing downward. We cannot achieve a true and comprehensive picture of man unless our images are capable of undergoing transformations.

We must keep our imagery mobile. If we look in an upward direction, our mental pictures will be different from those we find when looking downward. It is possible to recreate in one's imagery, the mobility characteristic of human nature. This is the beginning of an artistic activity which eventually will lead the investigator to what he finds outwardly in physical man. In this way one avoids the schism resulting from first looking at the material world outside and then forming abstract conceptions about it. Instead, one really dives down into human nature. One's conceptions become alive and they remain in harmony with what actually exists in the human being. There is no other way of gaining insight into man's true being, which is an essential prerequisite in the art of education. In order to know man, one has to become inwardly mobile and then one will rightly discover how these three members of the human organization work together in order to bring about a healthy equilibrium. One will learn to recognize how a disturbance of this equilibrium leads to all kinds of illnesses. One will be able to discriminate in a living way between what leads towards health or illness in human life.

This becomes specially important when one includes the entire span of human life in one's considerations, because these three members of the human organization are related together in different ways during the various stages of life. During childhood the soul and spiritual element works into the physical organization in a totally different way from what is happening during the older stages. It is essential to pay due attention to these subtle changes. However, if one is willing to develop the kind of mental imagery indicated above, one will gradually learn to broaden and deepen one's previous conception.

I seem to have offended many readers of my book *The Spiritual Guidance of Man and Mankind*, when I drew attention to the fact that in the child there lives a kind of wisdom which the adult no longer possesses. I certainly do not wish to belittle the wisdom and the abilities of the adult. But just imagine what would happen if—at the early stage when the brain and the other organs are still relatively unformed —it would depend on our personal wisdom only, to permeate and to shape the entire organization. I am afraid we should fare rather badly! Certainly, the child molds its brain and all the other organs entirely unconsciously, but great wisdom is at work there nonetheless. If you consider the entire course of human life, as described in the previous lectures, you will be able to recognize this wisdom, particularly so, if you have a sense for what children's dreams can tell you. Adults tend to dismiss such dreams as childish nonsense. But if you can experience their underlying reality, these dreams—so different from adult dreams—are actually most interesting. Of course the child is not able to express itself clearly when speaking about its dreams, but there are ways of finding out what it wants to tell us. And then we shall find that in its dreams, through images of spirit beings, the child dimly experiences the sublime powers of wisdom with the help of which it molds its brain and other physical organs. If we approach the child's dreams with reverence which is in tune with its own experiences, we will recognize in them an all-pervading cosmic wisdom at work. From this point of view—forgive this somewhat harsh statement—the child is much wiser, much cleverer than the adult. And when the teacher enters the classroom, he should really be aware of this abundance of wisdom in the child. He himself has already outgrown it and what he has gained instead, the knowledge of his own experience, is not in the least comparable with it.

Adult dreams no longer have the same quality. The adult carries his everyday life into them. I have already spoken about this from a different point of view. When an adult dreams, he carries his day wisdom into his night life, where it reacts upon him in turn. But when a child dreams, a sublime wisdom streams through it. Though quite unconscious of what is happening, the child nevertheless retains a dim awareness upon waking up. And when, during the day, it sits at its school desk, it still has an indistinct feeling of this cosmic wisdom. But it cannot find it in the teacher. The teacher, on the other hand feels superior to the child in matters of knowledge and wisdom. This is only natural, for otherwise he could not teach. He is conscious of his own wisdom and from this point of view, he is certainly superior. But his kind of wisdom is not as all-comprising and sublime as that of the child.

If one were to put into words what is happening when the young child, pervaded by wisdom, meets the teacher who has lost this primordial wisdom, the following picture would emerge: abstract knowledge, typical of our times, with which the teacher has been closely linked for so many years of his life, tends to turn him into rather a dry and pedantic adult. In some cases already his demeanor and outer appearance reveal these traits. The child, on the other hand, has retained the freshness and sprightliness which spring from spiritual wisdom.

When now the teacher enters his classroom, the child is made to control its high spirits. The teacher feels that he is intelligent and that his pupils are stupid. But in the subconscious realms of both teacher and pupils quite a different picture emerges. And if dreams were allowed to speak as well, the picture again would be quite different. Somewhere in their subconscious the children feel: How stupid the teacher is! And in his subconscious realm the teacher feels: How wise the children are! All this is part of the classroom atmosphere. It belongs to the imponderables which play a most important part in education. Because of this situation, the child cannot help confronting the teacher with a certain kind of arrogance, however slight, of which it remains completely unconscious. Its innate attitude towards the teacher is one of amusement, for it cannot help feeling how little of the flow of wisdom pervading its own body has survived in the teacher. Instinctively it contrasts its own wisdom with that of the teacher, as he enters the classroom somewhat stiff and pedantic, his expression grown morose from having lived long with abstract intellectual concepts, his coat so heavy with the dust of libraries that it defies the clothes' brush. The uppermost feeling of the child at this sorry sight is one of mild amusement.

This is how the teacher is seen with the eyes of the child, however unconscious the child may be. And we cannot help seeing a certain justification in its attitude. After all, such a reaction is a form of self-protection, preserving the child's state of health. A dream about its teachers would hardly be an elevating experience for the young pupil who is still able to dream of the powers of wisdom which permeate its whole being.

In the subconscious regions of the teacher, an opposite kind of feeling develops which is also very real and which, too, belongs to the imponderables of the classroom. In the case of the child we can speak of a dim awareness, but in the teacher, there lurks a subconscious desire. Though he will never admit this consciously, a yearning is rising up within him, a longing for the vitalizing forces of wisdom with which the child is blessed. If those who psycho-analyze human souls were more aware of spiritual realities than is usually the case, they would soon discover what an important part these vitalizing and fresh growing forces in the child, as well as the other human forces, are playing in the teacher's subsconscious life.

These are some of the imponderables pervading the classroom. And if one is able to look a little behind the scenes, one finds that the child turns away from the teacher because of a certain disenchantment. It dimly feels the unspoken question: what has become of all that streams and flows through me in this grown-up who is my teacher? In the teacher, on the other hand, subconscious longings begin to stir. Like a vampire he wants to prey upon the young souls in his charge. If one were to look a little closer, one would detect how strongly in many cases this vampire-like urge works underneath an outwardly orderly appearance. Herein lies the origin of various tendencies towards ill-health in young children. One only needs to look with open eyes at the psychological disposition of some teachers to recognize how such tendencies can result from daily life in the classroom.

As teachers, we cannot overcome these harmful influences, unless we are sustained by a knowledge of man which is imbued with love for humanity—a knowledge of man both mobile and alive, and in harmony with the human organism as I have described it. Only genuine love of man can overcome and balance the various forces in human nature which have become one-sided. Such knowledge of man also enables us to recognize not only how human nature expresses itself differently in different individuals, but also how it undergoes characteristic changes in childhood, maturity and old age. For the three members of the human being have a completely different working relationship during the three main ages of life, and each member has to adapt itself accordingly.

This needs to be borne in mind especially when the timetable is made. Obviously we must cater to the whole being of the child, to its head as well as to its limbs, and we must make allowances for the fact that in each of the three members processes springing from the other two are also going on all the time. For example, metabolic processes are continually happening also in the head.

If now the children have to sit still at their desks to do some head work—more of this later on, as also about the hygienic aspect of classroom desks—if their activities do not flow into their limbs and metabolism, we place them into a one-sided situation. This we must balance by allowing the head to relax later on, rightly so afterwards, by allowing them to enjoy moving about in gym lessons.

If one is conscious of the polar nature of the processes taking place in the head and in the limbs and metabolism, one will appreciate the importance of providing the right kind of change in the timetable. But if now, after a boisterous gym lesson, we take the pupils back into the classroom to continue our lessons, what do we do then?

You must realize that while a person is engaged in limb activities which stimulate the metabolism, any thoughts that may have been artificially implanted in the head during previous years no longer remain there. When the child jumps and runs about, when it is active in limbs and metabolism, any thoughts previously planted in the head simply fly away. But those forces which become manifest only in the child's dreams, the forces of supersensible wisdom, now enter the head region, claiming their rights. Well, if after a movement lesson we take the children back again to the classroom in order to replace these forces by something else which must appear inferior to their subconscious minds, a mood of resentment will make itself felt in the class. For during the previous lesson not only sense-perceptible but, above all, supersensible forces have been working upon the child. Pupils may not show unwillingness outwardly, but an inner resentment is certainly there. By resuming ordinary lessons after a movement lesson, we go against the child's nature and, by doing so, we implant potential seeds of illness in the child.

This is a fact which—so a physiologist assured me—has been known for a considerable time. Here I have given you an explanation from the anthroposophical point of view in order to show you how much lies in the teacher's hands to foster health in children, provided he has gained the right knowledge of man. Naturally, if we go about it in the wrong way, we will actually implant all kinds of illnesses in the child, and of this we must always be fully aware. As you may have noticed by now, I do not glorify in the usual kind of worldly wisdom, so often highly prized in our days. That kind of wisdom would hardly suffice to shape and mold the inner organs of the young for their years to come. Had we not become stiff in in our entire organization by the time we reach a mature age, with the result that all the knowledge we have impressed into our heads through naturalistic and intellectual concepts is thrown back in form of memory pictures, it would eventually stream down into our remaining organism. However absurd this may sound, if what under normal conditions belongs to the sphere of the head, should stream down into limb and metabolic regions, the human being would become ill. For these head forces act like poison when they enter the lower spheres. Brain wisdom indeed becomes a kind of poison as soon as it enters the wrong sphere, at least as soon as it reaches the metabolism. The only way in which we can manage to live with this brain knowledge of ours—and I mean this quite concretely and not in any sense as a moral judgment—is by preventing this poison from entering our metabolic and limb system, for here it would have a devastating effect.

But the child is not protected by this stiffness of the adult. If we impress our kind of knowledge into the child, we let our concepts invade and poison the child's metabolic and limb system. You see how important it is to realize from practical experience how much head knowledge we can expect a child to absorb without exposing it to the dangers of becoming poisoned in its metabolic and limb organization.

And so it lies in the teacher's hands to promote either health or illness in the child. If he insists on making pupils intellectually clever according to present-day standards, if he crams their heads with all kinds of intellectual content, he will actually prevent the unconscious forces of wisdom from permeating the child. Cosmic wisdom, on the other hand, is immediately set in motion when the child runs about, when it makes more or less rhythmical movements. Because of the unique position between head and limb-metabolism, this rhythmic activity brings about bodily union with these cosmic forces of wisdom. *Herbert Spencer* was quite correct when he spoke about the negative effects of a monastic education which aimed at making the young excel in intellectual achievements. For—so he pointed out—in later years these scholars would be unable to make use of their prowess of intellect because during their school days they had been impregnated with the seeds of all kinds of illnesses.

These are matters which cannot be weighed accurately by some special scales. They reveal themselves only to an open attitude of mind and to the kind of mobile thinking which can be developed through an anthroposophical schooling, a thinking which must always remain in touch with practical life.

So much about the importance of the teacher making himself acquainted with the fundamentals governing both health and illness in the human being. And here it must be emphasized once again that in order to avoid becoming entrapped by external criteria and by immobile and fixed concepts, one must learn to recognize the ever-changing processes in human nature which always tend towards either health or illness. These the teacher will meet in his classes and he must learn how to deal with them rightly. Further details will be given when we shall focus our attention on the changing stages of the child, of the growing human being.

LECTURE VII
Dornach, 29th December 1921

Anyone called upon to look after a very young child, either as a parent or in any other child-caring capacity, will experience the great responsibility such a task entails. He or she will feel morally obliged, through the way of looking after the child, to lay the best foundations for its future development. It therefore grieves me deeply that we in our Waldorf School in Stuttgart can accept only children who have already reached the official school age and it would give me the greatest satisfaction if we could also take in children of younger ages.* But apart from other difficulties, our aims at opening a nursery class have been thwarted by a lack of funds—as happened with so many other of our anthroposophical activities. This ever-present shortage of money at least leaves us with the hope that, if we can win the support of the general public, we shall eventually be able to build up a nursery class as an intrinsic part of our Waldorf School.

A very young child is the least accessible of all to us. The gates to its soul life are absolutely closed against the outer world. No outer influence can touch it. Anyone who has charge of an infant of this age, whilst it struggles and cries, is powerless. The child does what it wants. Thus an observant adult will accept the fact that the child's will is beyond

---

*The sixth year was the official school age in 1921. A Kindergarten was opened in the Waldorf School some four years after this lecture was given, i.e., in Easter 1926.

his control, even as far as later stages, and sometimes the latest stages of its future life are concerned.

You may know that early in 1890, well before publishing other anthroposophical literature, I published my book *The Philosophy of Spiritual Activity*. The purpose of this book was to put into the world a true assessment of that part in man which develops the impulse towards freedom of the full human personality, also seen within the social context. If one accepts its content, the problem of freedom on the one side, and that of destiny on the other, becomes relevant already when one is confronted by a babe in arms.

If one listens to what lives in the human heart, one can find that man's true happiness on earth depends on the awareness of his human freedom, on his appreciation of human values and on his feeling for human dignity. Anthroposophy shows us that—apart from what a person may have developed already before birth or conception while still living in the spiritual world, and apart from what he or she will meet again after death—the very purpose of earthly incarnation consists in bringing to life the impulse towards freedom. This impulse is totally dependent on man's plunging into an earthly body. It can be realized only in physical incarnation. We can attain to freedom only while living on earth, and we can take with us into other worlds only the degree of freedom which we have achieved down here on earth.

If one approaches the young child with such feelings—and feelings are the most potent source for those engaged in the art of education—the following question will be ever-present in the mind of a person who has charge of an infant: What must I do to enable this child to develop to the fullest extent the consciousness of human freedom, when it reaches maturity? And with this question another truth begins to dawn, a fact to which outer conditions of life are already clearly pointing and which, through anthroposophical in-

106

sight, can be understood with inner certainty, namely the fact that despite his freedom, each person has a destiny or, to call it by its eastern terminology, his or her "Karma."

Let us imagine that later in life someone meets another person whom he or she has known before, and that this other person exercises a profound influence upon the life of the first individual. Perhaps two such people might even enter into a partnership for life. At first it may appear to them as if their meeting were the result of mere chance. But when looking back over the previous years of their lives— even without any knowledge of anthroposophical spiritual science—the first individuality may well discover the strange fact that during the years prior to this meeting, he or she had unconsciously taken all kinds of steps which, eventually, led to the other person. What at first appeared the result of chance, with hindsight revealed an inherent pattern, an underlying plan. Looking back over his life, *Goethe's* old friend *Knebel* uttered these significant words from the depths of his soul: "If, in later years, one surveys one's previous life, everything seems to fall into a definite pattern. Everything fits together."—Since our will is woven into all our actions, we can see everywhere how destiny confronts us in the happenings of our life. One could quote many other personalities who, through purely outward observation of life, also reached the same conclusion. If we look at life's external happenings, we find confirmation of the hidden truths of Karma.

Anyone in charge of young children—especially those who are working in children's homes—who is aware of the working of destiny, must ask the question: Have I been specially chosen to fulfil the important task of guiding and educating this child, or these children? And then other questions will follow: What must I do to obliterate, as far as possible, my personal self in order to leave those entrusted in my care free from being burdened by my own subjective nature? How must I act so that I do not interfere with the child's destiny? And, above all, how can I best educate the child towards human freedom?

If one learns to understand what is going on in a child between birth and the change of teeth, that is during its first seven-year period of life—I shall speak about the embryonic development later on—one realizes how vulnerable such a child is and how deeply we can affect the being of such a young child.

The change of teeth represents a decisive turning-point in the life of the child. Upon close observation one will find that after the seventh year an entirely new interrelationship will emerge between the child's thinking, feeling and willing.

We have grown accustomed to apply certain concepts, gained from the observation of material processes, also to the life of man. For instance, if—when watching natural processes—we notice a sudden emergence of heat which had not been perceptible in a previous state and which had not been outwardly introduced, we speak of latent heat being set free. Just as latent heat can be set free by material processes, so soul and spirit forces are set free after the change of teeth, forces which hitherto have been bound up with the organism because they were instrumental to its growth. Freed from processes of growth and nourishment, these forces can now work in the child's soul sphere. They have become transmuted into soul forces.

Natural science today forms abstract conceptions about the relationship of body and soul and vice versa. Theories are made regarding the effects of one upon the other. One speaks of a psycho-physical parallelism, and so on. Instead of making exact observations, one philosophizes. But all this will lead us nowhere. If one wishes to fathom the secrets of human nature, one has to observe it with the same exactitude with which the phenomena of outer nature have been observed. And then one will discover that after approximately the seventh year forces, previously engaged in the building up of the child's physical organism, are being transformed into soul forces which then determine the child's relationship with the outer world.

If we wish to find out what the soul of a child is like between birth and the seventh year, we have to observe the child's development from the seventh year onward. For then, in the child's soul, we are able to observe the very same forces which previously were active in its physical organization. And we shall find that their hidden organic activity of molding and shaping the child's brain as well as its remaining organization is of a very special significance. For, through birth or conception, the child carries down into its physical organization what it has brought with it from the worlds of soul and spirit.

When the child is thus fully engaged in building up its physical organs, it must be left free to do so and consequently, the doors leading to the outer world remain closed. It is essential that we refrain from interfering in our clumsy ways with these inner activities of the child, for it is doing what it has to do, with the effect that it is not accessible to external will forces.

On the other hand we must also realize that despite the child's preoccupation with its own processes of growing, everything we do in its vicinity nevertheless makes a deep and incisive impression upon it. I shall go into further detail later, but we must never forget that what will work in the realm of the child's soul after the seventh year is directly involved in the organ-building processes before that age. This means that up to the seventh year any impressions coming from the outer world will directly affect its physical constitution—the lungs, stomach, liver and all kinds of other organs. Just because at this age the child's soul has not yet become emancipated from its physical organization—where it is still actively engaged—all impressions which come from us

109

through our conduct and general behavior will have a decisive effect upon its future constitution of health or illness.

You have come here with the expectation of learning something about our principles of education. But it is the practical application of these principles which is all-important. What really matters in education is the mood and attitude of soul, which the teacher carries in his heart with regard to the being of man. Only if we approach the growing human being with true insight shall we be good servants of the art of education. One could even go as far as saying: Each teacher is free to approach his subjects in his own individual way, for in any case he will have to prepare the relevant subject-matter according to what he has learned from life. What really matters is that each teacher carries within himself a true picture of man and if this picture stands there before his inner gaze, he or she will act rightly, though outwardly possibly in very different ways.—When, as the spiritual guide of the Waldorf School I visited parallel classes— because of our large numbers we already have parallel classes—and when I witness how each teacher treats the same subject very much in his or her own individual manner, I never object or insist that they all should follow the same set courses. Even if two versions of the same subject may outwardly appear contradictory, each one may nevertheless be right in its own way. In fact, if one teacher were to copy another, the results could be entirely wrong. It is not for nothing that our school is called "Free Waldorf School," not only because of our independence from the state system, but very much because of the atmosphere of freedom which pervades its entire constitution.

During the previous lecture I drew attention to the fact that a supersensible contemplation of man will reveal to us, apart from his physical body, another finer body which we have called the etheric body or the body of formative forces. From this etheric body spring not only all the forces sustain-

110

ing nourishment and growth, but it is also the source of the faculties of remembering and of making mental images, of ideation. It becomes an independent entity only during the change of teeth, at which time it is born in a similar way in which, at physical birth, the body is born from its mother. This means that up to the change of teeth the forces of the etheric body are entirely working in the processes of the child's organic growth, whereas after that time—though still remaining active in this realm to a great extent—they partly withdraw from these activities. These released forces of the ether body now begin to work in the soul realm of mental picturing and memory, as well as in the many other nuances of the child's soul life.

The change of teeth is a unique event. The forces needed to push out the second teeth existed prior to this event, but they are no longer needed afterwards. Once the second teeth have appeared, this particular activity of the etheric body becomes redundant. The final activity of pushing out the second teeth is an outward manifestation of the kind of working that is going on in the child's organism. Now, at the end of the first seven-year period, most of these etheric forces are released to flow into the child's soul and spiritual nature.

One can recognize such seven-year periods throughout the entire course of human life, and each of these periods again falls into three clearly differentiated shorter periods. If we observe the gradual withdrawal of some of these etheric forces until approximately the seventh year, we can see how in the first two-and-a-half years after physical birth the etheric body frees itself from the head region, how in the following two-and-a-half years it frees itself from the chest region and finally, up to the change of teeth, from the child's metabolic and limb system. Thus we can recognize three phases within the gradual withdrawal of etheric forces, and one can clearly recognize how, when the etheric body is still bound up with the head region, the child rejects any intentional influence coming from outside.

What the child learns during this first two-and-a-half year period is of utmost importance for its whole life. It does so, through an inward-bound activity, out of what it has brought with it from its prenatal existence. Only consider how during this first short period the child learns to speak and to walk, the two human faculties closely connected with an individual's maintaining a proper self-confidence, both from a personal and a social point of view. These two important faculties are achieved while the etheric body is still engaged in shaping the brain and while it is still raying out into the remaining organism. If these etheric forces ray out too strongly into the remaining organism so that they disturb the infant's still delicate processes of metabolism, of breathing and blood circulation, if they surge too powerfully within the baby's organism, scarlet fever and kindred children's illnesses may occur already at this young age. Fundamentally speaking, through all that is at work within a child at that stage, the child remains inaccessible to any conscious and will-directed approaches or demands coming from outside. It wants to be left to work on its own organism.

This inaccessibility to the outer world during the first two-and-a-half years is the one significant factor. The other is the fact that the child has a fine, instinctive perception for everything that is happening in its surroundings and especially for what is going on in the persons with whom it has established a certain rapport. Anyone looking after such a child naturally belongs to this category. I am not speaking now of the child's ability to use its senses in the way an older person does. It is not what it can see with its eyes that I am referring to, but to a general perceiving of a most intimate kind, of what is happening in its surroundings. This perceiving, however, excludes anything that seeks to impose

112

itself from outside, against which the child will defend itself instinctively during those first two-and-a-half years.

In order to understand better this susceptibility to the outer world at a time when its sense perceptions are still deeply immersed in feeling, it might help if we look at the creatures immediately below man, namely at the animals, for they display a similar sensitivity towards the outer world to a specially high degree. I am not here contradicting my remarks about senility, made to you in a previous lecture. One simply has to observe accurately. The animal is especially sensitive to its surroundings. I do not know whether those of you who have come from England or from the other European countries have ever heard of the horses which, a few years before the war, created a sensation because they seemed to be able to do simple arithmetical calculations. In Berlin there was the famous horse of *Herr von Osten* and in *Elberfeld* there were several horses which could reckon with numbers. Well, I cannot say anything about the Elberfeld horses, but I did make the acquaintance of Herr von Osten's horse in Berlin and I could observe the close relationship that existed between this horse and its master. It is quite true that the horse stamped with its legs: three threes are nine—which, for a horse, is quite a respectable achievement!.

All kinds of theories were advanced in order to explain the horse's reactions to the questions put to it by Herr von Osten. There was a certain university lecturer—a most erudite man—who even wrote a whole book about this horse. He wrote: "Of course the horse cannot calculate, but whenever Herr von Osten says, ''Three times three,'' he accompanies his words by hardly noticeable facial expressions. He does a kind of miming and when he pronounces the word ''nine,'' the horse which is capable of observing these facial expressions, will stamp accordingly.''—His was indeed a learned treatise! The author continued, ''I myself was not able to detect the miming on Herr von Osten's face and therefore I cannot guarantee that my theory is correct. But it must have been there and the horse was able to observe it.''—To me the author merely states that he, a university lecturer, considered the horse to be more capable of observation than he was himself. In my opinion the crucial point was Herr von Osten's procedure, for he had large pockets filled with sweetmeats which he shoved into the horse's mouth, thus maintaining an uninterrupted flow of sensation and gratification. The result was an intimate relationship between master and horse. All happenings were immersed in a feeling of sympathy, which made the horse, in accordance with its animal nature, extremely receptive to all that came from its master, even to his thoughts and all the shades of his feelings—but hardly to the play of mysterious expressions on his face. The processes of calculation going on in Herr von Osten's mind were transferred to the horse via the taste of sweetness.—This phenomenon does not become any the less interesting if interpreted in this way. It can teach us a great deal about the relationship of living beings. But it cannot be explained hypothetically by the observation of facial expressions which a horse could make, though not a university lecturer.

During the first two-and-a-half years the child, too, has a similar rapport with its mother or with other persons closely connected with it, as long as their attitude and conduct make it possible. And then the child becomes a perfect mimic, a complete imitator. This imposes upon the grown-up the moral duty to be worthy of imitation, which is a far less comfortable task then exerting one's will upon the child. The child will take in everything we do, the way we act or the way we move. It is equally susceptible to all our feelings and thoughts. It imitates us, and if this is not outwardly noticeable, it nevertheless does so by developing tendencies for imitation which, by means of its organ-bound

114

soul forces, it presses down into its physical organism. Therefore education during these first two-and-a-half years should be confined to the self-education of the adult in charge who should think, feel and act in a manner which, when perceived by the child, will cause it no harm. Fundamentally the stage of imitation continues up to the change of teeth and therefore the child will be strongly influenced by its surroundings also in later years, as the following example may show:

Two disconsolate parents once came to me, saying, "Our child has always been a good child, but now it has stolen money." Was this really so? At a superficial glance, yes, for it had taken money out of the cupboard where it was always kept by its mother. The child then had bought sweets with the money and even distributed some among other children. I reassured the parents that their child had not stolen at all, but that it had merely imitated its mother who regularly had taken money out of the cupboard in order to buy things. There never was any intention of stealing, the concept of which was as yet non-existent in the child's mind. But the child is an imitator. It will do what mother does and if one wishes to avoid confusion, it is up to the grownup to realize this fact and to act differently in front of the child.

We must also be careful not to harm the child's development when it is learning to speak. This can easily happen if we make it say words of our own choice which, again, amounts to imposing our will upon the child. It is best for us to speak naturally in front of the child—provided our talking is of a moral order—so that it has the opportunity of hearing us. In this way the child will find its own way into language.

Neither will the child learn to walk through our efforts at making it stand up and do all kinds of movements. Such instruction belongs to the gym lessons of a much later age. If

115

we intervene by making it stand and walk prematurely, we can do irreparable damage to its nerve processes. This damage may persist for the whole of its later life. If the child sees the adults in their upright position, as imitator it will raise itself to the same position when the right time comes. We must always regard the human being during the first stages as an imitating being and arrange our upbringing accordingly. This certainly can be very trying at times. We all know that there are babies who seem to be yelling all day long and who, apart from their ear-splitting noise, inflict all kinds of other provocations upon the adult. True, there are situations which have to be dealt with even quite drastically in order to avoid serious damage being done by the child. But such measures do not really belong to the field of education. Admittedly, it is hard to put up with a screaming child, but if we behave in the way indicated, our conduct will gradually sink into the deeper layers of the child's soul and spiritual forces—which are still closely bound up with organic processes—and will eventually bring about more positive results. If one observes small children without prejudice, one will find that their screaming and other unpleasant features come from the child's physical organization. Though the forces inherent in intense crying will remain with the child, the habit of crying will gradually pass. These forces certainly are of a great intensity. If we influence the child rightly by setting the right example and by acting morally, the forces underlying the baby's crying will reveal themselves as intensely moral forces in later life. A strong morality in adult life is the expression of the same forces which lived in intense crying during early childhood. On the other hand, if the persons close to the child have an immoral attitude, be it only in thoughts, these same forces will reappear later as intensely immoral forces.

You will now be able to appreciate the real point of what has been said so far, namely that one must not be tempted by a false kind of instinct—it is not even an instinct but something we may have brought with us through misguided customs—to make baby talk for the child's benefit. Nurses or others dealing with young children, should never speak to them in an artificial or childish manner. We really do a great wrong if we change our normal way of speaking to "suit" the child, for the child always wants to imitate us as we really are, and not as we pretend to be. It rejects anything that comes towards it as an expression of another person's will, such as childish and naive baby talk. The child has to put up with it, but it has a deep inner resentment towards such an approach. The aftereffects of this often well-meant folly may be so far-reaching as to come to light in later years as a weakened digestion. What is diagnosed in an older patient as symptoms of a weak digestion may well be nothing else but the result of the wrong approach of an over-zealous but misguided nurse during the patient's early childhood.

These are the main points regarding the first third of the first seven-year period, which need to be borne in mind.

At the age of two-and-a-half, the child's head organization is developed far enough for those forces of the ether body which have been working on it, to become released. This gradual withdrawal continues into the chest region up to about the fifth year, when breathing and blood circulation also have reached a certain stage of completion, so that by the time the child has learned to speak and to walk, the formative forces released from the head—acting now as soul and spiritual forces—join those which are being released in the chest region. This change can be recognized outwardly by the emergence of an exceptionally vivid memory which the child develops between two-and-a-half and five, as also by its wonderful imagination. However, great care must be taken when the child develops these two faculties, which are instrumental to the upbuilding of its soul. The child continues to live by imitation and therefore we should not attempt to make it remember anything of our own choice. At this stage it is best to leave the evolving forces of memory alone, allowing the child to remember whatever it pleases. On no account should one give it memory exercises of any kind. Otherwise in one's ignorance one might be responsible for consequences which can be observed if one looks upon the entire course of human life.

Sometimes one meets people who, around the age of forty or even later, complain of shooting pains, of rheumatism. This ailment certainly can have many different causes, but if research is carried far enough, it may reveal that the rheumatism is due to premature overloading of the memory during early childhood. The pattern of life indeed is very complex and only by trying to recognize its many hidden links can we engender the love which is the true basis of the growing human being.

Whatever one's attitude may be, as educators we must respond to the child's imagination or fantasy which seeks to express itself outwardly through its playing with toys, or in games with other children. This urge to play, between the age of two-and-a-half and five, is really nothing but the externalized activity of the child's powers of fantasy. And if one has the necessary ability of observation for such matters, one can foretell a great deal regarding the child's future soul life, its character, and so on, merely by watching it at play. The way in which such a young child plays is a clear indication of its potential gifts and faculties in later life. What is of utmost importance now, is that one meets this inborn urge to play with the right toys. People in past times have responded to this according to their own particular understanding.

I do not know whether this also happened in the West, but at one time a regular epidemic spread throughout Middle-Europe of giving children boxes of building bricks, especially at Christmastime. Out of separate cubic and quadrilateral stones the children were meant to build miniature architectural monstrosities. This kind of thing has a far-reaching effect upon the development of the child's imagination, for it begets an atomistic-materialistic attitude, a mentality which always wants to put bits and pieces together to form a whole. If one wants to come to terms with practical life, it is far better to allow full play to the child's ever mobile and living imaginative powers than to foster intellectual capacities which encourage the atomistic nature of present-day thinking. The child's imagination represents the very forces which have just freed themselves from performing similar creative work within the physical formation of its brain. It is for this reason that one must avoid, as far as this is possible, forcing these powers of imagination into rigid and finished forms.

Let us imagine two nurses who are looking after a child between two-and-a-half and five years old. One of them—she may be very fond of the little girl in her charge—gives it a "beautiful" doll, a doll that has not only painted cheeks and real hair, but even eyes that close and a moveable head. I believe there are dolls that can even speak! Well, she gives such a doll to the little girl, but as it is finished in every detail, there is nothing left for the child's imagination to create. Its yearning for creative mobility cannot be satisfied. It is as if its forces of imagination were put into a straitjacket. —The other nurse, who has a little more understanding for the inner needs of the child, takes an old piece of cloth which is of no use for anything else. She winds a thread around its upper end until something resembling a head appears. She may even ask the little girl to paint two black dots on the face, perhaps even more, for eyes, nose and mouth. Because now the child's imagination is stimulated, because it can be creative instead of having to put up with fixed and finished forms and contours, the child experiences

119

a far more lively and intimate response than with the so-called "beautiful" doll. Toys, as far as this is possible, should leave the child's power of fantasy free. And since intellect is not the same as fantasy or imagination, the activity of putting together many parts is hardly in harmony with the type of fantasy which is characteristic of a child of this age.

Anything that calls forth an inner feeling of liveliness and mobility is always most suitable for the young child. For example, a children's book with cut-out and tastefully colored figures which can be moved by pulling strings attached below, so that they will do all kinds of things, such as embracing or thrashing each other, always stimulates the child to invent whole stories and in this way is an extraordinarily wholesome means of play activity. In a similar way games with other children should not be too formal, but they should leave plenty of scope for the child's imagination.

All these suggestions spring from a knowledge of man which is founded upon reality and which enables the educator to acquire the necessary insights, especially as regards the practical side of life.

When the child approaches the fifth year, the forces of the etheric body which hitherto have been building up the breathing and the blood circulation, now become available for other activities. And likewise, up to the change of teeth etheric forces will struggle free which, after completing their task within the metabolic and limb system have now become redundant. At that time new spiritual and soul forces are gradually awakening which will emerge fully only after the seventh year and which we shall study in more detail later on. However, they already shine with a dawning light into this last and third period which concludes the first seven-year period of human life.

When etheric forces from the chest region reappear as soul and spiritual forces, the child is becoming amenable to exhortations, to what belongs to a sense of authority. Previously, unable to understand what it ought or ought not to do, it could only imitate, but now, little by little, it begins to listen to and to believe in what its elders say. Only towards the fifth year is it possible to awaken in a child the sense of what is right or wrong. We will educate the child rightly only if we realize that during the first seven-year period—that is up to the change of teeth—the child lives by imitation, and that only gradually will it develop imagination and memory as well as a first belief in what grownups say. This faith in the adult induces a feeling of authority, especially for the teacher with whom it has a very close relationship. However, at this stage, the child is still too young for any kind of formal education. It pains me to know that already the sixth year has been fixed as the official school age. Children ought not to enter school proper before their seventh year. I was therefore always glad to hear—and I don't mind if you consider this attitude quite uncivilized—that children of some anthroposophists had no knowledge of writing and reading even at the age of eight. What can be accomplished with forces available only at a later time, should never be crammed into an earlier stage, unless one is prepared to ruin the physical organism.

In the next few days I will show you how we try to treat our children without inflicting any harm upon them when they have entered the Waldorf School. Tomorrow I will make a beginning by introducing you to the Waldorf School, of course only by word of mouth.

LECTURE VIII

Dornach, 30th December, 1921

Looking back over the past meetings of this conference, I feel it necessary to digress a little from our planned program in order to tell you something about the practical aspects of Waldorf Education. From all you have heard so far, you will have gathered that the key to this education, both with regard to its curriculum and the methods employed, lies in the understanding of man's physical, soul and spiritual constitution, as it develops throughout the course of life. In order to follow this principle, a new look at schooling in general was necessary, with the result that in many ways the Waldorf School is run very differently from traditional schools.

The first point we had to consider was how to make the best use of the available teaching time, especially with regard to the development of the pupil's soul life. The usual practice today is to split up the available time into many separate lessons, but this method does not allow for sufficient depth and concentration of the various subjects. Let me give you an example: Imagine that you wish to bring something to your pupils which is to be of lasting value for them, something which they can take into later life. I will choose my example from a subject which is taught in practically every school, namely from history. Imagine that you wish to introduce to your pupils the time of Queen Elizabeth I, including all the main events and personalities that are usually taught to children. This could be done by the teacher talking about the relevant facts of this historical period during the history lessons which might take, let us say, half a year.

But one can also proceed in a different manner. After a methodical preparation at home, the teacher can cultivate in himself a fine feeling for the salient facts, which then become a kind of framework for this period. These the teacher allows to work upon his soul, in this way remembering them without much difficulty. All other additional material will then fall into place more or less naturally. If one has mastered the subject matter in this way, it is quite possible—and this is no exaggeration—to bring to one's pupils in only three to four lessons what otherwise might well take half a year, and this even in greater depth, so that the pupils retain a lasting impression of the subject.

If you survey in detail all that children are supposed to learn at school at the present time, you will agree with the method indicated just now. For what, in our present state of civilization, our children are supposed to have learned already at the age of fourteen, is such an accumulation of material, that it is simply beyond their capacity to absorb it all. No school really succeeds in imparting so much learning, but this fact is generally ignored. One merely pretends that the present system is working and the curricula are set accordingly.

The aims of Waldorf Education are to arrange the entire teaching in such a way that within the shortest time the maximum amount of content can be given to the pupils with the simplest means possible. This helps the children to retain an overall view of their subjects, not so much intellectually, but very much with regard to their feeling life.

It is obvious that such a method makes great demands upon the teacher. I feel convinced that if a teacher applies this method—which I should like to call a teaching based on "soul-economy"—he or she will have to spend at least two or three hours of concentrated preparation in order to teach for about half an hour. And this he must be willing to do if he wishes to avoid inflicting harm upon his pupils. Such preparation may not always be practically possible, but if the teacher wishes to succeed in carrying into the classroom a comprehensive and living presentation of the subject, this kind of private preparation is of fundamental importance. It certainly makes great demands upon the teacher, but such obligations are intrinsic features of his calling which have to be accepted with the best possible response.

In order to put into practice such a fundamental educational principle, it was necessary to create a suitable curriculum and timetable, when the Waldorf School was founded. Today I should like to give you an outline of this curriculum and of its application without, however, having to go into details, for this will be our task during the coming days.

And so the teacher, having duly prepared himself in the way just indicated, enters the school building in the morning. The pupils arrive at school a little earlier in summertime, i.e, at eight o'clock, and a little later during the winter. When they are assembled in their classrooms, the teacher brings them together by speaking a morning verse in chorus with the whole class. This verse, which could also be sung and which embraces both a general human as well as a religious element, unites the pupils in a mood of prayer. It can be followed by a genuine prayer. In our "Free Waldorf School" such details are entirely left to the discretion of each individual teacher.

Then begins our so-called main lesson, occupying nearly two hours which, in the traditional timetables, are so often cut up into smaller sections. But the principle of "soul-economy" in teaching makes it necessary to change the conventional structure of the timetable. This means that during the first two hours of the morning our pupils are taught the same subject in block periods, each lasting from four to six weeks. It is left to the class teacher to introduce a short break during the main lesson, which would be essential in the younger classes. In this way, subjects like geography or

124

arithmetic are taught for four to six weeks at a time. Thereafter another main lesson subject is studied, again for a block period, and not in shorter lessons to be given at regular intervals through the year.

In this way the various main lesson subjects are introduced to the pupils according to principles agreed by us, principles which include a carefully planned economy of the child's soul life. At all costs must we avoid too much stress upon the child's mind and soul. It should never feel that lessons are too difficult. On the contrary, there should always be a longing in the child to move on from one step to the next. Never should the pupil experience an arbitrary breakoff in a subject, but one thing should always lead to another. During the four to six weeks of a main lesson block period, the class teacher will always endeavor to present the content as a complete chapter, as an artistic whole, which the child can take into later life.

It goes without saying that towards the end of the school year, before the approaching summer holidays, all the main lesson subjects taught during the year should be woven together into a short but artistic recapitulation.

Just as we provide children with clothing wide enough to allow for their limbs to grow freely, so should we as teachers respond to their inner needs by giving them content not only suited to their present stage, but also capable of further expansion. If we give the child concepts which are fixed and finished, we do not allow for this inner growth and maturing. Therefore all concepts which we introduce, all feelings which we invoke and all will impulses which we give, must be treated with the same care and foresight with which we clothe our children's limbs. We must not expect them to remember abstract definitions for the rest of their lives. Just as, at the age of forty-five, our little finger will not be the same as it was when we were eight, so concepts introduced at the age of eight should not remain unchanged when the pupils reach the age of forty-five. We must approach the child's organization in such a way that its various members are capable of growing and expanding. We must not "clothe" our content in such fixed and stiff forms that when a pupil reaches the age of forty-five, he will remember it exactly as it was given to him in his eighth or ninth year. This, however, is only possible if we present our subject matter with what I called soul economy. During the remaining hours of the morning, non-main lessons subjects are taught and here modern foreign languages play the most important part. Foreign languages are introduced already in class one, when the children enter the Waldorf School in their sixth and seventh year, and they are presented in such a way that the child really can live itself into them. This means that while teaching the foreign language, the teacher will try to avoid using the child's mother tongue.

The teacher of foreign languages naturally has to take into account that his pupils are older now than they were when they learned their own mother tongue, and he will arrange his lessons accordingly. This is essential if he aims to be in harmony with the pupil's particular age and development. The children should be able to live themselves into the language in such a way that they will not inwardly translate from their mother tongue into the foreign language every time they wish to say something. This continual jumping from one language into the other is to be avoided at all costs. If, for example, the teacher wants to introduce a particular word, such as "table" or "window," he will not mention the parallel word in the mother tongue at all, but will point at the object in question while calling it out with a clear pronunciation. In this way the child will learn the new tongue directly and well before learning to translate, if this latter activity should be considered desirable at all. We have certainly found that by avoiding, in the early stages, the usual grammar teaching with all that it entails, the children

126

find their way into a new language quite naturally and in a living way. More details will be given later on, when we shall speak about the different ages. So far I only wished to give you a general picture of the practical arrangements in the Waldorf School.

Another subject of paramount importance at this stage is handwork, which includes several crafts. As the Waldorf School is a coeducational school, both boys and girls share these lessons and it is indeed a heartwarming sight to see the young lads and girls sitting together busily knitting, crocheting and engaged in other similar activities. Experience has shown that, although boys have a different relationship to knitting from girls, they do enjoy it and they benefit from such an activity. Their working together has certainly proved advantageous to the general development of all the pupils. In other craft lessons, involving heavier physical work, girls also take part fully. In this way the development of manual skills is nurtured and practiced in our school.

A further subject taught during the morning sessions is one which could be called "World Outlook." You must realize that the Waldorf School or any other school which might spring from the anthroposophical movement, would never wish to teach its pupils Anthroposophy in the form in which it exists today. This I should consider the very worst thing one could do. For Anthroposophy in its present form is a subject for grownups and, as one can see by the color of their hair, often for quite mature adults! Consequently it is presented through its literature or by word of mouth in a form appropriate only to the adult. I should consider any passing on to pupils of content taken from my *Theosophy* or from my book *Knowledge of the Higher Worlds and Its Attainment* as the very worst misuse possible. Such a thing simply must not happen. For if we were to teach content which is totally unsuitable for school-agers, we should—forgive this somewhat trivial expression used in the German language—

we should make the young folk want "to jump out of their skin."* Naturally, in class lessons they would have to submit themselves to what the teacher brought, but inwardly they nevertheless would experience such an urge. Anthroposophy itself is not to be taught in a Waldorf School. What matters is that its teaching should not become mere theoretical knowledge, or a world outlook based on certain ideas, but it should become a way of life, involving the entire human being. If therefore a teacher who is an anthroposophist enters school, he must have so worked upon himself that he has become a many-sided and skilful person, someone who has developed the art of education. And it is this latter achievement which is important, but never a wish to bring anthroposophical content to pupils.

Waldorf Education is meant to be pragmatic. The Waldorf School is meant to be a place where anthroposophical knowledge can find practical application. And if one has made such a world outlook—so linked to practical life—one's own, one will not turn into a theorizer who is alienated from life, but into a skilled, capable person. By this I do not mean to assert that all members of the anthroposophical movement have actually reached these aims. Far from it! I happen to know that there are still some men among our members who are not even capable of sewing on a trouser button which may have dropped off. And no one suffering from such a shortcoming could be considered a full human being. Above all, there are still members who do not fully accept the contention that one cannot be a real philosopher unless one is able to put one's hand to anything—such as mending one's shoes—should the need arise. This may sound a little exaggerated, but I hope that you know what I am trying to say.

---

*This German saying is often used when a person cannot bear an annoyance any longer.

Whoever has to deal with theoretical work ought to stand in practical life even more firmly than people who happen to be tailors, cobblers or engineers. In my opinion, any passing on of theoretical knowledge is acceptable only if the person concerned is also well versed in all practical matters of life, for otherwise his ideas will remain alienated from life. By acting out of anthroposophical knowledge in the classroom, the teachers, as artists, should develop the ability of finding the right solutions to whatever the needs of the children may be. If teachers carry into the classroom such an attitude together with the fruits of their endeavors, they will also be guided in particular situations by a sound pedagogical instinct. This, however, is hardly the case in the general teaching situation of today.

Please do not mistake these remarks as criticism against some teachers. Those who belong to the teaching profession will be the first ones to experience the truth of what has been said. In their own limitations they may well feel that they are the victims of prevailing conditions. The mere fact that they had to suffer the martyrdom of a high school education, may be enough to prevent them from breaking through many great hindrances. What matters most during actual teaching is an ability to meet the ever-changing classroom situations, which result from the immediate response of the pupils. But who in this wide world trains teachers to do that? Are they not trained to decide beforehand what they are going to teach? This often gives me the impression that the child is not considered at all during educational deliberations. Such an attitude would be tantamount to making papier-mâché masks of each pupil as he enters school in order to deal with these masks rather than with the actual children.

As mentioned before, it is not at all our aim to teach an ideology in the Waldorf School, though such a thought might easily occur to people upon hearing that the anthroposophists have founded a new school. Our aim is to carry insights gained through knowledge of Anthroposophy right into actual teaching.

This is the reason why I did not mind handing over the responsibility of giving religion lessons to representatives of the various religious denominations. Religion, after all, represents the very core of a person's world outlook. And so, in our Waldorf School, a Roman Catholic priest was asked to give Roman Catholic religion lessons to pupils of this denomination, and a Protestant priest was given the task of teaching the Protestant religion lessons. When this decision was taken, we were not afraid of being unable to balance any outer influence brought into the school by these priests, influence which might not be in harmony with what we were trying to do. But then a somewhat unexpected situation arose. For when our friend, *Emil Molt*, founded the Waldorf School, most of our pupils came from the homes of the workers employed at his factory. Among them were many children of atheistic parents, children who, had they been sent to another school, would not have received any religious instruction at all. Gradually among these children—in the way such things happen when one is dealing with children and their parents—there arose the wish that they too, should receive some form of religion lessons. And this is how our "free"—that is, non-denominational—religion lessons came about. They were given by our own teachers, just as the other religion lessons were given by the respective priests. These teachers were recognized by us as religion teachers of the Waldorf curriculum. In this way, anthroposophical religion lessons were introduced in our school. These religion lessons have come to mean a great deal to many of our pupils, but particularly to the children of the factory workers.

However, all this brought specific problems in its wake, for Anthroposophy is there for the adult. If, therefore, the teacher wants to bring the right content into his anthroposophical religion lessons, he has to create it anew and this is no mean task. For it means a remolding and transforming of anthroposophical content in order to make it suitable for the various age groups. In fact, this task of changing a modern philosophy to suit young people occupies us a great deal. It means working in depth on fundamental questions, such as: What is the effect upon pupils of our using certain symbols? Or: How do we deal with the imponderables inherent in such a situation? More of this later on.

I am sure that you will appreciate that a school like ours, which aims at basing its curriculum upon the needs of the growing child in the light of anthroposophical knowledge of man, has to make compromises of the most varied kinds. For today it would be quite impossible to educate children according to abstract educational ideas, to be subsequently labelled as the Principles of Waldorf Education. The result of such a misguided approach would be that our graduates would not be able to find their way into life. It is all too easy to criticize life at the present time. Most people meet displeasing aspects of it every day and one could easily feel tempted to make clever suggestions about how to put the world in order. But it simply won't do to educate pupils in such a way that, when they leave school to enter life, they can only criticize the senselessness of all they find there. However imperfect life may be when judged by abstract reasoning, one nevertheless must be able to play one's full part in it. Waldorf pupils who have been treated as individuals perhaps more than is usually the case elsewhere, have to be sent out into life—otherwise there would be no sense in having a Waldorf School at all. But they must not become estranged from contemporary life to the extent that they can only criticize what they meet outside. This I can only touch upon here. Right from the start the most varied compromises had to be made, also with regard to our curriculum and our pedagogical aims. As soon as the school was founded, I sent a memorandum to the education authorities in which I made the following request: From their sixth or seventh year up to the completion of their ninth year, that is, to the end of the third class, our pupils are to be schooled according to the principles of Waldorf Education without any outside interference. By this I meant that the planning of the curriculum and the standards to be achieved, as well as the methods of teaching, were to be left entirely in the hands of our teaching staff or College of Teachers, which would bear the ultimate responsibility for the running of the school.

For us it is not only important that each teacher knows the pupils of his class well, but also that a corresponding relationship exists between the entire body of teachers and all the pupils of the school, so that pupils can feel quite free to contact any teacher of their choice for guidance or advice. It is a real joy to witness, every time one enters the Waldorf School, how friendly and trusting the pupils are not only with their class teachers, but with all the teachers, both in and out of lesson time.

To return to my letter to the education authorities: I stated that on completion of the third school year our pupils should have reached the same standards with regard to the Three R's as those achieved in other schools so that they would be able to change schools without encountering any difficulties. This implied that a child who had had a wider educational background than the pupils of his new class, nevertheless would be able to fit into new surroundings, and that it had not lost touch with life in general.

In a similar way I stated that our teaching between the end of the pupils' ninth year and twelfth year, that is from the end of class three to the end of class six, again was to achieve standards comparable with those of other schools, so that our pupils would be able to enter a seventh grade in another school without falling behind.

We do not wish to be fanatical and therefore we had to make such compromises. Waldorf teachers must always be willing to cope with the practical problems of life. And if a pupil has to leave our school at the age of fourteen, he or she should be able to enter a high school or any other school leading up to university entrance examination. In this way we try to put into practice what has been indicated.

And now, having established our school up to the age of fourteen plus, every year we are adding a new class, so that eventually we shall be able to offer the full range of secondary education, leading up to higher education. This means that we have to plan our curriculum in such a way that our young people will be able to take their school-leaving exams. In Austria this exam is called "Maturity Exam," in Germany "Abitur" (Latin for: Leaving) and in other countries there will be other names for these institutions. In any case, our pupils are to be given the possibility of entering other schools of higher education. There exists as yet no possibility of our founding a vocational school* or university, for whatever we might be trying to do in this direction would always bear the stamp of a private initiative and no government would grant us permission to issue our own certificates of education based on non-existing exam results. For we should never want to hold official examinations.

And so the general situation forces us to make compromises in our Waldorf plan and we are perfectly willing to acknowledge this fact. What matters to us is that—despite all compromising—the genuine Waldorf spirit lives in our teaching, and this as much as possible.

---

*The German word used here is Hochschule, translated literally as high school, but signifying a school for those who have finished their secondary education (but have not necessarily taken the school-leaving exam) and who wish to learn a trade or skill, ranging from manual labor to secretarial or bookkeeping skills to crafts or household management.

As we wanted to have a complete junior school at the opening of the Waldorf School, we naturally had to take in pupils from other schools also and this gave us ample opportunity of witnessing the fruits of the so-called "strict discipline" characteristic of other schools. We now have a little more than two years of "Waldorf discipline" behind us which, to a large extent, consists of our trying to get rid of the ordinary kind of school discipline. I should like to give you an example of what I mean: Only a few weeks ago we laid the foundation stone for a larger school building—for up till now we had to make do with provisional classrooms only. To my mind it seemed right that all our children should take part in this stone-laying ceremony. And—as so often happens in life—things took a little longer than anticipated so that, by the time we were only just getting ready for the actual ceremony, all our pupils were already in the building. First I had to meet teachers and several other personalities, but all the children were there already! We grownups had to meet in our so-called staffroom. What were we to do with all those children? The chairman of the College of Teachers simply said, "We'll send them to their classrooms. They now have reached a stage when we can leave them unattended without untoward consequences. They won't disturb us."

So—despite the dubious "discipline" which had been imported from other schools, and despite our having got rid of so-called "school discipline," it had become possible to send the pupils to their classrooms without their disturbing us. Admittedly, this peace was somewhat ephemeral so that over-sensitive ears might have been offended, but that did not matter. Children who do not* disturb oversensitive ears are not generally well-disciplined. At any rate, the effects of imponderables in the Waldorf School became ap-

---

*Here the shorthand text is not clear

parent in the children's good behavior under these unusual circumstances.

As you know, various kinds of punishment are administered in most other schools and we, too, had to find our ways with regard to this problem. When we discussed the question of punishment in one of our teacher meetings, one of our teachers reported the following interesting incident: He had tried to find out the effects which certain forms of punishment had upon his pupils. Among his pupils, who had experienced our kind of discipline for some time, there were a few notorious scamps. These little good-for-nothings, as such pupils are called in Germany, had produced very poor work and they were to be punished according to usual school discipline. They were to be given detention, they were told to stay in after lessons to do their sums properly. However, when this punishment was announced in class, lo and behold! all the other pupils protested that they, too, wanted to stay in to do extra sums, for arithmetic was so much fun!

So you see, the concept of punishment had undergone a complete transformation, it had changed into something desirable for the whole class. Such matters rarely happen if the teacher tries to bring them about directly, but they can become the natural consequence of the right approach. I am well aware that the problem of school discipline occupies many people's minds today.

I once had the opportunity of observing closely the importance of the relationship of a teacher with his pupils, a relationship which is the natural outcome of the characterological disposition of both teacher and pupils. One could go as far as saying that whether pupils profit from their lessons, or how much they gain, depends on whether the teacher evokes sympathy or antipathy in his pupils. And it is absolutely open to discussion whether an easygoing teacher who does not even work according to proper educational principles, may in effect achieve more than another teacher who, intent on following perfectly sound but abstract principles, is unable to realize them in the classroom. There are plenty of such abstract principles to be found these days. I am not even trying to be sarcastic by calling them clever and ingenious—one could argue about their merits. But if a slovenly and indolent teacher who nevertheless radiates warmth and affection for his children, enters the classroom, he may give more to his pupils for their later lives than a highly principled teacher whose personality calls forth antipathy. Even though the pupils of a genial but untidy teacher are not likely to grow into models of orderliness, they at least will not have to suffer from so-called nervousness in later life. Nervousness can be the result of antipathy felt towards a teacher of even excellent educational principles who is not able to make the right kind of contact with his pupils.

Such points are open to discussion and they ought to be discussed if one takes the art of education seriously. For this reason I once had to act in a case of this kind and my decision may well evoke strong disapproval among some people. During one of my visits to the Waldorf School I was told of a boy in one of the classes who was causing great difficulties. He had committed all kinds of misdemeanors and none of the teachers of this class was able to deal with him. I asked for the boy to be sent to me because first I wanted to find out the root of the trouble. You will admit that in many other schools such a boy would have received corporal punishment or possibly less drastic forms of punishment. Well, I examined the boy carefully and came to the conclusion that he should be moved up into the next class above. This change was to be his punishment. I have not heard of any complaints since. His new class teacher has confirmed that the boy has even become a model pupil and that everything seems to be in order now. This, after all, is what really matters. The important thing is that one penetrates the very

136

soul and nature of such a child. The cause of the trouble was that there was no human contact between him and his teacher and since he was intelligent enough to cope with the work of the class above him—there was no parallel class in his case—the only right thing was to move him up. Had we put him down into the next lower class, we would have ruined that child.

If one bears in mind the well-being and inner development of the child, one will find the right way of acting pedagogically. This is why it is good to look at specific and symptomatic cases. We have no intention of denying that in many ways the Waldorf School is built upon compromise, but as far as it is humanly possible, we shall always try to educate out of a true knowledge of man.

To continue: The morning sessions are arranged in the way already indicated. Because it is essential for our pupils to be able to move on to higher forms of education, we had to include in our curriculum certain other subjects, such as Greek and Latin, which are also taught in morning lessons. In these ancient languages "soul-economy" is of particular importance.

The afternoon lessons are given over to more physical activities, such as gym and eurythmy, and to artistic work which plays a very special part in a Waldorf School. I will give further details in the coming days.

We try, as far as this is possible, to teach the more intellectual subjects in the morning and only when the children's headwork has been done, are they given movement lessons —in as far as they have not let off steam already between morning lessons. However, after these movement lessons they are not taken back to the classroom in order to do more headwork. I have already indicated that this has a destructive effect upon life. For while the child is engaged in physical movement, supersensible forces are unconsciously working through it. And the head, having surrendered itself to physical movement, is no longer in a position to resume its headwork. It is therefore quite erroneous to believe that by sandwiching a gym lesson between other more intellectual lessons, one is providing a helpful change with its attendant benefits. The homogeneous character of both morning and afternoon sessions has shown itself to be beneficial to the general development of the pupils. If one constantly bears in mind the characteristic features of human nature, one will best serve human inclinations.

I have already mentioned that we found it necessary to give some kind of anthroposophical religion lessons to our pupils. Soon afterwards, arising out of these lessons, another need was felt which led to the introduction of a Sunday Service for our pupils. This Service is in the nature of a cult in which the children take part with deeply religious feelings. We have found that such a ritual, performed before the children's eyes every Sunday morning, has greatly deepened their religious experience.

The Sunday Service had to be enlarged for the sake of those pupils who were about to leave our middle school. In Germany it is the custom for pupils of this age to be confirmed in a special ceremony which signifies their having reached a stage of maturity at which they are ready to enter life. We, too, have made similar arrangements for a ceremonial which, as experience has shown, has made a lasting impression upon our pupils.

In an education based upon knowledge of man, many needs become apparent which may have gone unnoticed in the more traditional forms of education. For instance, in Germany all pupils receive school reports at the end of each school year, for it is considered essential to give them something of this kind before they go into their summer holidays. But in this case, too, we felt the need of an innovation. For I must admit that I should find it extremely difficult to accept the usual form of school reports in a Waldorf School, for the

138

simple reason that I could never appreciate the difference between a "satisfactory" or "near-satisfactory" mark, or between "fair" and "fairly good" marks, and so on. These marks are then converted into numbers, so that in Germany some reports show the various subjects arranged in one column, and on the opposite side there is a column of figures, such as: 4½, 3, 3-4, and so on. I have never been able to develop the necessary understanding for these somewhat occult relationships! And so we decided to find other ways of writing our school reports.

When our pupils go into their holidays at the end of the school year they, too, receive reports. But these contain a kind of mirror picture, a kind of biography of their progress during the year, written by their class teachers. And we have found again and again that our children accept these reports with inner approval. In them they can read what impression they have created during the years. They will feel that, although such a description has been written with sympathetic understanding, it will not tolerate any whitewashing of less positive aspects of their work. These reports, which are recieved with deep inner satisfaction, end with a verse, specially composed for each individual child. This verse is a kind of guiding motive for the coming years. Our kind of reports, so I believe, have already proved themselves and will retain their value in the future, even though in some parts of Germany they have already been nicknamed as "Ersatz," as report substitute!

The pupils' response to life in the Waldorf School is an entirely positive one. To show how much they like their school, I should like to tell you what I recently heard from one of our mothers, for such an example helps to illustrate more general symptoms. She said, "My boy was never an affectionate child. He never showed any tender feelings towards me, his mother. After his first year in the Waldorf School—while still quite a young child—his summer holi-

139

days began. When they were nearly over and I told him that soon he would be going to school again, he came and kissed me for the first time.'' Such a little anecdote could be considered symptomatic of the effects of an education which is based on knowledge of man and which is practiced in a human and friendly atmosphere. And our school reports also help to contribute towards this atmosphere.

In order to introduce you to life in the Waldorf School, I felt it necessary to digress a little from our planned program. Tomorrow we shall continue with a more detailed account of the child's development after the change of teeth. I did want to include in our study a description of what by now has become the outer framework of practical life in the Waldorf School.

LECTURE IX

Dornach, 31st December 1921

An important and far-reaching change is taking place when the child begins to shed its milk teeth. This change is not only a physical event in the life of a human being, for the entire human organization undergoes a metamorphosis. A true art of education demands a thorough appreciation and understanding of this metamorphosis. What in our previous meetings I have called the etheric body, or the refined body of formative forces, is becoming freed from certain of its functions during the time between the change of teeth and puberty. Previously the etheric body has been working directly into the physical body of the child, but now it is beginning to function also in the realm of the child's soul. The effect of this is that the child's physical body is being gripped from within in quite a different manner from that of the previous stage. Previously, the situation was more or less as described by exponents of a materialistic outlook who see in the physical processes of the human body the foundation of man's psyche. They look upon his soul and spirit as something emanating from the physical and related to it much as the candle flame is related to the candle. And this is more or less correct with regard to the young child up to the change of teeth. During these early years the soul and spiritual life of the child is entirely bound up with its physical and organic processes and all physical and organic processes are at the same time of a soul and spiritual nature. All the shaping and forming of the body which is going on at that age, is conducted from the head downwards. This stage finds its conclusion when the second teeth are being pushed

141

through in the head. At that time the forces working in the head cease to predominate, while soul and spiritual activities are entering the lower regions of the body, namely the rhythmical activities of heart and breathing. Previously, these forces, working especially upon the formation of the child's brain, were also streaming down into the remaining organism, shaping and molding, and entering directly into the physical substances of the body. Here they brought about physical processes.

All this changes with the coming of the second teeth, when certain of these forces begin to work more in the child's soul and spiritual realm, affecting especially the rhythmical movement of heart and lungs. They are no longer active to the same degree in the physical processes themselves, but now they also work in the rhythms of breathing and blood circulation. One can observe this even physically, in that the child's breathing and pulse beat become noticeably stronger at this time. The child now has a strong desire to experience within its own body its emerging life of soul and spirit on waves of rhythm and beat, quite unconsciously of course. It has a real longing for this interplay of rhythm and beat in its own organism. Consequently the adult must realize that whatever he or she brings to the child after the change of teeth, has to be given with an inherent quality of rhythm and beat. Everything addressed to the child at this time must be imbued with these qualities. The educator has to be able so to live himself into the element of rhythm and beat that whatever he brings will make an impact upon the child because it is allowed to live in its own musical element.

All this is also the beginning of something else. If, at this stage, the rhythm of breathing and blood circulation is not treated in the right way, the resulting harm may extend irreparably into later life. Many weaknesses and unhealthy conditions of the respiratory and circulatory system in adult life are the consequences of a wrong education during these early school years. Through the change in the working of the child's etheric body, the limbs begin to grow rapidly, with the effect that the life of the muscles and bones, that of the entire skeleton, begins to play a predominant role. The life of muscles and bones strives to become attuned to the rhythms of breathing and blood circulation. At this stage the child's muscles vibrate in sympathy with the rhythms of breathing and blood circulation, so that the entire being of the child takes on a musical character. Whereas previously the child's inborn activities were akin to those of a sculptor, now the inner musician begins to work, albeit beyond the child's consciousness. It is essential for the teacher to realize that, when the child enters class one, he or she is dealing with a natural, though unconscious musician. One must meet these inner needs of the child, demanding a somewhat similar treatment—metaphorically speaking—to that of a new violin responding to the playing of a violinist, adapting itself to the characteristic pattern of his sound waves. Through maltreatment, a violin may be ruined once and for all. But in the case of the living human organism it is possible to implant principles harmful to its growth, which will increase and develop until eventually they can ruin the entire life of the individual concerned.

When one has embarked on the study of man which throws light both on educational principles and methods, one will find that the characteristic features just indicated roughly occupy the time between the change of teeth and puberty. One will also discover that this period of time again falls into three smaller phases: The first one lasts from the change of teeth until approximately the end of the ninth year, the second one roughly until the end of the twelfth year and the third one from the thirteenth year until sexual maturity has been reached.

If one observes how the child lives entirely in a musical element, one can gain insight also into how these three phases differ from one another. During the first phase, that is until approximately the end of the ninth year, the child wants to experience everything that comes toward it within its own inner rhythms—in what belongs to beat and measure. It will relate everything to the rhythms of breath and heartbeat and, indirectly, also to the way its muscles and bones are shaping themselves. But if the outer influences do not synchronize with its own inner rhythms, the young person will eventually grow into a kind of inner cripple, even if this may not be outwardly discernible in the early stages. Up to its ninth year the child has the strong desire to experience inwardly in form of beat and rhythm everything that comes toward it. When a child of this age hears music—and anyone able to observe what goes on in a child's soul will be able to perceive it—it transforms all the outer sounds into its own inner rhythms. It co-vibrates with the music. It reproduces within what it perceives from without. For at this stage, at least to a certain extent, the child has retained features which are characteristic of its previous stages. Up to the change of teeth, fundamentally, the child is like one sense organ, unconsciously reproducing outer sense impressions, as most sense organs do. The child lives, above all, by imitation, as already shown in previous meetings. Observing the human eye, leaving out of account any mental images resulting from the eye's sense perceptions, you will find that it reproduces outer stimuli by forming after-images. These after-images are then taken hold of by the activity leading to mental representation. In as far as the very young child inwardly reproduces all it perceives, especially with regard to the people around it, it is like one great unconscious sense organ. But the images reproduced within do not remain mere images, for they act at the same time as forces, forming and shaping the child even physically.

And now, at the time when the second teeth appear, these after-images enter only as far as the rhythmic system, the system of movement. Something of the previous formative activity remains, but now it is accompanied by a new element. There is a definite difference in the way a child responds to rhythm and beat before and after the change of teeth. Before it, by way of imitation, rhythm and beat directly affected the shaping of bodily organs. After the change of teeth it is transformed into an inner musical element.

On completion of the ninth year and up to the twelfth year, the child develops an understanding of rhythm and beat, of what belongs to melody in its own right. It now no longer has the same urge to reproduce inwardly all that belongs to this realm, but it begins to perceive it as something outside itself. Whereas, earlier on, the child experienced rhythm and beat unconsciously, it now develops a conscious perception and understanding of it. This continues up to the twelfth year, not only with regard to music, but also to everything else coming to meet it from outside.

Towards the twelfth year, or perhaps a little earlier, the child develops the ability of leading into the thinking realm the elements of rhythm and beat which, previously, it had experienced only imaginatively.

If, through insight, one is able to perceive what happens in the realm of the soul, one can also recognize the corresponding effects in the physical body. I have just spoken of how the child wants to shape its muscles, its bones, in accordance with what is happening within its organs. Now, towards the twelfth year, the child begins to be no longer satisfied with living solely in the elements of rhythm and beat; now it wants to lift this experience more into the realm of abstract and conscious understanding. And this coincides with the hardening of those parts of the muscles which lead over into the tendons. Whereas previously all movement was oriented more towards the muscles themselves, it now is oriented towards the tendons. Everything happening in the realm of soul and spirit has its counter-effect in the physical realm. And this inclusion of the life of the tendons, that is, of the link between muscle and bone, is the outer physical expression for the child's sailing out of a feeling approach to rhythm and beat into what belongs to the realm of logic, which is devoid of rhythm and beat. A discovery of this kind, an offshoot of a real knowledge of man, needs to be made into a guideline in the art of education.

Most adults who think about something in a general way, be it plants or animals—and as teachers you will have to introduce such general subjects to your pupils—will remember what they themselves once learned in botany or zoology, but at a later age than that of the children we are talking about here. Unfortunately, what you find in most textbooks on botany or zoology, is most unsuitable material for teaching the young. Some of these textbooks may be of great scientific merit—though usually this is not the case—but as teaching material for the age which concerns us here, they are of no use at all. For everything which we, as teachers, bring to our pupils in plant or animal study has to be woven into an artistic whole. We must aim at highlighting the harmonious configuration of the plant's being. We must describe the harmonious relationships of one plant species with another. What children can appreciate through a rhythmical, harmonious and feeling approach, has to be of far greater significance for Waldorf teachers than what the ordinary textbooks can offer us. The usual methods of classifying plants is particularly objectionable. Perhaps the least offensive of all the various systems is that of *Linné*, who looks only upon the blossom of the plant, that is to that part where the plant ceases to be merely plant and where it stretches forth its forces into the entire cosmos. But any of these plant systems is unacceptable for use at school at all. We shall see later what needs to be done in this respect.

A teacher who, textbook in hand, enters the classroom to teach to younger classes what he himself had learned in botany or zoology, is a pitiful sight. If he now strides up and down in front of the desks, reading from his textbook—which, in itself, is totally unsuitable—in order to refresh his memory of what, long ago, he himself once learned, he becomes a mere caricature of a teacher. It is absolutely essential for us to learn to talk about plants or animals in a living and artistic way. Only then will our content be attuned to the child's inner musical needs. We must always bear in mind that our teaching must spring from an artistic element. Our lessons must not be merely thought out. Even a correct but abstract kind of observation is not good enough. Only what is imbued with a living element of sensitive and artistic experience will provide the child with the soul nourishment it needs.

When children enter class one and we are expected to teach them writing as soon as possible, we might be tempted to introduce the letters of the alphabet as they are used today. But the forms of these letters are something which which the child of this age—just after the onset of the change of teeth—has not the slightest inner connection. How was it then, at the time when such a direct human relationship to the written letters still existed? To find the answer we need only look at what happened in early civilizations. In those ancient days primitive man engraved images on tablets or painted pictures which still bore a resemblance to what he had seen in nature. There still was a direct human link between outer objects and their written forms. As civilization progressed, these forms became more and more abstract until, after having undergone many transformations, they finally emerged as today's letters of the alphabet, which no longer bear any direct human relationship to the person writing them.

But the young child who, in many ways, shows us how men of earlier civilizations experienced the world, needs a direct connection with whatever we demand from its will activities. Therefore, when introducing writing, we must refrain from teaching today's abstract letter forms straight away. Especially at the time of changing teeth must we offer the child a human and artistic bridge to whatever we teach. This implies that we allow the child to link what it has seen with its eyes to the result of its own will activity on paper which we call: writing. Experiencing life through its own will activities is a primary need of the child at this stage. We must give it an opportunity to give vent to this innate artistic drive by, for example, letting it run a curve (see diagram).

When we draw the child's attention to the fact that its legs have run such a curve on the floor, we lift up its will activity into a semiconscious feeling. The next step would be to ask the child to draw the curve it had run into the air, using its arm and hand. Now another form could be run on the floor, again to be "written" into the air.

Thus the form which in the first instance was made by the entire body of the running child, was subsequently repro-

148

duced merely by the use of its hand. This could be followed by the teacher asking the child to pronounce words beginning with the letter "L." Gradually, under his or her guidance, the child will find the link between the shape it has run and drawn, and the sound of the appropriate letter "L."

Only after the experience of its own inner movement is the child led to the drawing of the actual letters. This would be one way of proceeding, but there is also another possibility. After the change of teeth the child inwardly is not only a musician but, as an echo from earlier stages, it has remained also an inner sculptor. Therefore one can begin by talking to the child about the fish, gradually leading over artistically to its outer form, which the child will draw. Then, appealing to its sense of sound, one directs its attention from the whole word "fish" to the initial sound "F," in this way relating the shape of the letter to its sound.

This method, at least to a certain extent, even follows the historical development of the letter "F." There is, however, no need to restrict ourselves to actual historical examples, it is certainly right for us to use our own imagination. What matters is not that the child recapitulates the evolution of the actual letters, but that it finds its way into writing through the artistic activity of drawing pictures which final-

149

ly will lead to today's abstract letter forms. For instance, one could remind the children of how water makes waves, drawing a picture of this kind,

and gradually changing it into

Repeating words such as, "Washing Waves of Water—Waving, Washing Water," while at the same time drawing the form, one links the sound of the letter "W" to its written form. Taking one's start with the child's own life experience, one leads over from the activity of drawing to the final letter forms.

Following our Waldorf method, the children won't learn to write as quickly as they do in other schools. In the Waldorf School we hold regular meetings for parents without their children, in which they are invited to discuss the effects of Waldorf education with their teachers. In such meetings some parents have expressed their anxieties about the fact that their children even at the age of eight, are still unable to write properly. We have to show them that our slower approach is really a blessing, because it allows the child to integrate the art of writing with its whole being. We try to convince them that in our school the child learns writing at the right age and in a far more humane manner than if it had to absorb something essentially alien to its own nature; alien because it represents the end product of a long

150

cultural evolution. We must help our parents to see the importance of an immediate and direct response in the child to the introduction of writing. Naturally we have to provide our pupils with the tools of learning, but we must always do so by adapting our content to the nature of the child.

One aspect, so often omitted nowadays, is that of the relationship of a specific area to life as a whole. In our advanced stage of civilization everything has come to depend on specialization. Certainly for a time this was necessary, but we now have reached a stage where, for the sake of mankind's healthy development, we must never lose sight of the totality of life. To do so, we must keep an open mind for what spiritual investigation has to tell us about the human being. To believe that anthroposophists are always railing against new achievements of technology would be a serious misunderstanding of what this movement could contribute towards knowledge of man. For it is necessary to look upon the complexities of life from a holistic point of view. To give you an example: I have not the slightest objection to the use of typewriters. Typing, of course, is a far less human activity than writing by hand but, as just said, I do not remonstrate against it. Nevertheless I find it important for us to realize its implications, because everything we do in life has its repercussions. Therefore you must forgive me if, in order to illustrate my point, I say something about typewriting from the point of view of anthroposophical spiritual insight. Anyone unwilling to accept it, is perfectly free to dismiss this aspect of life's realities as foolish nonsense. But what I have to say does accord with actual facts.

You see, if one is aware of spiritual processes which, like those in ordinary life, are always happening around us, typewriting creates a very definite impression. After I have been typing—as you see, I am not fulminating against it at all, but am only pleased if I have time for it—when during the day I have been typing, this activity continues to affect

151

me for quite a long time afterwards. This in itself does not disturb me, but the aftereffects are noticeably there. And when, finally, I reach a state of inner quietude, the activity of typing, seen in imaginative consciousness, becomes transformed into self-beholding. This seeing of oneself stands there before the seer, who is then able to witness outwardly what is happening inwardly. All this must occur in full consciousness which enables one to recognize that what has thus appeared in form on an outer image is nothing but the projection of what is, or has been, taking place—possibly at a much earlier time—as an inner organic activity. One can clearly see what is happening inside the human body when one has reached the stage of clairvoyant Imagination. In such objective beholding, every pressing of a typewriter key is changed into a flash of lightning. And what appears during the state of Imagination as a human heart, is constantly being struck and pierced by these flashes of lightning. Now, as you know, the typewriter keys are not arranged according to any spiritual principle, but only according to frequency of use in order to facilitate greater speed in typing. The result is that, whenever the fingers hit the various keys, these flashes of lightning become completely chaotic. In short, a frightful thunderstorm is raging when typewriting is seen with spiritual eyes!

And what does this mean? It means nothing less than that here we have an explanation of why so many people walk about with weak hearts, for they were unable to balance the damaging effects of typing by appropriate counter measures. This is specially the case if people started typing at too early an age, at a time when the heart is most liable to be adversely affected. And if typing should spread more and more, one will soon see how all kinds of heart complaints will be on the increase.

Causes and effects of this kind are part of the pattern of life. There is no wish on our part to run down any of the new technical inventions, but one ought to be able to look with open eyes at what they do to us. One ought to find the means of compensating for any possible harmful effects. Such matters are of special importance for teachers because they have the task of relating education to practical life. What we do at school or in the company of children is not the only thing that matters. What is of paramount importance is that school and everything pertaining to education is related to life in the fullest sense. And this implies that whoever chooses to be an educator must be familiar with what is happening in the big wide world, must know and recognize life in its widest context.

In Germany the first railway was built from Fürth to Nürnberg in 1835. Before this happened, the health authorities of Bavaria were approached for their opinion as to whether, from a medical point of view, the building of such a railway could be recommended. Before embarking on major projects of this kind, it had always been the custom to seek expert advice. In answer, the Bavarian health authorities stated—and documentary evidence is available—that expert medical opinion could not recommend the building of railways because of the severe strain upon the nervous system which travelling on trains would inflict upon passengers and railway staff alike. However—so the report continued—should railways be built despite the warning of the authorities concerned, all railway lines should at least be fenced off by high wooden walls in order to protect farmers in fields or any others likely to be near travelling trains from suffering concussion of the brain.

These were the findings of medical experts employed by the Bavarian health authorities. Today we laugh about them and many other similar examples could be quoted. Nevertheless, there are at least two sides to each problem and from a certain point of view one could even agree with some aspects of this report, made not so long ago, in fact not even a century ago. The fact is that people have become more nervous since the arrival of rail travel. And if we were to make the necessary investigation to find out the difference between people living in our present age of the train and those who still travelled in the old, venerable but rather philistine stagecoach, we would definitely be able to ascertain that the constitutions of the latter were different. Their nervous system behaved quite differently! Though the officials of the Bavarian health authorities have made fools of themselves, from a certain point of view they were not entirely wrong.

When new inventions make their impact on modern life, we must take steps to balance any possible ill effects by finding appropriate countermeasures. We must aim at compensating for any weakening of man's constitution due to outer influences, by strengthening him from within. But, in this age of ever-increasing specialization, this is only possible through a new art of education, based on true knowledge of man.

The only safe way of introducing writing to the young child is the one advocated just now, because at that age all learning must proceed from the will sphere, and the child's inclination towards the world of rhythm and measure springs from the will sphere. We must satisfy this inner urge of the child by allowing it controlled will activities and not by appealing to its sense of observation and an ability to make mental images. From this it follows that it would be wrong to teach reading before the child has been introduced to writing, for reading already represents a transition from a will activity to an abstract observation. The first step is to introduce writing artistically, imaginatively, and then to let the child read what it has written. The last step, since modern life demands it, would be to help the child to read from printed texts. Only by applying a deepened knowledge of man, based upon the realities of life, is the teacher able to discern what needs to be done.

When the child enters class one, it is certainly ready to learn how to reckon with simple numbers. But also in the introduction of arithmetic one must be careful to meet the inner needs of the child. These spring from the same realm of rhythm and measure, and from a sensitive apprehension of the harmonizing element inherent in the world of number. However, if we begin with what I should like to call the additive approach, if we start by teaching the child to count, we again fail to understand the nature of the child. Of course it must learn to count, but additive counting in itself is not in harmony with the child's inner needs.

Only during the course of civilization has our way of dealing with numbers gradually developed into one of synthesizing, that is, of putting numbers together. Today we have the concept of one unit, of a oneness. We have a second unit, a third unit, and so on, and when counting, we mentally place one unit next to the other and add them up. But the child's nature does not experience number in the same way, for human evolution did not proceed according to this principle. True, all counting began with a unit, with number one. However, the second unit, number two, was not an outer repetition of the first unit, but it was felt to be contained within the first unit. Number one was the origin of number two, the two units of which were concealed within the original number. The same number one, when divided into three parts, gave number three, the three units of which were felt to be part of the one. Translated into contemporary terms: When reaching the concept two, one did not leave the bounds of number one, but an inner progression within number one was experienced. The twoness was inherent in the oneness. Also three, four and all other numbers were felt to be part of the all-comprising first unit and all numbers were experienced as organic members arising out of it.

Due to its musical—rhythmical nature the child, too, experiences the world of number in a similar way. Therefore, instead of beginning by adding in a rather pedantic way, it would be better to call out a child and give it some apples or any other suitable objects. Instead of giving it, say, three apples, then four more and finally another two, asking the child to add them all together, one begins by giving it a whole pile of apples, or whatever is convenient. This would be the start of the whole operation. Then one calls out two more children and says to the first one, "Here you have a heap of apples. Give some to the other two children and keep some for yourself. But each one of you must have the same number of apples." In this way you help the child grasp the idea of sharing by three. One begins with the total amount and leads to the principle of division. Following this method, the child will respond and apprehend this process quite naturally. According to our picture of man, and in order to be attuned to the child's nature, we do not begin by adding numbers, but by dividing and subtracting them. Then, retracing our steps and thus reversing the first two processes, we are led to multiplication and addition. Moving from the whole to the part, we follow the original number experience which was one of analyzing, that is, of a divisional quality, and not the contemporary method of synthesizing, of putting things together, of adding.

These are some examples to show how one can read in the development of the child what and how one ought to teach during the different stages. Breathing and blood circulation are the physical bases of the life of feeling, just as the head is the basis for mental imagery, for thinking. With the change of teeth the life of feeling becomes liberated and therefore, at this stage one can always reach the child through the element of feeling, provided that the teaching material is artistically attuned to the child's nature.

To sum up: Before the change of teeth the child is not yet aware of its separate identity and consequently it cannot appreciate the characteristic nature of other persons whose gestures, manners of speaking and even whose sentiments it imitates in an imponderable way. Up to the seventh year the child cannot yet differentiate between its own self and that of another person. It experiences others as something with which it is intimately connected, similar to the way in which it feels connected with its own arms and legs. It does not yet make a distinction between self and the surrounding world.

With the change of teeth new soul forces of feeling, linked to breathing and blood circulation, come into their own, with the effect that the child begins to distance itself from other people, whom it now experiences as individual characters. And this creates in the child a longing to follow the grownup in every way and to look up to the adult in shy reverence. The child's previous inclination to imitate the more external features changes after the second dentition. True to the child's nature, a strong feeling for authority begins to develop.

You will hardly expect a ready sympathy for general obedience to authority from someone who, as a young person, published *The Philosophy of Spiritual Activity* early in the 1890s. But this sense for authority in the child between the change of teeth and puberty must be respected and nurtured, because it represents an inborn need at this age. Only those who have experienced shy reverence and a feeling of authority for the adult between their change of teeth and puberty can, in later life, use their freedom rightly. This is another example showing how education must be seen within the context of the social life in general.

If you look back a few decades and see how proud many people then were of their "modern" educational ideas, some strange feelings will begin to stir in you. After the vic-

157

tory of Prussia over Austria in 1866, one often heard a remark in Austria, where I spent half of my life. People expressed the opinion that the battle had been won by the Prussian schoolmaster! Austria, where the education act was implemented later than in Prussia, was always considered to have an inferior education system and the Prussian schoolmaster was hailed as having won the victory. However, after 1918, one no longer sang the praises of the Prussian schoolmaster! This is an example to show how "modern" educational attitudes have been praised for the most extraordinary successes. And today we witness some of the results, namely our chaotic social life which threatens to become more and more chaotic because so many people have replaced a will-controlled and morally strong sense of freedom by indulgence and license. Many of them have forgotten how to make use of their real, inner freedom. Whoever is able to observe life will find definite links between the general chaos of today and educational principles which, though highly satisfying to intellectual and naturalistic attitudes, will fail to bring about the full development of the human being. One must become aware of the polar effects in life, such as that man in his later life can become free in the right way only if, as a child, he has gone through a stage of looking up to and of revering his elders. It is wholesome for the child to believe that a thing is beautiful, true and good—or ugly, false and evil—if and because the teacher says so.

With the change of teeth the child gains a new relationship to the world. As the life of its own soul gradually emerges—which the child now experiences as something in its own right—it has to meet the world first of all supported by the feeling of authority. At this stage the educator represents the world at large and the child has to meet it through the eyes of its teacher. Therefore we have to say:

From birth to the change of teeth = instinctive imitation
From the change of teeth to puberty = principle of
  authority

But by authority we mean the child's natural response to its teacher and never an enforced authority. It is the kind of authority which, in quite intangible ways, creates the right rapport between child and teacher.

And here we enter the realm of imponderables. I should like to show you by way of an example how they work. Let us imagine that we wish to give the child a concept of the immortality of the soul, a task whch is a good deal more difficult than one may suppose. At the age we are speaking of, an age in which the child is so open to the artistic element in education, we cannot communicate such a concept by abstract reasoning or by means of ideas. We must clothe it in pictures. Now, how might a teacher—one who feels drawn to the more intellectual and naturalistic side of life— proceed? Subconsciously he may say to himself: Naturally, I am more intelligent than the child who in reality is stupid. Therefore I must invent a suitable picture in order to give the child an idea of the immortality of the human soul. The chrysalis from which the butterfly emerges offers a good metaphor. The butterfly is hidden in the chrysalis. In the body, the human soul is hidden. The butterfly flies out of the chrysalis. This is a visible picture of what happens in death, when the supersensible soul leaves the body to fly into the spiritual world.

This is the kind of idea which a skillful, though intellectually inclined person might have thought out in order to pass on to the child the concept of the immortality of the soul. But with such an attitude of mind the child will not feel inwardly touched. It will accept this picture and soon afterwards forget it again.

However, one could approach the same task in a different manner. For it is quite wrong to feel, "I am intelligent and the child is stupid." We have already seen in the course of our deliberations how cosmic wisdom is still working directly through the child and that from this point of view, it is the child who is intelligent and the teacher who is stupid. This I can bear in mind and I can fully believe in the picture of the emerging butterfly. A spiritual attitude to the world teaches me to believe in the truth of this picture which tells me: The same process which, on a higher plane, signifies the soul's withdrawal from the body, is repeated on a lower level in a simplified and sense-perceptible form when a butterfly emerges from the chrysalis. This picture is not an invention of mine, but it has been placed into the world by powers of cosmic wisdom. Here, before my very eyes, I can behold what, on a higher plane, happens when the soul leaves the body in death.

If this picture makes a deep impression upon my soul, I cannot but feel convinced of its truth.—If the teacher has such an experience, something begins to stir between his pupils and him or herself, something which can be assigned only to the realm of the imponderables. If, with the warmth and inwardness of his belief, the teacher brings this picture to the child, it will create a deep and lasting impression. It will become part of the child's being.

If one can look upon the effects of natural authority, leading to an obedience of a most inward kind, in a similar light, then authority will be accepted as something wholesome and positive. Then it will not be resented by a mistaken idea of freedom.

And so the teacher as artist in the field of education has to stand before the child as an artist of life also, because, after the change of teeth, the child approaches him as an artist, too, namely as a sculptor and a musician.

In certain cases these unconscious and inherent gifts of the child are developed to a specially high degree, namely in those children who in later life become virtuosi or geniuses. Such individuals never lose these former artistic gifts. But inwardly, though entirely unconsciously, every child is a great sculptor. Children retain these gifts from the time before the change of teeth. After this, the inner musical activities are woven together with the inner sculptural-formative activities. As educators we must learn to cooperate in a living way with these artistic forces working through the child.

Proceeding along these lines, it is possible to prevent rampant growth in the young human being. Then we shall enable him to develop his potential in the widest possible sense.

LECTURE X

Dornach, 1st January 1922

When the child has completed the ninth year, there follows an important moment in its development. In order to appreciate the significant change taking place during the ninth to the tenth year, one has to remember that the child's inborn feeling for authority, which began with the change of teeth, was of a general, undifferentiated kind. The child accepted the dictates of authority as a matter of course and it felt an inner need to conform to them without being as yet aware of the individual character of the adults concerned. With the completion of the ninth year, however, the child wants to experience an inner justification for authority.

Do not misunderstand my meaning. The child would never inwardly reason about whether authority is justified or not. Yet something emerges in its soul, seeking assurance that the authority of the grownup will stand the test of quality, that it is properly founded in life and that it carries an inner certainty. At this time of life the child has an acute awareness for these qualities and this awareness manifests itself in a subtle, yet quite objective change in its soul condition. Any sound education must take cognizance of this change and act accordingly. Up to this point in time the child was unable to discriminate fully between self and surroundings, for the world and self were experienced as one unity.

When trying to characterize such matters, one sometimes has to make rather radical statements and I must ask you to accept such a statement with the right attitude. For instance, if I say that before the ninth year the child does

162

not yet make a proper distinction between humans, animals, plants and stones, and that everything surrounding it appears to be alive in a general kind of way, it would be completely wrong to declare dogmatically that the child could not appreciate the difference between a human being and a lily. And yet, in a certain respect, my statement is correct. A real art of education will know how to appreciate the meaning of such apparently radical statements without turning them into dogmas. Life itself shows us everywhere that there are no sharp and rigid contours, so popular among pedantic minds.

The end of the ninth year is also the end of a characteristic feature which has frequently been misinterpreted by child psychologists. For example, when a child accidentally knocks itself against a table, it will hit back at it. This has been explained by them as the child's "personifying" the table. According to child psychology the child endows an inanimate object with a living soul which it wants to punish. But this interpretation shows only a superficial understanding of the child's feelings. In reality the child does not personify the table at all, but the fact is that it has not yet learned to discriminate between an inanimate object and a living being. The child responds to the situation in this way because it cannot yet separate itself from its environment.

Towards the end of the ninth year whole ranges of questions come up in the child's soul, which all arise from a new feeling of differentiation between the self and the outer world and also from a feeling of separateness from the person of the teacher. It is this new way of confronting the world which makes this age into such a turning point in the child's development. Up till now the child was hardly aware of whether the teacher was a clumsy sort of fellow who would knock against desks or tables, or who dropped pieces of blackboard chalk on the floor. It would not have occurred to the child under nine to react to a certain situation, as once

163

did a congregation during a church service. For the preacher had the habit of touching his nose every time he had completed a sentence of his sermon, and this habit caused ripples of laughter in church. True, the child would notice such an idiosyncrasy already before the completion of the ninth year, but it would pass by without making a deeper impression. It would be wrong to think that the child does not notice such things, but after the ninth year it becomes acutely aware of them. Already one or two years later, in the tenth and eleventh year, the child will pay far less attention to such matters. But what, at this particular time, is observed so keenly, becomes wrapped up in an entire system of inner questions which burden its soul. These questions may never be voiced, but they are there nonetheless. The child wonders whether the teacher is skilful in all matters pertaining to life, whether he knows what he wants and, above all, whether he or she is firmly rooted in life. The child has a sensitive perception for the general background of a teacher's personality. Consequently a teacher who is a sceptic will make a totally different impression from one who is a genuine believer, no matter what words he or she may be speaking.

These are the kind of things that are of a real concern to a child between the ninth and tenth year. Here many individual features of the adult play an important part. An orthodox Protestant teacher will arouse an entirely different impression in the child from a Catholic one, simply because of the differences of their soul situation. Here other factors need also to be considered, such as the fact that this turning point manifests itself at varying ages according to race and nationality, that is, earlier in one nationality and later in another. In each individual case this change may appear now earlier, now later, so that all forms of generalizations could be misleading. All one can say is that it is up to the teacher to perceive this subtle change in the child's soul. As

164

in so many other aspects of education, here a great deal depends on the teacher's penetrating and objective observation of all the pupils in his class.

This latter aspect is of special importance to us in the Waldorf School. In our regular teachers' meetings we discuss every single pupil and we try to learn as much as we can through each child's individuality. Naturally, if our numbers continue to grow, we may have to make other arrangements. But it is certainly possible to learn a great deal in these meetings, especially if one endeavors to study the more hidden aspects of the growing human being. And here one can make rather surprising discoveries. For example, for a time I made careful observations in our coeducational school regarding the effects of whether boys or girls were in the majority in the various classes, or whether their numbers were more or less balanced. Leaving aside more obvious features resulting from the general class life of the pupils, features which could be explained rationally, I found that classes where the girls were in the majority had an altogether different quality from others where there were more boys than girls. Here the imponderables are very much at work in the social sphere. However, it would be very wrong to draw the most convenient conclusion from what has been said by suggesting the abolition of coeducation. Such a retrograde step would merely increase the problems of life. The only answer is to learn how to deal with the problems posed by the majority or minority of boys or girls in the various classes.

The way in which a teacher is able to observe each individual pupil as well as the class as a whole is always of great importance. Here deeply philosophical questions arise. For example, in the Waldorf School we have observed that teachers made the best progress if they were able to relate themselves in the right way to the lessons they were giving, and also that with the passing of time their way of teaching had to change. Here again, unconscious and subconscious elements play their dominant part.

From all that has been said so far, you will have seen that at this crucial point the child will approach the teacher with all kinds of inner questions. Neither the content of these questions, nor the answers given to them matter as much as a certain inner awareness which gradually dawns upon the child's soul. This awareness springs from an indefinable element which, at this particular time, has to develop between the teacher as the guide and the pupil. This is what the pupil feels: "Up till now I have always looked up to my teacher. Now I can no longer do so, unless I know that he, too, looks up to something higher than himself, to something which is safely rooted in life." Specially inquisitive children will even pursue their teacher out of school time, noticing well what he does outside school. Everything depends on the teacher recognizing the significance of this stage and on his realizing that the child's tender approach is now longing for renewed confidence and trust. And the way in which a teacher responds to this situation may be a decisive factor for the child's entire life. Whether it will grow up into an unstable character or into a person strongly integrated in life, may well depend on whether the teacher is acting with inner certainty and understanding during this crucial time. If we realize the importance of the teacher's conduct and response during the child's ninth to tenth year, we may well wonder in what way the human being is dependent on his environment. However, light cannot be shed upon this important question unless we include in our deliberations other fundamental factors, deeply linked with a person's destiny or karma, questions which will occupy us more towards the end of this conference. Nevertheless, what has been stated here is absolutely relevant and true for any serious discussions on education. What matters is that at

166

this moment in life the child can find someone—whether this be one person or possibly several persons is of less importance—whose picture it can carry through life.

Only few people are able to observe a phenomenon of life which I should like to describe to you: During certain periods in a person's life the effects of childhood experiences will surface again and again and the images, springing from this particular turning point, are of the greatest importance. Whether they emerge only dimly in later life, whether in dreams or in the waking state, whether they are viewed with feelings of sympathy or antipathy, all this is of great importance, not the sympathy or antipathy in itself, but the fact that something passed through the child's soul which in one case evoked sympathy and in another case antipathy. I am not implying that these reminiscences, arising from the turning point during the ninth to tenth year, are experienced in clear consciousness. In some cases they remain almost completely hidden within the subconscious, but nevertheless they are bound to occur. People who have vivid dreams may see, at regular intervals, a certain scene or perhaps even the personality, the guide himself, who came to his aid in childhood, helping, admonishing, reassuring and awakening a personal relationship with them. This is the kind of soul experience which everyone needs to have met between the ninth and the tenth year. It is all part of the objective change taking place in the child which, previously, was not yet able to distinguish itself from its surroundings and which now feels the need to find its own identity, to become a separate individuality, able to confront the outer world.

From what has been said it follows that the subject matter to be taught at this age must also be adapted to this particular period in the child's development. Especially in our present times it will become more and more necessary to deal with all educational matters out of real insight into the human being. Just think for a moment of how many children, after their change of teeth, have the possibility of seeing all kinds of machines at work, such as railway engines, tram cars and so on. Here I can speak out of personal experience, for as a young child I grew up in a small railway station where every day I could watch countless trains passing by. And I must state quite categorically that the worst possible thing for a child before the end of the ninth year is to gain a mechanical understanding of a locomotive, a tram or any other mechanical contrivance. That such matters can affect the entire constitution right down to the physical body you will understand if you observe other related phenomena of life. For example, you need only think of what it means to the life experience of several generations, if a whole nation adopts a new language. Why, for instance, do the Bulgarians appear a Slavonic people? According to their racial origin they are not Slavs at all, for by race they belong to the family of the Finns, of the Huns. According to their race they belong to the Mongolian-Tartar stream. But early on in their history they adopted a Slavonic idiom and, because of it, they gradually changed into a Slavonic nation. All that they imbibed with their new language and with their new culture penetrated their entire inner being. I have met people who considered the Bulgarian element as one of the purest of all the Slavonic elements which, from the anthropological point of view, it certainly is not. All too often one fails to realize the potent effects of soul and spiritual influences upon the children's entire constitution, working right down into their physical organization.

And so I have to make a rather drastic remark. After the change of teeth a child would experience a conceptual method of thinking as if spikes were being driven through its whole being, especially if such concepts came from the inorganic or lifeless realm. Anything taken from the soulless realm in itself, will estrange the child. Therefore those whose task it is to teach children of this age need an artistic ability of imbuing everything they bring with life. Everything must live. The teacher must let the plants speak, he or she must let the animals act as moral beings. The teacher must be able to turn the whole world into a fairy tale, into fables and legends. And in this context something else of great significance also must be taken into account.

What would an easygoing teacher do, when faced with such a pedagogical challenge? Most likely he would go to libraries to find books containing legends, animal stories and other kindred subjects. These he or she would read up for use in the classroom. Of course, sometimes one has to make do with second-best arrangements, but this method is far from ideal. The ideal would be for the teacher to have prepared himself so well for his task—and this kind of approach does need very thorough preparation—that a conversation between plants—or a fairy tale about the lily and the rose—will come to the children as his own creation. Ideally, such a conversation between the sun and the moon should be the product of the teacher's individual imagination. And why should this be so? Let me answer in a picture. If one tells pupils what one has found in books—however lively one may be as a person—if one tells them what one has read and possibly even memorized, one talks to them like a dry and dessicated individual. It is as if one did not have a living skin, but were covered with parchment instead, for there always remain death-like traces in one's own being of what was thus learned from the past. If, on the other hand, a teacher is creative in his work, his content will radiate growing forces, it will be fresh and alive, and this is what feeds the souls of the children.

There has to be a creative urge to clothe the world of plants and animals, of sun and moon, into living stories, if the teacher wishes to reach children of this age. And when—having engrossed himself in such imaginative work which

169

demands a great deal of inner effort—he hurries to school, his steps already betraying his eagerness to share his offering with his class, the effects of his endeavor will doubtlessly be wholesome for all the children. Such a teacher knows only too well that his story will remain incomplete until he has seen the radiant faces of his young listeners.

Up to the end of the ninth year everything the child learns about plants, animals and stones, about sun, moon and stars or clouds, mountains and rivers, should be clothed in such a picture form, for the child feels at one with the world. In those young days, child and world are one united whole.

But with the arrival of the great change a new situation arises. The child now begins to experience itself as a self-contained being. It learns to distinguish itself from the surroundings, and this offers a new possibility, indeed the necessity, of introducing the child to the world in new terms. Now the teaching should bring out the fundamental difference between the plant world and that of the animals, for the child needs to be introduced to these two kingdoms of nature each in its own different way. It is certainly possible to introduce children in their tenth to twelfth years to the plant and animal kingdoms, but each of these two subjects must be taken from a different point of view.

To introduce pupils of this age to a plant by showing them a specimen, pulled out of the earth, as if it were complete in itself, is really a dreadful thing to do. Right from the start there ought to be a feeling that a single plant torn out of the earth—not unlike a human hair pulled out of the body—does not represent a reality. It could never exist on its own. Likewise—once it has been pulled out of the earth —the plant cannot exist independently. The plant belongs to the surface of the earth, as the human hair belongs to the head. Plant and earth belong together. We shall see in a moment that something else is needed here, but to begin with we awaken in the children a feeling of how plant and earth belong together. We let them experience how in the root the plant is more earth-like, the root adapting itself to the varying nature of the soil. Such an observation, however, must never be abstract, nor should it be simply taught as a fact, but the pupils should gradually develop a feeling of how, for instance, the roots are different in dry or in wet soil, or whether they grow close to towering rocks or near to the sea. First of all the child has to learn to look upon the plant as belonging to the earth's soul, and upon all sprouting vegetation as rising up out of the soil.

Then one has to develop a feeling in the children for the contrasting nature of earth-like root and the blossom and fruit which are closely allied to the sun. When talking about blossom and fruit, one has to lead the children from the earth sphere to the sun sphere. The pupil ought to gain a feeling of how the blossom unfolds in the warmth and light of the sun's rays and how in blossom and fruit the plant is becoming emancipated from the fetters of the earth. Earth, plant growth and the influence of the sun all have to be looked upon as being part of a complete whole. I should even like to say that the child's idea of the plant should be so steeped in feeling that, were one to talk about it without referring both to the earth as a whole and to the sun, the child should inwardly experience a twinge of pain not unlike one caused by seeing a plant being torn from its earthly home.

Here again we must not look upon the subject to be taught merely in the abstract, but we ought also to consider its social implications. Only think of what it means for the development of our civilization that a large proportion of our population is now living in urban surroundings, with the effect—and people who have left the countryside to live in towns will confirm this—that generations of city children have grown up who are unable to distinguish wheat from rye. Although this may sound grotesque, in my opinion a person who has not learned to distinguish rye from wheat cannot be considered a full human being. I would even go as far as saying that a city dweller who knows the difference between these two grains only through handling them, still does not attain to the ideal. Only he who has stood on the very soil on which rye and wheat were growing and who has learned to recognize them there on the spot, has made the right inner connection with those two plants.

As teachers we should avoid collecting specimens on our own in order to show them to our pupils in the classroom. It would be far better to take the children out into nature so that there, in the real and living situation of earth, sun and weather conditions they may gain an understanding of plant life. This would also give us an opportunity of showing them something else of importance, namely, what a potato really is. For the potato is not part of the root, as it may appear, but in reality it is a bulbous stem. The dry soil on which the potato plant grows, draws back into the earth what really belongs to the green leaves and stems. Looking at these green parts of a plant one should be able to recognize to what extent the plant's growth is governed by the forces of the earth and in how far the soil makes its impulse felt in the plant. One ought to be able to experience how in the case of the potato the stalks demean themselves by creeping under the dry ground. And again one ought to have an eye for how the moist meadowland and the slanting rays of the autumn sun create the lilac-colored cups of Colchicum Autumnale, the autumn crocus.

If we thus present a picture of how the plant grows out of the earth as out of a living organism, showing how it adapts itself to the varying kinds of soil, to different climates and other influences, we can easily find a transition to geography. Other aspects of this subject will fit into the picture quite naturally. And yet, when talking about the earth, what kind of picture is usually presented nowadays? So

often the earth's green mantle, the plant world, is completely left out of account. People talk as if the earth were nothing but a globe moving in outer space, controlled by the
laws of gravity which explain the mutual effects between
heavenly bodies. It is as if this mathematical—mechanical
aspect were all that mattered. But who has the right to isolate
the mathematical and mechanical laws of gravity affecting the
earth from what belongs to it so intimately, namely the growing plant? When talking about the earth as a sphere moving
through the universe, one ought to pay at least equally
much attention to what the earth contributes to the plant in
its root, as we do to the purely mathematical and mechanical
relationships resulting from gravitation and so on.

It is important to let all lessons be pervaded by the
fulness of life. Now, just as we related the plant world to the
surface of the earth, so—when introducing animal study—
should we link the animals to the human being. When calling forth ideas about the plant world in the way I have indicated, the teacher will notice that all kinds of questions as to
the why and wherefore of the world will come up in class
conversations. It is really much healthier if such questions
of causality come up during the study of the plant than if
they are brought about by mechanical concepts or through
the study of lifeless minerals. And just as we should allow a
feeling for causality to develop through the study of the
plant, so it is right to introduce the study of animals by comparing them with the human being, an analogy which will
remain valid throughout the pupils' lives.

In order to facilitate a clear understanding of the principles underlying the introduction to the study of animals, I
should like to pass on to you certain ideas—far too often ignored nowadays—which, however, are definitely addressed
to the adult world and which would have to be specially
adapted for use in the classrooms of pupils aged ten to twelve.

If we look at the human being from a morphological and

173

physiological point of view, we see that the head in its outer appearance is rounded off and roughly spherical. Within it there is the grey matter of the brain which is only slightly differentiated from cellular ganglia, and deeper within there is the fibrous white matter. Now, is it possible to find an analogy to the formation of the human head in the animal world? And if so, where do we find it? We have to look for it among the lowest grades of the animal kingdom. The human head is of course a highly complex organ, but its most characteristic feature consists in that a soft mass within is enclosed by a hard outer shell, and this fundamental feature can be found, though in a primitive state, among the lower animals. Anyone willing to look at nature without prejudice will recognize in the crustaceans the principle of the human head in its most primitive form and, consequently, will relate the human head to the shellfish. From this point of view an oyster resembles the human head far more than an ape. If you look at any of the soft-bodied animals encased within a hard shell, you have before you the simplest form of the human head.

If we now move on to the human chest system, to that part of our body which mainly comes under the influence of the spine, we are led to higher animals, for example the fish. And how is the fish constituted? In the case of the fish, the head is hardly more than a continuation of the spine, despite the fact that the head is more differentiated. The entire fish is a spine creature. And if we look upon the organization of the fish as a creature belonging to the middle group of the animal kingdom, we have to compare it with the human lymph organization, with man's middle system.

If we look at yet higher animals, the mammals, we cannot but compare what they have developed to a specially high degree to the human metabolism and limb system. Take the lion or the camel: Their entire being is dominated by the specially developed organization of limbs and metabolism.

174

Looking at the animal kingdom from this point of view, a remarkable relationship emerges between the three animal groups and the human organization:

Organization of the head—lower animals

Organization of the rhythmic system—intermediary animals

Organization of the metabolism and limbs—higher animals

Such an approach gives us also a real insight into the evolution of man and animal. Human development began with something which finally emerged as the head, but this happened during very ancient times when outer conditions of the earth were entirely different from what they are today. There was as yet plenty of time and opportunity for these early stages—which, oyster-like, were depending on impulses coming from their surroundings—to develop into what has become the present head. Now the head, parasite-like, sits on top of the remaining organism from which it draws what the oyster still draws from its environment. During the course of evolution man replaced external earthly surroundings by developing the head as part of the human organism. One can follow this development if one looks at human embryology which shows that, with regard to his head organization, man has undergone a long evolution. The head organization began at a time which is still represented by today's mollusks. Today's mollusks, however, are late arrivals in evolution. As they now have to develop under less favorable outer conditions, they cannot achieve the density of the human head, but have to remain at the stage of a soft-bodied animal surrounded by a hard shell. In today's completely different external conditions they still represent early stages of man's head organization.

The organization of the fish, on the other hand, occurred during a later period of earth evolution than that of man, and it already met different outer conditions. At that time man had already reached a stage when he could draw from his own rhythmic system impulses which the fish still had to draw from its surroundings. The organization of the intermediate animal group was added to that of the evolving human being who by that time had reached a certain stage of development. And finally, when man had already begun to develop his limb and metabolic system in its present sense—when his metabolism had become differentiated, leaving only a residue in the head and chest organization—the higher animals began to appear on the earth.

This point of view will enable you to understand that the current theory of man's descent is correct, but only with regard to the head. For the head does stem from forebears who had a remote resemblance to the lowest animals of to-day. And yet, these forebears were again quite different from our present day crustaceans because these latter creatures have to exist under such different external conditions.

Regarding the organization of his middle system, man is descended from forebears who quite definitely were already on the way towards becoming human and who, regarding their physical organization, resembled the fish. However, the fish species itself arrived too late and consequently it had no longer enough time to develop the head fully, especially since the fish was restricted to living in the watery element.

In this way, we obtain a theory of man's descent which is in accordance with reality. On the other hand, if one does not take into consideration man's threefold organization, one can reach only a one-sided theory which, however ingenious it may be, simply does not stand up to a thorough and searching investigation. And so we can say: In the ascending order of today's animal species we can recognize the one-sided development of one particular system of the human organization. The shellfish is a one-sided head animal, the fishes are one-sided chest animals and the higher mammals have specialized in their development of the metabolic and limb system. We can understand every animal form, if we look at each major animal group as having specialized—onesidedly—in one of the three main systems of man's bodily organization.

At the turn of the eighteenth to nineteenth century there were still some people who had a natural feeling for such ideas. But as there was not sufficient knowledge to work them out thoroughly and realistically at that particular time, only the underlying feelings were correct. *Oken*, one of the German nature philosophers now held much in contempt but who, nevertheless, was a very ingenious personality, once made a grotesque-sounding statement. It is of course all too easy to ridicule it today, but it was made out of a certain right feeling. *Oken* declared that the human tongue was an octopus. Well, the human tongue is definitely not an octopus. It is easy enough to make this judgment. But behind *Oken's* statement there was a general feeling that one has to look at the lower animals if one wants to gain an understanding of the various forms of the organs in the human head.

What I have told you was given for your information, but it is quite possible to present these ideas so that children can also understand them, for children are receptive to the morphological approach to the human being. One can study the various human forms and then find the appropriate analogy to forms in the animal world. In this way it is definitely possible to awaken in children the feeling that the entire animal kingdom is like a human being spread out into all the manifold animal forms, or that man is the synthesis of the animal kingdom.

In this way the teacher links the animal world to the human being, as the plant world was related to the earth. Introducing each of these two subjects according to its own individual character, we shall awaken a healthy feeling for the world when, after the age of nine, the child has learned to appreciate the distinction between inner self and outer world. The aim is not so much that the pupils should accumulate a great deal of knowledge, but that we prepare the

177

ground for them to acquire the right feeling for the world.

Just think of the kind of things which are done in the name of education, not only as far as pupils are concerned, but also with regard to the training of teachers. Quite dreadful things are happening in teacher training centers where, in order to pass their exams, candidates are often expected to carry an unnecessary burden of factual knowledge in their heads. In most instances examination questions demand the kind of knowledge which could be looked up equally well in an encyclopedia. Such memorized facts are of little real value. What is important is that the examiners gain the conviction of a candidate's suitability for the teaching profession because he or she is capable of teaching out of a real knowledge of man.

The question of memory and our attitude towards its development in children is another point of great importance. We must not forget that up to the change of teeth memory, or the ability to remember, is directly linked to the child's organic development. What a child of that age remembers so easily is brought about by forces which are working at the same time in the process of nutrition and growth. Up to the change of teeth, the child's soul-spiritual and its physical forces are simply one unity. Therefore we could make the greatest mistakes if, by artificial means we were to try to strengthen the child's memory before it has shed its teeth.

We must be clear that before the change of teeth the child is an imitator, also with regard to the development of its memory. This means that if we behave rightly in its presence, the child will develop its memory according to its predisposition towards physical growth and nutrition. Physical care, of which we shall have to speak later on, and the child's hygiene are the best means for cultivating the child's memory forces.

One of the characteristic traits of our materialistic age is that people try to interfere with the young child's natural development by using artificial educational means. Appealing to the child's soul and spiritual element, they want to train its memory already before the seventh year. Some of them even want to go further—which only goes to show how out of touch with reality a materialistic attitude can be. There are mothers—and here I speak from personal experience—who not only ask how they should teach their children before the change of teeth in a manner befitting only a later age, but who even go as far as asking how one should educate a child before it is born. They ask how the embryo should be educated! All one can say in answer is: Let the mother look after herself and her conduct. If she lives healthily and treats herself rightly, the child will develop in a healthy way. Its growth will have to be left to the Creator.

This may be rather a radical way of putting it, but it is nevertheless a justifiable one in view of the sophisticated questions about educational principles which really belong to an older age.

On the other hand we must be clear that with the change of teeth the soul and spiritual part of the child becomes emancipated from the physical to such an extent that now is the right time for us to plan educational principles which are to aid the child's faculty of remembering. For this faculty, too, becomes emancipated at this stage. When the child reaches school age, it is right to do something about strengthening its memory, but this needs to be done according to a definite plan. If one burdens the child's memory, that is, if one tries to strengthen it by overloading it, the child's faculty of remembering will only be weakened. Such misdirected efforts will encourage a certain rigidity in later life and a proneness towards prejudices which such a person will find hard to overcome. If, on the other hand, memory development is disregarded altogether, the child will be deprived of certain means towards developing physical

179

strength. If, when a child reaches school age, nothing is done to train its memory, the consequences will be a tendency towards inflammatory conditions in adolescence. Such a person will easily suffer from inflammations and be liable to catch colds.

Causal links of this kind once again show how one has to consider both the physical and the soul-spiritual aspects together. Therefore memory development demands a certain tact from the teacher who must avoid doing too much or too little about it. It would be equally wrong to drill the child's memory excessively, as it would be to overlook the question of memory altogether. The answer is neither to damage the child's living interest by enforcing mechanical memorizing, nor to neglect memory building altogether.

Let us look at ways of putting these ideas into practice. We can introduce children to the four rules of Arithmetic as described in the last lecture. We can give them some understanding of number relationships according to whether we subtract, divide, add or multiply, as shown yesterday. But there is always an opportunity of letting the pupils memorize their tables, as long as these are related to the four rules in the right way. This will also help them to deal with more complicated number relationships to be introduced at a later stage.

In this respect it is easy to commit sins by introducing the so-called object lessons. Calculators* have been introduced. I do not wish to be fanatical in any way and the calculator may have its usefulness. From certain points of view everything in life is justifiable. But much of what can be gained from the use of thought-out calculating machines can equally well be achieved through the use of the ten fingers or, for example, through taking the number of pupils in the class. Do not take it amiss if I tell you that when I see calculators in classrooms, from a spiritual point of view it strikes

---

*Here Rudolf Steiner was referring to various forms of the abacus.

180

me as if I were in a medieval torture chamber! It really is not right to delegate learning processes to mechanical devices simply in order to bypass apparently mechanical memorizing. This is an area where we are facing a specially difficult task in the Waldorf School. I have already told you that we aim at achieving "soul economy" in our teaching and, consequently, we believe it to be beneficial for our pupils if we restrict learning to the classrooms. This means that we give the pupils as little homework as possible. This principle is prompted by yet another motive. Certainly one should aim at developing in the child a feeling of duty, of responsibility and, later on, we shall speak about how one can try to bring this about. But what is very damaging is, if the teacher makes certain demands upon the pupils which they do not fulfil. And homework—as any other learning done at home —is very conducive to this effect. Parents often complain to us that their children are not given enough homework to do. But we have to consider the fact—and this is absolutely clear to anyone with sufficient insight—that too much homework will cause some pupils to be overtaxed, while others will be tempted to produce slipshod work or simply to evade such tasks. Sometimes it is simply beyond the children's abilities to fulfil the teacher's demands. But the worst thing to happen is that children do not carry out what the teacher has told them to do. Therefore it would be better to ask less of them than to risk letting them get away with not fulfilling their set tasks. All expectations and demands regarding the training of memory as well as those involving homework need to be dealt with by the teachers very tactfully. The development of the pupil's memory depends especially upon the teacher's sensitive perception and it is largely due to this quality that the right relationship between the teacher and his class will develop.

Tomorrow we shall go into further details about the right attitude towards memory training.

LECTURE XI

Dornach, 2nd January 1922

At the end of yesterday's lecture I tried to speak to you about the development of memory during the early school years. If we now look at the attitude regarding this question as shown by most contemporary educational theorists, we cannot but notice a total lack of awareness of how certain impulses in the early years of pupils continue to play into their later lives and how these then reappear in a transformed condition. This, at any rate, is what a true knowledge of man reveals to us. What so often happens nowadays is that the adult, when he tries to understand the ways of his own physical organism and of his psyche, reaches certain conclusions. Although he may not be conscious of it, he then assumes that these conclusions also apply to the varying ages and stages of childhood. Such an attitude, however, is very misleading for—as I pointed out already—the forces working throughout the child's development need to be recognized and supported if our education is to be sound. We must meet the inner needs of the child, as the example of the importance of authority in the life of a young child was meant to convey.

Let us take a hypothetical example of someone who, in his fortieth year, undergoes certain vague soul experiences. Outer circumstances may suddenly shed light upon what has thus arisen in his soul. He may recognize that what was in his mind was something which, at the age of eight or nine, he had accepted simply on the authority of a beloved teacher. At such a tender age he could only entrust it to his memory, for the maturity of a forty-year-old person may

182

have been necessary for its full comprehension. (I say this although not many people will believe my interpretation.) However, children cannot always wait until they are forty before they understand what they may have been told at the age of eight and this is the very reason why they have an inner longing for authority. And when, at the age of forty, new light suddenly flashes upon what had been accepted merely on the basis of authority at the age of eight, this happening brings an experience of new inner life forces which have a refreshing effect upon the entire person. New inner strength, badly needed in later life, is developed through such a process. And if one has accepted on authority plenty of content which, through outer circumstances, will reappear as if by magic out of one's organism, one is blessed with a revitalizing source of strength for the remaining years of one's life. Nowadays, many people age prematurely, both in body and in soul, because they are denied access to this vivifying force. Too many years have gone by since memory, during the early school years, was systematically strengthened through right and reasonable methods, and since it was based upon faith and belief in the authority of an adult.

Memory training apart, there are always plenty of other opportunities for cultivating the children's faculties of comprehension, as I mentioned yesterday. But between the change of teeth and puberty it is absolutely essential for teachers to work out well thought out and sensible methods for developing the pupils' memory, because without this aid they will be deprived of too much in their later lives.

If my intention were to please my listeners, I should have to speak quite differently about many things. But I wish to convey only what a true knowledge of man has revealed after decades of anthroposophical research. Consequently many things I have to say will sound paradoxical when compared with currently accepted opinions. Some of my findings will create an impression of being old fashioned, while others may appear "avant-garde." But all this is quite unimportant. The only thing that matters is whether what I have to say will stand the test of a real knowledge of man.

If one examines the general picture of man, as seen by so many people today, one can't help feeling that it has been arrived at by observing the human being from the outside only. It is as if one were trying to understand how a clock works merely by looking at it from the outside. In this way one can read the time. One can recognize whether a watch is made of gold or silver, but one will never learn to become a clock maker. What today goes under the name of biology, physiology or anatomy shows us only what man is like when viewed externally. Human nature will become transparent to our understanding only if we learn to penetrate man's body, soul and spirit. Only by including these three members in our investigations are we in a position to treat the human being in accordance with his real nature. And if, with insight into the whole human being, we now look at a certain question lately much discussed in educational circles —it is the question of fatigue in the child's organism—we have to say the following: Experiments are being made today to establish the causes of fatigue or tiredness in children. The results of these investigations are then made use of in new teaching techniques which aim at reducing strain in pupils. This sort of thing is done all over the world and yet the whole question is based upon the wrong premise. A real knowledge of man would never lead to such a question at all. You only need to consider something which has been pointed out here during our last few meetings, in order to find it so. You will remember that a strong plea was made repeatedly that all teaching during the younger years should appeal to the rhythmical and musical element in children which, first and foremost, works upon their breathing and blood circulation.

And now I ask you: Can the source of fatigue ever lie in the children's breathing and blood circulation? Can it ever lie in the middle region of the human being, in the very region to which we always give our special attention and treatment during the child's school age? Never! For, don't we all breathe continuously, both during sleep and waking life, from the moment we are born until we die, without ever feeling tired of breathing? Does not our blood circulate tirelessly from birth to death? Never is its flow interrupted through fatigue, for if this were to happen, the consequences would be serious indeed. Does this not show that teachers working out of a real art of education are constantly appealing to the very organs which are never subject to fatigue? This whole question has to be considered from quite a different angle. We must formulate it differently and ask: Where do the real sources of tiredness lie in the human being? We find them in the head region and in the limb system. It is to these two systems we have to turn our attention if we wish to understand the nature of tiredness in children which, according to whether it emanates from the head or from the limbs and metabolism, bears a completely different character.

The forces working from the head downwards into the remaining human organism deposit a very fine metabolic residue which wants to permeate the whole human body with fine salt-like deposits. This process, which affects also the breathing and blood circulation, is the cause of fatigue because of the head's direct contact with the external world and because of its arrhythmical and non-musical relationship with the outer world. The rhythms of breathing and blood circulation, on the other hand, are so strongly bound to the human organism that they retain a state of equilibrium, obeying their own laws. And what in the middle system acts like a self-contained unit, is not subject to fatigue, at least not to any marked degree. It is of course

185

possible to damage the inner rhythms of both children and adults by a wrong kind of treatment. But there is one thing we may be sure of, and that is that the rhythmic system, which is of such primary importance in any true art of education, never suffers from tiredness or fatigue.

The limbs and metabolism, like the head, do get tired. You can observe this by watching a snake after it has eaten. The limb and metabolic system tires, or at least it can become a source of tiredness, affecting the whole human being. Yet this form of tiredness is of a totally different kind from that of the head. The head system causes tiredness through depositing salts, through a precipitation of mineral substances in the human organism. The limb and metabolic system, on the other hand, always has the tendency to dissolve physical substances through its creation of warmth. Here, too, despite its polar opposite effect from that of the head, the cause of tiredness is to be found in the comparative independence of this system from the inner rhythms of the human organization. This tiredness stems from the limbs' activities in the external world and from the metabolism's responding to the intake of food. Eating and drinking usually happen at irregular intervals, for there are only very few people who adhere to a strict and fixed rhythm of eating and drinking. Therefore, though both head and metabolism share the same cause of tiredness, their effects are of a polar-opposite nature.

What follows from all this? The whole question of fatigue in pupils needs to be put differently. If the child tires easily we ought to ask: What is it we have done wrongly? Where do our mistakes lie? For we have no right to assume that our teaching methods are always correct. As long as we proceed by testing the child's liability to make so and so many more errors per line after half an hour of writing than before, as long as we check its lack of awareness of meaningless words inserted in the text after a certain time of

186

reading, we shall never reach human nature. This we shall do only by asking the right question which, in the case of fatigue in children, should be: Have I overburdened either the child's head or its limb system? We must find ways of not placing too much strain upon either of these two systems.

However, it would be erroneous to believe that this could be achieved simply by adjusting the sequence of lessons in the timetable, for neither will gym lessons in themselves balance out too much head work nor, conversely, would arithmetic lessons directly work into the metabolism, though they do so indirectly. It is not possible to achieve the right balance merely by readjusting the timetable, but only by an artistic presentation of all lesson content, at least during the early school years. This in turn means that we have to appeal—in the way I have indicated—above all to the rhythmic system, the one system of the human being that never tires. When doing so, we also involve the other two systems—that of the head and the metabolic and limb system—in the activity of learning. Naturally, this needs to be done in the right way.

I hope that by now you may have realized that certain doubts with regard to new ideas and methods of education—so frequently expressed by people who are prejudiced—do not apply to Waldorf Education at all because, in every respect, it is founded upon a true knowledge of man. And as it also endeavors to shed light upon man's soul and spiritual nature, it is able to lay the foundations of educational methods which will work upon the entire human being. And so, to give an example, it is important to recognize that the head system of man is the bearer of forces which—most strongly during childhood and to a lessening degree during successive ages—penetrate the entire human organism, shaping it, forming it and giving it strength. What is working as a thought-directing capacity in the head is something which the human being, with all his predispositions, brings with him into this world at birth or conception. Eventually these forces take on the task of forming the entire human being. If the head were not in direct touch with the external world and if, in consequence, the inner rhythms of the human being were not disturbed all the time, then—if I may express it in this way—what has incarnated at birth in the head, would be fully satisfied with the physical organization of man. The human being would flow into his physical organization which would claim his entire being. He would be completely absorbed by it. He would not be able to make any contact with the supersensible world. As man would thus become separated from the spiritual world, his inner life would become more and more artificial and false. And, conversely, if through his limb and metabolic system man would not be in constant touch with the external world, he would not be able to permeate with glowing warmth what is streaming down from the head. He would be unable to counteract these forces which would be working towards a more and more artificial state of perfection.

Here we have two marked polarities. The head always wants to cut us off from the spiritual world by shaping our body in a way which would prevent us from gaining a right relationship to the spiritual world. For the head, with all that belongs to it, has completed its development a long time ago during man's pre-earthly existence, and the process of materialization, issuing from the head, always has to be counteracted by the activities of man's metabolism and limbs, which stream upwards from below. In this way a balance is achieved in our corporeality. And between these two poles, as our middle system—like an organism complete in itself—there lies our respiration and blood circulation, our rhythmic system. This rhythmic system is like a separate world in itself, like a real microcosm. However, despite its comparative independence, it must be protected from extreme influences coming from the head, as can happen under certain circumstances when the lungs become invaded by all kinds of foreign organic processes. This we can observe in the hardening of lungs, in new growth in the lungs of people suffering from lung diseases.

Man needs this polarity between the head on the one side and the metabolism and limb systems on the other. The latter is always trying to dissolve the hardening processes issuing from the head and this situation can be utilized also medically. For if one recognizes the interplay between what descends from the head and what ascends from the metabolism, one is able to cure, for example, pathological symptoms in the larynx, the trachea or also in the lungs, by treating the metabolic system, even if the source of illness lies in the head. Especially in the case of children's diseases quite spectacular results have been achieved by treating a patient's metabolism for the symptoms of illness which appeared in the head organization. The human being is one organic entity and has to be treated accordingly. This rule applies to all aspects of man, not only to a well-founded therapy, but especially to the field of education.

If you look at the great progress in general knowledge made during the last centuries, it becomes very noticeable how little has been achieved with regard to knowledge of man. This is mainly due to the fact that the methods applied took into consideration only the physical, the external aspect of man. It really is of utmost importance for anyone engaged in the art of education to be able to recognize quite realistically what is happening in the body, soul and spirit of the growing child, especially during the time which falls between the great turning point at nine plus and the coming of puberty. It is essential for the educator to be able to see how the physical, soul and spiritual forces work upon and affect each other in the children he is dealing with.

If, with real insight, we observe a child aged nine to ten,

we shall find that everything that enters its soul is absorbed and transmuted in such a way that the muscular system, permeated by forces of growth, becomes actively involved. At that time of life the muscular system always responds to and cooperates with the soul nature of the child, especially where the more intimate forces of growth are at work. The interior swelling or stretching of the muscles mainly depends upon the development of the child's soul forces. And the characteristic feature of the age between ten to twelve consists in the muscles having a specially intimate relationship with respiration and blood circulation. They are attuned to the middle system of breathing and blood circulation. And as Waldorf Education appeals so strongly to this very part of the child's being, we indirectly promote the growth and development of the child's muscles.

Towards the twelfth year a new situation arises. The muscles no longer remain so intimately connected with the child's respiration and blood circulation; they now incline more towards the bony system, adapting themselves to the dynamics of the skeleton. Their forces of growth are fully engaged in the movement of limbs in walking, jumping and grasping, in fact in all limb activities in their relation to the skeleton. The muscles, previously closely allied to the rhythmic system, now become entirely oriented towards the bony system. In this way the child adapts itself more strongly to the external world than was the case before the twelfth year. Formerly the muscular system was more directly connected with the child's inner being, and the rhythmic system, because of its relative independence, played a dominant part in the growth of the muscles. The child moved in harmony with the muscular system, and the skeleton, embedded in the muscles, was simply carried along. Now, towards the twelfth year, the situation changes rapidly. The muscular system begins to serve the mechanics and the dynamics of the bony system.

Everyone who is able to observe and understand what is happening within the child—how before the twelfth year the child uses its muscles which simply carry the bones along, and how afterwards it begins to relate itself directly to the skeleton and, in doing so, also to the external world—has really gained a deep insight into the development of human nature. Such insights free us from abstract and intellectual modes of investigation so prevalent today, which so easily creep into the field of education. These insights also help the educator towards a truly human approach to the child. If one allowed such things to work upon one's soul, one would never impose the kind of treatment on a child, such as *Marsyas* had to endure. It is of course possible that some people are frightened off when they witness how transparent the human being becomes in the light of this kind of knowledge of man. They may well feel that the human soul is being dissected, but this is not the case, for the anthroposophical approach is both artistic and at the same time a deed of knowledge. The whole way of looking upon man is an artistic one and it is this quality which is necessary if one wants to grasp the significance of the child's stage up to puberty or, as we can now describe it, the transition from the intimate affinity of the muscles to the breathing and blood circulation up to the twelfth year, and the subsequent kinship of the muscles to the bones from the twelfth year to the coming of puberty.

Can you see now how the incarnating human being gradually adapts himself to the world? In the very young child the formative forces are centered in the brain. They ray out from the head. Then the center of activities shifts to the muscular system, and after the age of twelve, the human being pours himself into the skeleton, as it were. Only then is he ready to enter the world fully. The incarnating human being first must penetrate the body before he can establish a relationship with the external world. First the forces of the head are at work. Later on, these forces are poured into the muscles, then into the bony system and after sexual maturity is reached, the adolescent is able to enter the world. Only then can he stand properly in the world.

This gradual process of incarnation needs to be taken into consideration if one wants to find the right choice and presentation of subject matter, especially for this age. But unfortunately nowadays educators are hardly blessed with a sound knowledge of man. And now I must ask you to forgive me if I confront you with something which may appear to you completely absurd. Often I feel compelled to do such a thing because I have to stand up for anthroposophical truths. Contemporary physiologists, biologists and anatomists will look upon what I am going to say as pure heresy, but nevertheless it represents the truth.

When people speak or think about the human being today, they first of all turn their attention to the head. Although the head in itself always has the tendency to push us into what is material, although it would want to kill us every day if it were given free rein, it has nevertheless become the focus of attention among the general public of today, and this is what is so unhealthy in our present evaluation of the human being. It is the natural consequence of our modern scientific outlook. The general idea is that in the head there is the brain which is a kind of absolute ruler over everything we think or do. I wonder how such a theory could have been explained before the time of the telegraph, for this invention offered such a plausible analogy to what is happening in our brain. However, this need not concern us here. The theory of the human nervous system was postulated only after the use of telecommunications had made such an analogy possible. And so the brain was compared to a telecommunication center stationed, let us say, in London. (Here Rudolf Steiner made a drawing on the blackboard.) If this is the center in London, then here could be Oxford, and

Dover over there. If London is the center, then we could say: Here is a line running from Oxford to London. And here in London messages coming from Oxford are switched over to Dover. Under given circumstances we could well imagine it to be like this.

And now one imagines that the human brain functions in a similar way. The nerves go from the brain to the sense organs where sense perception takes place, and this perception is conducted back to the brain. Here in the brain there is the central station, the human "London." Then, so one imagines, there are the motor nerves which go from the brain to the organs of movement where they bring about the will impulses of movement in accordance with the thoughts of the brain which, somehow, are also part of such a will activity.

Once such a theory has been thought out, one can present the relevant facts in such a way that they seem to substantiate it. Take any book on physiology and in it you will find descriptions of how experiments are made in cutting nerves and of how various physical reactions in the human body lead to definite logical conclusions. Unless you have strong reservations from the outset—for all these things look so very plausible—everything seems to fit together beautifully. The only snag is that it does not stand up to what a penetrating knowledge of man has to say about it. There it is not acceptable.

I will disregard the fact that, anatomically, the sensory nerves and the motor nerves are practically indistinguishable from one another. At most the one kind is a little thicker than the other, but with regard to their structure, there is not really any significant difference between them. According to anthroposophical research—and this I can only indicate, as otherwise I should have to give whole lectures on anthroposophical physiology—both types of nerves are uniform organs. It is quite absurd to talk about two different kinds of nerves, about sensory and motor nerves. As both the element of sensation and that of will are omnipresent in the human soul, I leave everybody free to call these nerves sensory or motor nerves, but they must be recognized as being but one unified entity, for there is no essential difference between them. The difference lies entirely in the direction in which they function. The optic nerve—a sensory nerve— is open to the light impressions upon the eye, and what is happening at the periphery again affects another nerve which present-day physiology calls a motor nerve. If now this other nerve goes from the brain to the remaining organism, its function is to perceive what is happening during physical movement. A correct treatment of Tabes Dorsalis would confirm this statement.

It is the function of the so-called motor nerve to perceive the motor impulses, to perceive what is happening when physical movement takes place, but not to initiate them. Nerves, wherever they may be, are organs for transmitting impressions. The sensory nerves transmit external impressions and the motor nerves internal impressions. There is but one kind of nerve. Only a scientific materialism could have invented the analogy of the nerves with the telegraphic system. Only a materialistic science could believe that, apart from the nerves which transmit sense impressions during the process of perception, there must also be other nerves whose special function it is to initiate will impulses. This, however, is not the case. Will impulses have their origin in man's soul and spiritual domain. Here they begin and they work directly into the limb and metabolic system, but not via any other kind of nerves. Nerves which enter the metabolism and limbs only transmit the impressions of what a person is doing in response to soul and spiritual impulses. Through them we perceive the consequences of soul-spiritual will processes in the blood circulation, in the remaining metabolism and also in the movement of the limbs. These we perceive. The so-called motor nerves do not initiate physical movement, they only allow us to perceive the consequences of our will impulses. Unless we are clear about these relationships, we will not come to a proper understanding of man. On the other hand, if you can see the truth of what I am saying, you will also appreciate why I have to insist on making such apparently paradoxical statements, for they are instrumental in showing how the soul and spiritual part of man always works upon the entire human being.

Approximately up to the twelfth year the effects of what has just been described are found in muscular activity which is so intensely bound up with the child's breathing and blood circulation. From the age of twelve until puberty they are linked more to the forces working in the skeleton. This means that before the twelfth year the child perceives with its so-called motor nerves more what is living in the activity of its muscles, whereas after the twelfth year its perceptivity tends more toward the processes taking place between muscles and bones. If you now consider that in every process of thinking something of a will nature is also involved—for when linking together or synthesizing certain mental images, or when separating or analyzing them from each other, one is also using will forces—you have to look for this will element in the appropriate region of the organism into which it works from out of the domain of the human soul and spirit. And the will forces involved in the process of thinking are connected with the organism in the way just described. Therefore, when entering the twelfth year, the child develops the kind of thinking which, in its will nature, is taking place within the bones, within the dynamics of the skeleton. At this point of time the important transition is taking place from the soft muscular system to the hard boney system which—as I should like to put it—places itself into the world like an objective system of levers. And herein lies the heresy, the paradox, which I have to put before you:

When a person thinks about something belonging to the external, inorganic nature, he does so primarily with his skeleton! Naturally, anyone used to the accepted ideas of present-day physiology, is liable to laugh at such a statement coming from someone living in Dornach who maintains that when a man thinks abstractly, he does so with his bones. But this is how it is. It would be more comfortable for me not to proclaim it, but it must be said because a correct knowledge of man is so necessary today. The thoughts in our brain are only the pictures of what is really going on during the process of thinking. The brain is only the instrument which produces the passive mental pictures of the real processes which are going on in the activity of thinking. In order to become conscious of our thinking, we need these mental pictures. But these images which the brain reflects for us, lack the inner force inherent in pure thinking; they lack the element of will. The real nature of thinking has no more to do with the mental images produced by the brain, than a picture of a certain Mr. X, which you may see hanging on a wall, has to do with the actual Mr. X himself. We must learn to distinguish the picture of a Mr. X from the real Mr. X. In the same way the real process taking place during the activity of thinking must be distinguished from the mental images derived therefrom. When thinking is directed towards outer physical nature, the entire human organism is involved to a certain extent, but particularly so the bony system, the skeleton. And in the twelfth year the child's thinking enters the sphere of the skeleton. This is the signal for us to lead over from the teaching of subjects characterized yesterday—from the plant in its relation to the earth and from the animal kingdom in relation to man—to a new range of subjects.

Our awareness of what is happening in the soul and spiritual domain of the child must lead to the appropriate choice and planning of lesson content. The way in which the soft muscular system with its kinship to respiration and blood circulation plays its part, is an indication that the child, from the tenth to the twelfth year, should be introduced to plants and animals in the way indicated. For these subjects are more directly related to the inner nature of man than the more distant subjects, such as mineralogy, dynamics, physics, and so on. Therefore, at the approach of the twelfth year, the teaching content which previously had mainly a pictorial character, and which included the living plant and the sentient animal, should now appeal more to the intellectual grasp of inorganic nature.

Only now the point is reached when the young adolescent can place himself as an earthly being into the world of dynamics, of mechanics, and when he can experience their forces. Only now the possibility offers itself of introducing him to the first principles of physics and chemistry which are subject to definite natural laws, and to a knowledge of what belongs to the realm of the mineral world. If these subjects are taught at an earlier age, one interferes with evolving human nature, unconsciously damaging the pupil's healthy development.

The ability to grasp historical connections, to gain an overall view of historical developments with their underlying impulses and social implications, represents the other side of the stage at which the pupils are able to comprehend the physical and mineral aspects of life. Only towards the twelfth year do they become mature enough for both of these aspects. For historical ideas and impulses, which find outer expression in definite historical periods and which directly affect social life and social forms, are like the skeleton of history, although—when seen in a purely historical context—they can also be something quite different. The flesh or the muscles, as it were, are represented by the historical personalities themselves, by their biographies and also by concrete historical events. Therefore, if we have to introduce history already between the tenth and the twelfth year, we must bring it in the form of pictures which engender warmth of feeling and which inwardly uplift the pupils' souls. This is possible through telling the children of biographical events and through characterizing certain concrete happenings which form a self-contained whole. But we must refrain from introducing abstract ideas and impulses underlying certain historical epochs. These the pupils should meet in their twelfth year, which is the time when they begin to take their stand in the external world. Here again you can see how an inner development gradually extends in an outward direction. Only now is the pupil ready to grasp how historical impulses, manifesting in outer events, affect the lives of people.

It is important to realize this as otherwise there is always the danger of our approaching the child from an adult point of view. When dealing with the education of the young, it is all too easy to draw a parallel to an adult study of the sciences, where one begins with simpler content in physics and chemistry in order to move on gradually to more difficult parts. In a similar way—so one may think—should the subjects taught at school also be graded. But this is not in accordance with the child's nature. What to an adult appears to be the simplest content, such as we find it in the mineral kingdom and in the inorganic physical world, the child is able to grasp only when it has penetrated the sphere of its bony system, when it moves about in the external world according to the dynamics of the skeleton, as if it were obeying the laws of the lever.

Many people today have become accustomed to looking at practically every aspect of life as if it ought to belong to the domain of natural laws. We find historians who try to interpret social phenomena accompanying historical impulses as if they, too, should be subservient to the laws of nature. This attitude is encouraged already in childhood if

198

physical and chemical laws are taught before the twelfth year, that is, before the other subjects, more closely allied to human life, are studied in lessons. If school subjects are introduced in their wrong order, pupils will project their own experiences and their understanding of purely physical laws also into the social sphere and into their understanding of history. And since such a way of looking at the world has already deeply penetrated educational practice, the general public is only too willing to look for natural laws operating in practically every sphere, so that one may no longer speak of historical impulses as having their origin directly in the spiritual world. And this, in turn, is again reflected in our present principles of education. The child is encouraged to develop such a firm belief in what it has been taught in physics and chemistry that later on, as an adult, he or she will carry this limited outlook into the entire world outlook.

What I have written on the blackboard comes from America: "Nature's Proceedings in Social Phenomena." This phrase has become almost a slogan for an educational principle which postulates that the child should be educated in such a way that it will look upon processes in social life as if they were the results of natural laws. The child is to regard occurrences in the life of the community as mere processes of nature.

People have come to me again and again to tell me that this phrase should read differently in English, that it should read: "Progress of Nature," or something similar. However justified their criticism may be from the point of view of use of language, what matters is that the quotation in question has actually become a catchword for a definite principle in educational science. Whatever the correct wording may be, we must realize that its message needs to be corrected, and this is what I wish to do from a worldwide point of view. Merely correcting the wording is not good enough, for the meaning implies that one can find only natural laws working

199

through social impulses. And this is the kind of attitude which we inculcate in our children. We must begin to experience natural laws working in the processes of nature, and higher, spiritual laws working within the social sphere. And this is not happening. We ruin our pupils' future world-outlook if we introduce them prematurely to what belongs to chemistry, mineralogy, physics, dynamics and so on. As I have pointed out so many times already, one has to keep an eye on the entire milieu of our culture in order to know where to promote the impulses of the art of education. Forgive me if once again I have raised an objection against what has become common practice, but in my opinion it is a justified objection.

If one approaches present-day science with the knowledge and insight which can be gained by following the paths outlined in my book, *Knowledge of the Higher Worlds and Its Attainment*, one is under the impression that the world as described by natural science—which explains everything in terms of mineral and physical laws only—is not a world in which we as human beings of flesh and blood can live. Theirs is a different world altogether. If one looks with eyes, opened by imaginative knowledge, at the kind of world described by exponents of modern natural science, and if one sees how their picture of the world is meant to affect the people of today, one cannot find any human beings of flesh and blood there at all. One sees only walking skeletons, only little bone men and bone women. Theirs is a strange world indeed. I once made an interesting experiment. The younger ones among you won't remember a certain Swiss philosopher called *Vogt*—known as "Fat Vogt"—, a typical thinker of recent times who in the fifties of the last century somehow managed to knock together a rough and ready materialistic world philosophy which, spectre-like, still haunts all kinds of world views of today. Well, I tried to imagine what would happen if a real human being of flesh and blood were to find his way into this world of walking skeletons. Any healthy person of flesh and blood could not possibly bear to live in such a world. But what would happen—so I asked myself—if someone with at least a modicum of flesh and blood were to stray into this world of walking skeletons? The effects of living in a world as described by a purely materialistic outlook and the intentional influences upon people emanating from it, would make such a person suffer from both neurasthenia and hysteria of the worst kind. He would never be able to free himself from all the influences surrounding him. Fundamentally speaking, natural science of today describes a world in which we all could become neurasthenic and hysterical. Mercifully, the world of the natural scientist is not the real world in which we live. Quite other forces, undreamt of by them, are at work in the real world. Nevertheless, it is necessary for us to extricate ourselves from this falsely uniform world of illusion, from which we take almost everything that contributes to the general civilization of today. We must reach a true and real knowledge of man, for only then will we be able to educate in the right way.

LECTURE XII

Dornach, 3rd January 1922

From what you have heard so far, you may have gained the impression that the art of education based on anthroposophical knowledge of man seeks to nurture above all a healthy and harmonious development of the child's physical body. You may have noticed that the following questions could be looked upon as guidelines for our educational aims: How can we assist the free unfolding of the formative forces, issuing from the head and working upon and shaping the young organism? How do we work in harmony with the child's developing breathing and blood circulation during the middle years? What must we do in order to cultivate in the widest sense possible the forces working throughout the child's muscular system? How can we rightly support the processes of the muscles growing onto the bones through the tendons, so that the young adolescent can place himself properly into the external world? All these questions imply that whatever we do to enhance the development of the child's soul and spirit is directed, first of all, towards the best possible healthy and normal development of its physical body. And this, indeed, is the case. We do aim in full consciousness to aid and foster the healthy development of the child's physical body, for in this way the child's soul and spiritual nature is given the best means of unfolding freely and out of its own resources. By damaging as little as possible the spiritual forces working through the child, we give it the best possibility of developing healthily. Not that we have our preconceived ideas of what a growing human being should be like. Whatever we do in our teaching is an attempt to create the most favorable conditions for the children's physical health. And because we have to pay attention also to the soul and spiritual element, because the physical must ultimately become its outer expression, its manifestation, we have to come to terms also with the soul and spiritual aspect in the way best suited for the healthy development of the child.

You may ask: From which educational ideal does such an attitude spring? It is the outcome of a total dedication towards human freedom. It springs from the ideal to place the human being into the world in such a way that he can unfold his individual freedom or, at least, that no physical hindrances should prevent him from doing so.

What we are specially striving for in our education with its emphasis on the promotion of the physical development of the child, is that our pupils should learn to make full use of their physical powers and skills in their later lives. Waldorf Education rests upon the knowledge and the confidence that life in general will have the best chance of developing if it is allowed to develop freely and healthily. Naturally, all this has to be taken in a relative sense which, I hope, will be understood.

A child which, through educational malpractice during the school years, has been prevented from breathing rightly and from using its bony system with its tendons properly, will grow into an unfree person. Likewise a pupil into whose head fixed ideas and conceptions were crammed because they were deemed important for later life, will also become inwardly unfree. Only he, whose childhood needs, imposed by his physical development, were both understood and catered for by the use of appropriate educational principles and methods, will grow into a free human being. Naturally, the soul and spiritual needs of the child must also be recognized and met by the right educational means.

Far from leading to any kind of false or lofty idealism,

203

Anthroposophy wishes to prove itself by enabling its followers to deal with the practical problems of life between birth and death, that is, during the span of time in which they should have developed their physical bodies in accord with their souls and spirits.

So you see that even if we, the educators, wanted it, we have no influence over the development of what belongs to the realm of soul and spirit. The soul and spiritual part of man exists in its true being only from the moment of his falling asleep until the time of wakening. This means that if one wanted to educate a person's soul and spirit, one would have to do so during his sleep. In fact, it is not possible for us to do so. The belief that one has to educate a person's soul and spirit, the belief in indoctrinating certain conceptions, is something we meet so strongly in a time like ours. All one can do is to help towards a free use of physical capabilities by means of the soul and spirit.

As I have often said before, it is not possible to deal with educational matters without taking into full account the entire life situation of our times, without considering the general milieu into which education is placed. I will certainly refrain from introducing any extraneous matter into our considerations here, but what I wish to say now definitely belongs to our theme.

News has come to us that in Eastern Europe a new pedagogy is being worked out for the benefit of those people who are still recognized there, namely for the people who belong to the Radical Socialist Party. Because anything that was acceptable prior to the revolution is no longer regarded as right, a new pedagogy is being worked out there now. And this is done by purely outward means. How? We are told that one of the leading personalities in present-day Russia has been commissioned to write the History of the Communist Party. The new government has given him one month in which to complete his task. During this month he is also to do some practical work at the Moscow Center. As a result of these activities a book is to be published which is to become the officially accepted model for the reeducation of all those who are being recognized as proper Russians. A second party member has been commissioned to write a History of the Western Workers' Movement and a History of International Communism. While compiling his authoritative account, this person, too, has been given some other work to do, and after six weeks he is to have completed his set task. Again, every genuine Soviet Russian is to occupy himself with this book.—Forgive me, I believe that the second writer was actually given two months' time. A third person was commissioned to publish the Theory of Marxism, and it was he who had been given six weeks to deliver the book with the aid of which every true Russian is to familiarize himself with the new conditions in the East. According to these same methods several other personalities have been given the task of creating the new Russian Literature. Everyone of them has been allotted a fixed time schedule in which to complete his order. Everyone of them has been told what other work he has to perform during the time of writing. The party member selected to write the book about Marxism has also been made co-editor of *Pravda*.

Why should I bring this up in today's lecture? Because, fundamentally, what is happening in Soviet Russia today is the ultimate consequence of what lives in all of us, inasfar as we are representatives of our present-day civilization. People will not admit that what is happening in Russia is but the final consequence of our own situation, taken to extremes in Eastern Europe. The absurdity of communist ideology lies in the fact that it is decided and laid down officially what a citizen has to know, instead of the question being asked, "How must a human being behave in order to be a true human being, that is, one who is rightly integrated into the entire world fabric?"

The teacher is called upon to carry into his lessons the utmost respect for soul and spirit. Without it he will succeed as little as if he were lacking an even fundamental artistic and scientific background. Therefore the first prerequisite of a Waldorf teacher is to have reverence for the soul and spiritual potential which each child brings with it into the world. When confronted with the child, the teacher must be imbued with the awareness that he is dealing with an innately free human being. With this attitude he will be able to work out educational principles and methods which will safeguard the child's inborn freedom so that in later life, when a pupil looks back upon his school days, he will not find any infringement upon his personal freedom, not even in the aftereffects of his education.

In order to make clearer what these statements imply, we might ask ourselves the following question: What will become of a person, if his physical peculiarities are not dealt with properly during childhood? Childish idiosyncrasies continue their existence into later life. And if you wonder what kind of effect they will have on an adult, I have to make what may appear as rather a surprising and a somewhat paradoxical statement: Peculiar physical habits in early childhood, if left untreated, will degenerate and become causes of illnesses in later life. One has to know in all seriousness that characteristic physical tendencies in childhood, if allowed to continue unchanged, become causes of illness. This knowledge will give one the right impulse for a proper hygiene which in no way conflicts with the deepest respect for human freedom.

By way of comparison, let us imagine somebody who, right down to the deepest fibers of his being, is filled with enthusiasm for the inner freedom of man. Let us imagine that such a person falls ill and that he has to call the doctor. The doctor cures him with the aid of all the best modern means available to the art of healing. Would such a person

206

ever feel that his personal freedom had thereby been interfered with? Never. What comes towards such a person in this way would never impinge upon his inner freedom.

A similar feeling must also be present in those who are engaged in the art of education. They ought to be willing and able to look at their calling in the light of the relationship between doctor and patient. Education obviously exists in its own right. It certainly is no mere therapy in the true sense of the word. But there is a certain kinship, a certain similarity between the work of a doctor and that of a teacher, which justifies a comparison with the therapeutic situation.

When the pupil leaves school at the age of fourteen plus*, it is time for us to examine once more whether, during his school years from the change of teeth to the coming of puberty, we have done our utmost to help and equip him for later life. (During the coming days, when dealing with the aesthetic and moral aspects of education, we shall look more closely at the stage of puberty. Just now we will consider the more general human aspects.) We must realize that during his past school years we have been dealing mainly with his etheric body, with his body of formative forces, and that the soul life—of which more will be said a little later—was only beginning to manifest itself towards the approach of his school-leaving age. We must consider the next stage, which begins with the fourteenth to fifteenth year and which continues right up to the beginning of the twenties, a time in which the young man or woman has to face the task of fitting himself or herself more and more into external life. We have already seen how, gradually, the child takes hold of its body, finally incarnating right into its skeleton, and how, by doing so, it grows together more and more with the external world, how it learns to adapt to outer circumstances. Fundamentally, this process continues up to the early twenties,

*In 1922 the school-leaving age was fourteen.

207

after which there follows a most important period of life. Although as teachers we now no longer have any direct influence over the young person, we have in fact already done a great deal in this direction during the previous years and this will become apparent from the early to the late twenties.

After leaving school, the young person has to undergo a training for a particular vocation. Now he or she no longer receives what has mainly come out of human nature itself, but rather what has become part and parcel of the civilization we live in, at least with regard to a chosen trade or profession. Now the young person has to be adaptable to certain forms of specialization. In our Waldorf School we try to prepare this stepping out into life by introducing practical crafts, such as spinning and weaving, to our fourteen and fifteen year olds. To gain practical experience in such crafts, is not only important for a future spinner or weaver, but for every person who wishes to be able to turn his hand to anything that a given situation may demand. However, it is important to introduce the right activities at the right time.

Now, what has been cultivated in a child's etheric body, or body of formative forces, during the early school years, reemerges in the soul sphere of a young person during his or her twenties, that is, at the time when he or she has to enter a profession. The way in which he was treated at school will be largely instrumental in his responding to outer conditions either clumsily, reluctantly, full of inhibitions, or skilfully and with an inner strength to overcome obstacles. During his twenties the young person will certainly become aware of how the experiences of his school years first went underground, as it were, while he was training for a trade or profession, only to surface again in form of capacities, such as being able to handle certain situations or to fit oneself into life in the right way. A teacher who is aware of these facts will pay due attention to the critical moments in the life of the pupil between the change of teeth and puberty.

During the ninth to tenth year there occurs the important turning point of life of which I have repeatedly spoken. Towards the twelfth year another important change takes place which I have already mentioned. The six- to seven-year-old child, on entering school, is what I have previously called one great sense organ. At that stage a great deal has already been absorbed by imitation. The child has also been engaged in the inner process of molding and sculpting its organs, the result of which it brings to school. And now, everything the teacher does with the young pupil until the turning point at nine plus, should have a formative effect, but in such a way that the child feels stimulated to participate freely and actively in this inner shaping or forming. I have already indicated this by my strong appeal for an artistic approach during the introduction to reading, writing and arithmetic. The artistic element is of particular importance at this age.

Everyone who knows that all teaching during the early school years has to proceed from the child's will sphere, and that only gradually should it lead over towards the intellect, will pay special attention to the education of the child's will. He will know that the child must learn to drive out its will forces from its own organism, but in the right way. In order to bring this about, the child's will activities need to be tinged with an element of feeling. It is not enough for the teacher to do different things with his children, he must also develop sympathy and antipathy in accordance with what they are doing. And the musical element—quite apart from music in its own right—offers the best means for achieving it. Therefore, as soon as the child is brought to us, we ought to immerse it in the element of music, not only through singing but also by letting it experience music-making with simple instruments. In this way the young pupil will not only nurture an aesthetic sense but, above all, though in a roundabout way, he or she will learn how to use and to control will forces in a harmonious manner.

The child brings many inborn gifts to school. Inwardly it

is a natural sculptor and we can draw on these sculptural gifts, as well as on its other hidden talents. For instance, we can let children do all kinds of things with liquid paints on paper—even if this can be inconvenient for the teacher—and in this way we can introduce them to the secrets of color. It is really fascinating to observe how a child will relate itself to color, when left to cover a white surface with various patches of color. What it produces in an apparently haphazard manner is not at all meaningless, for in all the blotches and smears one can detect a certain color harmony resulting from an inborn kinship to the world of color. Only one must be careful not to let children use the kind of solid blocks of color which are sold in children's paint boxes, where they are supposed to paint directly from the blocks onto the paper. This always has a damaging effect, even in the case of painting as an art. One ought to paint with liquid colors, with colors already dissolved in water or any other suitable liquid. It is important to develop an intimate relationship with color, especially in the case of children. If one uses thick paints from a palette, one does not have the same intimate relationship to color as one does if one is using liquid colors out of paint jars.

In a painting lesson you could say to the child, "What you have painted here is really beautiful. You have put red in the middle, and all the other colors around it go well with the red. Everything you have painted fits well together with the red in the middle. Now try to do it the other way round. Where you have red, paint blue, and then paint around it all the other colors so that they also go well with the blue in the middle."

Not only will the child be tremendously stimulated by an exercise of this kind, but by working out such a transposition of colors—possibly with a certain amount of help from the teacher—it will gain a great deal in establishing an inner relationship to the world in general.

However inconvenient it may be for the teacher, he or she should always encourage the young pupils to form shapes of all kinds out of any suitable material he can lay his hands on. True, one should avoid letting children get unduly dirty and messy, for this can be a real nuisance. But what children gain in these creative activities is worth far more than that they should remain clean and tidy. In short, especially during the early years, it is of great value for them to gain experience of the artistic element.

Anything that has to come from the child, first has to be induced in a way appropriate to its nature. And if artistic activities are introduced in the way indicated, the learning of other subjects will also become easier. Foreign languages, for example, will be learned with far greater ease, if pupils have done artistic work beforehand. I have already mentioned that learning of foreign languages should begin at a very early age, if possible as soon as a child enters school.

Nowadays one often encounters rather fanatical attitudes, so that something which in itself is quite right and justifiable, tends to become exaggerated to the point of a fanatical one-sidedness. And the teaching of foreign languages is no exception. The child learns its mother tongue naturally, that is, without any grammatical consciousness, and this is how it should be. And when it enters school, it should learn foreign languages in a similar way, namely without any grammatical awareness, although this time the process of learning a language will naturally be a more mature and conscious one.

However, during the tenth year, at the turning point of life mentioned already several times, the new situation calls for the introduction to the first fundamentals of grammar. These should be taught without any pedantry whatever. It is necessary to take this new step for the benefit of the child's healthy development, for at this age it has to make the transition from a predominantly feeling approach to life

211

to one in which it has to unfold its ego consciousness. Whatever the young person is doing, has now to be done more consciously than hitherto. Consequently we must introduce a more conscious and intellectual element into the language which, meanwhile, the pupil has learned to speak, write and read. But when doing so, we must avoid pedantic grammar exercises. Instead, we should give the children stimulating practice in recognizing and applying fundamental rules. At this stage the child really needs the logical support which a knowledge of grammar can give, so that it does not have to puzzle time and again over how to express itself correctly.

We must realize that language contains two main elements which always play into each other, namely an emotional or feeling element and an intellectual, thinking element. I should like to give you an illustration of this with a quotation from *Goethe's "Faust"*:

> Grey, dear friend, is every theory
> And green the golden tree of life.

I am not expecting from you, our guests who have mainly come from the West,★ that you should study all the commentaries on Goethe's *Faust*, for there are enough of them to fill a whole library. However, if you did so, you would make a strange discovery. When coming to this sentence in *Faust*, most likely you would find a remark at the bottom of the page, duly equipped with yet a new number—at least a four-figure number because of all the many previous explanations already given—you would find there a comment about the lack of logic inherent in this sentence. Despite the poetic license granted to any reputable author—so the commentator might point out—the colors of the tree in this stanza do not make sense. A golden tree—does this mean an orange

---

★These repeat lectures were given to foreign visitors, most of whom had come from Western countries.

tree? But then it would not be green. If it were an ordinary tree, it would not be golden. Perhaps Goethe had in mind an artificial tree? At any rate—so a typical commentary would continue—a tree cannot be golden and green at the same time. Then there is this other problem of a grey theory. How can a theory be grey if it is something invisible? In this way many commentaries point out the lack of logic in this sentence.

There are of course also other, more artistically inclined commentators who take delight in the apparent lack of logic in this passage. But what is really at the bottom of it all? It is the fact that in this sentence on the one side the emotional, the feeling element in language predominates, whereas on the other the more thoughtful, image-like aspect is stressed. When Goethe speaks of a golden tree, he implies that one would love the tree as one loves gold. The word gold here does not bear an image-like quality, but it reveals the warmth of feeling engendered by the glow of gold. Here only the feelings are portrayed. The adjective green, on the other hand, refers to an ordinary tree, such as we see it in nature. This is the logic of it.

With regard to the word "theory": A theory is of course invisible. Yet, rightly or wrongly, the mere word may conjure up certain feelings in some people, which are reminiscent of those in a London fog! It is quite possible to transfer such a feeling to the concept of theory. The purely feeling element of language is again expressed in the adjective "grey."

The feeling and thinking quality in language intermingles everywhere. In contemporary languages much has already become lamed, but during their earlier stages there lived everywhere an active and creative element through which the feeling and thinking qualities came into existence.

As mentioned already, before the age of nine the child has an entirely feeling relationship to language. Yet, unless we also introduce the thinking element inherent in language, the child's self-consciousness cannot develop properly, and this is the reason why it is so important for us to bring to the child the intellectual aspect of language. This can be done by a judicious teaching of grammatical rules, first of all in the mother tongue and subsequently also in foreign languages, whereby the rules should be introduced only after the child has already begun to speak the language. And so, in accordance with the indications given, the teacher should arouse the feeling in the pupil aged nine to ten that he or she is now beginning to penetrate the language more consciously. This is how a proper grammatical sense could be cultivated in the child.

By the time the pupil reaches the age of twelve, he should have developed a feeling for the beauty of language, that is, an aesthetic sense of the language. This should stimulate him to aim at what one might call "beauty in speaking" without, however, his ever falling into any mannerisms. From then on, until the time of puberty, the pupil should learn to appreciate the dialectical aspect of language, he should develop the faculty of convincing another person through his command of language. This third element of language should be introduced only when the pupil is approaching school-leaving age.*

Briefly summarizing the aims of language teaching one could say: First the child should develop, step by step, a feeling for the correct use of language, then a sense of beauty of language and, finally, he should learn to experience the power inherent in linguistic command.

It is far more important for the teacher to find his way into such an approach to language teaching than for him merely to follow a fixed curriculum. In this way he will soon find out how to introduce and deal with what is needed for

---

*In 1922 the official school-leaving age was fourteen

the various ages. After a predominantly artistic approach, in which the pupil up to nine plus is involved very actively, the teacher should begin to dwell more on the descriptive element in language without, however, neglecting the creative aspect. This is certainly possible if one chooses the kind of syllabus which I have tried to characterize during these past few days, where the introduction of nature study leads to geography and where the animals are seen within the context of man. The most effective way of including the descriptive element would be if the teacher appealed mainly to the child's soul sphere rather than claiming its entire being. This should be done by his clothing the lesson content in a story form, told in a vivid and imaginative style. In like manner, at this stage of life, the teacher should present historical content by giving lively accounts of human events which, in themselves, form a whole, as already indicated.

Having gone through the stage of spontaneous activity, which was followed by an appreciation of the descriptive element, the pupil approaching the twelfth year is ready for what could be called the explanatory approach. Now cause and effect enter general considerations and content can be given which will stretch the powers of reasoning.

Throughout these stages the mathematical aspects in all their manifold forms need to be presented, naturally in a way appropriate to the pupil's age. The mathematical element, such as it is taught in arithmetic and geometry, is liable to cause quite special difficulties to a teacher. Before the ninth year, this work is introduced in its simpler forms, to be subsequently expanded—for the child is well able to take in a great deal if one knows how to proceed in the right way. Now, it is a fact that all mathematical content which is taught throughout the entire time spent at school, must also be presented in a thoroughly artistic and imaginative way. By all kinds of means the teacher must contrive to introduce the arithmetical and geometrical content artistically and

215

here, too, between the ninth and tenth year he has to go over to a descriptive method. The pupil has to be taught how to observe angles, triangles, quadrilaterals and so on, through a descriptive method. Proofs should not enter the work before the twelfth year.

A boring math teacher will achieve extremely little, if anything at all, whereas a teacher, inspired by this subject, will succeed in making it into a stimulating and exhilarating experience for his pupils. For, after all, it is by grace of mathematics that, fundamentally, we are able to experience the harmonies of ideal space. If a teacher can wax enthusiastic over the theorem of Phythagoras or over the inner harmonies between planes and solid bodies, he will bring something into these lessons which is of immense importance for the child, also with regard to its soul development. Through his contributions he will counteract the element of confusion with which life presents us everywhere.

You see, language could not exist without the constant intermingling of the element of thought and feeling. Once again I have made a very radical statement, but if you were to examine the various languages, you would discover everywhere how feeling and thinking are constantly interwoven. This in itself, as well as many other factors, could easily introduce a certain chaos into our lives, where it not for the inner firmness which mathematics especially can bestow upon us. Anyone able to look more deeply into life will know that many people have been saved from falling victim to neurasthenia, hysteria and even worse afflictions simply because they learned how to observe triangles, quadrilaterals, tetrahedra and other geometrical realities in the right way.

Perhaps I may be allowed here a more personal note because it may help to clarify the point I am making. I have a special love for mechanics, not only because of its objective value, but very much for personal reasons. And I owe this love of mechanics to the enthusiasm for this subject dis-

played by one of my teachers in the Vienna High School—
for such things live on into later life. This teacher glowed
with excitement when searching for the resultants from giv-
en components. It was so interesting to witness the joy with
which he was looking for the resultants and with which he
would take them apart again in order to fit them back into
their components. While doing this, he almost jumped and
danced from one end of the blackboard to the other until,
full of glee, he would finally call out the formula he had
found, such as: $c^2 = a^2 + b^2$. Captivated by his findings,
which he had written on the board, he would look around at
his audience with a benign smile which in itself was enough
to kindle enthusiasm for analytical mechanics, a subject
which usually hardly evokes such feelings in people. It is
really important that mathematics, which is taught in its
various forms and aspects right through the school, should
pour out, as it were, its own special substance over all the
pupils.

And so we can speak of the two poles in human development: The rhythmic-artistic pole and the mathematical-
conceptual one. And if, in the way indicated, the young soul
is worked upon from within in an outward direction, the
pupil will gradually grow into the world in the right way.

At the approach of the school-leaving age*, the teacher
will feel an inner need once more to survey the most significant moments in the development of his or her pupils during the last few years, this time in retrospect. The pupils
entered school in Class I at the age of six or seven. A few
years later they are sent out into the world again and—as I
indicated at the beginning of today's lecture—it is the teacher's aim to enable them to adapt themselves to the life of the
world. When we receive the young pupil in Class I, he is
like one great sense organ. Within, he bears a kind of a copy

*The official school-leaving age at that time was fourteen

or a stamp of his parents, of other people in his surroundings and of his entire social background. It is our task to transmute these adopted and specialized features into more general human features. This we can do by appealing above all to the child's middle system of breathing and blood circulation, which is not so much bound up with the more personal sides of the human being. Yet, apart from these adopted features which the child, unconsciously, has copied from its environment, it also bears its very own individual characteristics when it enters school. These are less pronounced than similar characteristics found also in adults, features which we associate with the melancholic, sanguine, phlegmatic or choleric temperaments. Nevertheless, the child's nature, too, is definitely colored by what could be called its temperamental disposition, so that we can speak of children with melancholic, phlegmatic, sanguine and choleric tendencies. It is essential for teachers to acquire a fine perception for the manifold symptoms and characteristics resulting from the children's temperamental dispositions and to find the right way of dealing with them.

The melancholic child is the one to depend most strongly on the conditions of its physical body. Due to its special constitution it tends to feel weighed down by its bodily nature. It easily becomes self-centered and generally little interested in what is going on around it. Yet it would be wrong to think of the melancholic child simply as being inattentive, for it is so only with regard to its surroundings and to what comes from the teacher. It is very attentive to its own inner conditions and this is the reason why a melancholic child tends to be so moody.—Please note that what I am saying about the temperaments applies only to children whose symptoms cannot be automatically transferred to grownups of the same temperament.

The relationship of the phlegmatic child to its environment is one of complete, though entirely subconscious, surrender to the world at large. And as the world is vast and so full of things to which it has surrendered itself, it shows only little interest for what is near at hand.—(Again, my remarks about this temperament refer only to the child, otherwise they might be looked upon as being a compliment to the phlegmatic adult and this they certainly are not meant to be.)—Making rather a sweeping statement, one could say: If a child with phlegmatic tendencies did not happen to live on earth, if it were living out there in the heavenly world, in the cosmos, it would be full of the deepest interest in its surroundings. For the phlegmatic child really feels at home in the periphery of the world. It is open for what is immense and for what does not make an immediate impact because of its vastness and remoteness.

To a certain extent, the sanguine child displays opposite characteristics to those of the melancholic or phlegmatic child. The young melancholic is immersed in his bodily nature. The phlegmatic child feels drawn outwards to the spheres of infinity because it is so strongly linked to its etheric body, or body of formative forces. The etheric body is always inclined to strive outwards towards an infinite totality. It disperses itself into the cosmos already a few days after death. The sanguine child lives in what we call the astral body or the "soul body." This member of the human being is different from the physical or etheric bodies inasmuch as it does not concern itself with what is of a temporal or spatial nature. It exists beyond the realm of time and space. It is due to the astral body that during every moment of our lives we have an awareness of our entire life up to the present moment, even though our memories of earlier experiences are generally weaker than those of more recent ones. The astral body is mainly instrumental in directing our dreams. These, as you know, bear little relationship to the correct sequence of time. We may dream about something that happened only yesterday yet, mixed up in the dream, people may appear whom we met already in early childhood. The astral body mixes up all our life experiences. It has no regard for the element of time and space, but in its chaotic ways it has its own dimension which is totally different from what is temporal and spatial.

The sanguine child surrenders itself to its astral body and this becomes evident in its entire pattern of behavior. It responds to outer impressions as if what lies beyond time and space were directly transmitted to us through the outer world itself. It quickly responds to impressions without digesting them inwardly, because it does not care for the time element. It simply surrenders itself to its astral body. It makes no efforts to retain outer impressions. Or, again, it does not like to live in memories of earlier happenings. Because it pays so little heed to the element of time, the sanguine child lives in and for the present moment. It brings to outer expression what, in reality, is the task of the astral body in the higher worlds, and this gives the sanguine child a certain superficiality.

The choleric child is most directly linked to its egocenter. Its very build shows a strong will nature which, permeated by the forces of its ego, is apt to enter life aggressively.

It is really important for the teacher to cultivate a fine perception for the characteristic features of the various temperaments in the growing children. In a twofold way he must try to deal with them. First by introducing a certain social element in the classroom, which is based on the various temperaments. When he has got an idea of his pupils as a whole, he should place them in groups according to similarity of temperaments. There are of course children of mixed temperaments and this, too, has to be considered. But in general it has a salutary effect if children of the same temperament are seated together, for the simple reason that then the temperaments rub up against each other. The melancholic child, for example, will have a neighbor who is also a melancholic. It will become aware of how this neighbor is suffering from all kinds of discomforts arising out of the physical constitution. The melancholic pupil will recognize similar symptoms in himself and the mere looks of his neighbor will have a healing effect upon his own nature.

If phlegmatic children sit next to other phlegmatics, they will become so bored with them that in the end their own phlegma becomes stirred up to the extent that they will try to shake off their own lethargy.

The sanguine child, when seated among other sanguines, will see how they flutter from one impression to the next, being momentarily interested now in one thing and then in another, until it feels like brushing them away like flies. Experiencing its own traits in its neighbors, the sanguine child becomes aware of the superficiality of its own sanguine temperament.

If the colerics are seated together, there will be such a constant exchange of blows, that the resulting bruises which they give each other will have an extraordinarily healing effect upon their temperament.

You must observe these things and then you will find that by introducing, through your choice of seating, a social element in the classroom, the result will have a wholesome and balancing effect upon each child. In this way the teacher's relationship to each of the temperaments can also find its rightful expression. The second point to be borne in mind is that it would be not at all helpful to treat a melancholic child—or that of any other temperament for that matter —by going against its inherent disposition. On the contrary, one should develop the habit of treating like with like. If, for instance, one were to force a choleric child to sit still and to be quiet, the result would be an accumulation of suppressed choler which would act like a poison in its system. It simply would not work. On the other hand, if, for example, a teacher shows continued interest and understanding for

221

the doleful moods of a melancholic child, his attitude will finally bring about a beneficial and healing effect. When dealing with a phlegmatic child, outwardly one should appear also rather phlegmatic and somewhat indifferent, despite one's real inner interest in the pupil. The sanguine child should be subjected to many quickly-changing sense impressions. In this way one would increase the tendencies of its own temperament, with the result that the child will try to catch up with the many fleeting impressions. It will develop a stronger intensity. The sheer number of sense impressions will bring about an inner effort of self-intensification in the child. It is by treating like with like that one can really come to grips with the different temperaments. As for the choleric children, if conditions at school would allow it, I should like it best to send them out into the garden during the afternoons and let them run about until they were exhausted. I should let them climb up and down the trees. When one of them had reached a treetop, I should let him shout across to his playmate sitting on top of another tree. I should let them shout at each other until they were tired out. If one allows a choleric child to free itself in a natural way from pent-up choler, one exercises a most healing influence upon its temperament.

In getting to know the nature of the different temperaments, one can learn to work effectively as a teacher. However, there is one thing which is essential. It really is no good at all if a teacher enters his classroom with a morose demeanor which, already at a comparatively early age in his life, has engraved deep wrinkles on his face. He must know how to act with a great sense of humor in the classroom. He must be able to enter into everything that comes towards him from the class. He must be able to let his own being flow into that of his children.

LECTURE XIII

Dornach, 4th January 1922

When pupils reach the official school-leaving age*, they have already entered puberty. Teachers need to bear this in mind with great intensity well before it actually manifests itself. We only have to look with open eyes at what is happening in the growing human being both before and during the time of sexual maturity, in order to appreciate the importance of being prepared to meet this challenge.

We have already seen during the course of our studies that up to the change of teeth the child is an imitator and that, while there exists as yet no clear differentiation between organic functioning and the activities of soul forces, the child is inwardly given over to those soul and spiritual forces which are streaming downwards from the head, forces which still work organically, permeating its entire organism. The way in which these soul-spiritual forces work together with the bodily forces is the most characteristic feature of this particular stage.

In order to give you a clear description of what is happening in a young child at this time of life, I find it necessary once again to make use of insights gained through clairvoyant consciousness. I do so, not because I believe it necessary to formulate ideas in some particular way, but simply because this may best help us to reach an understanding on the basis of all that has been presented so far.

When a young child sleeps, its soul and spiritual members leave the physical sheaths—just as happens in a

---

*fourteen plus

223

grownup person—and they reenter the body during the moment of waking. But in the case of the child there is as yet no great difference between the conscious experiences in the waking state and the unconscious experiences during sleep. Under normal conditions, that is, if no reminiscences of what happened during the day enter the child's world of sleep—and this hardly happens in childhood—the child's life of sleep moves about in spheres lying far beyond the earthly realm. It is from these higher worlds that the active forces are drawn which, during the waking state, work from the brain downwards into the child's entire organism.

During the second dentition, certain soul and spiritual forces in the child are released from working entirely in the organic sphere. They begin to assume an independent soul and spiritual character. Between the change of teeth and puberty the child develops a freer thinking, feeling and willing than was the case previously. No longer is it only an imitator, but through its natural feeling for authority, it develops the degree of consciousness, necessary for it to make contact with the world. This faith in the authority of a grownup is essential, for the outer conditions of life are not sufficient in themselves to ensure the child's necessary contact with the world. The way in which one adult confronts another, whether by verbal or by other means of communication, is very different from the way in which a child meets an adult. The child simply needs the additional support which a sense of authority can give. As a consequence, more and more experiences from the child's waking state will enter its soul and spiritual life also during sleep. And to the same extent to which earthly experiences enter its sleeping state, replacing those of the spiritual world, is the possibility given to us teachers to reach the child between the change of teeth and puberty through our educational endeavors.

With the onset of puberty, an entirely new situation arises, with the effect that, fundamentally, the emerging adolescent is a totally different being from what he was before sexual maturity. In order to characterize the situation, it may be useful to refer to what was spoken of at the end of yesterday's lecture. Up to the change of teeth, it is normal for a child to live entirely within the physical body. However, if this state is extended beyond its normal time—and in later life such a situation would no longer represent normal conditions—the consequences will be a markedly melancholic temperament. During childhood it is natural to have the kind of relationship between the soul-spiritual and physical organization which is characteristic of an adult melancholic. We must always bear in mind that what is right and good for one stage of life, becomes abnormal for another.

During the second dentition certain soul and spiritual forces are freed from their previous organic activities and they flow into what I have called the body of formative forces, or the ether body. This member of the human being is entirely linked to the external world and it is right for the child to live in it during the time between the change of teeth and puberty. If, already before the change of teeth there was an excess of these etheric forces, that is, if the child has lived too much in its etheric sheath before the second dentition, the outcome is a markedly phlegmatic temperament. However, it is quite possible for a child to have a normal and balanced relationship with the etheric body and this is absolutely essential between the seventh and the fourteenth year, that is, between the change of teeth and puberty. Again, if this condition is carried over too far into later life, a decidedly phlegmatic temperament will develop in the grownup.

The next member of the human being which, under normal circumstances gains its independent existence in puberty and which yesterday I called the astral body—the member of the human being which lives beyond space and time—is the real birthplace of the sanguine temperament. And if,

225

during the time between the change of teeth and puberty, a child draws too much upon what should come into its own only when sexual maturity is reached, the sanguine temperament comes into being. Only with the arrival of puberty does the growing human being become inwardly mature for sanguinity. Thus everything in life has its right or normal period of time. The various abnormalities come about if that which is normal for one particular time of life is pushed into another period of life. If you can survey life from this viewpoint, you learn to understand the human being in depth.

And now, what is actually happening during the time of sexual maturity? Our considerations of the last few days have already shed some light on it. We have seen how, after the change of teeth, the child is still working inwardly with those forces which, to a certain degree, have become emancipated soul and spiritual forces. During the subsequent stages the child incarnates via the system of breathing and blood circulation to where in the tendons the muscles grow onto the bones. It incarnates from within outwards towards the human periphery and at the time of sexual maturity, the young adolescent breaks through into the external world. Only then does she or he fully stand in the world.

This dramatic development makes it imperative for the teacher to approach the adolescent, who has passed through sexual maturity, quite differently from the way in which he had dealt with him or her prior to this event. For, fundamentally, the previous processes involving the emancipated soul and spiritual forces before puberty had as yet nothing to do with sex in its own realm. True, boys or girls show a definite predisposition towards their sexes, but this cannot be considered as actual sexuality. Sexuality only develops after the breakthrough into the external world, when a new relationship with the outer world has been established.

But then, at this particular time, something is happening within the realm of the adolescent's soul and bodily nature,

226

which is not unlike what happened previously during the second dentition. During the change of teeth forces were liberated to become actively engaged in the child's thinking, feeling and willing, forces which were directed more towards the memory. The powers of memory were then released. Now, at puberty, something else becomes available for free activity in the soul realm. These are powers which, previously, had entered the rhythms of breathing and which, subsequently, were striving to introduce rhythmical qualities also into the muscular and even into the bony system. This rhythmical element now becomes transmuted into the adolescent's receptiveness for all that belongs to the realm of creative ideas, for all that belongs to fantasy. Fundamentally speaking, genuine powers of fantasy find their birth only during puberty, for they can come into their own only after the astral body has been born. It is this same astral body which exists beyond time and space and which links together past, present and future according to its own principles, as we can experience it in our dreams.

What is it that the adolescent brings with him when he "breaks through" into the external world via his bony system? It is what originally he had brought down with him from pre-earthly existence and what, gradually, had become interwoven with his whole inner being. And now, with the onset of sexual maturity, the adolescent is being cast out of the spiritual world, as it were. Without exaggerating, one can really put it that strongly, for it represents the actual truth; with the coming of puberty the young human being is cast out from the living world of the spirit, and thrown into the external world which he or she can perceive only by means of the physical and etheric body. And though the adolescent is not at all aware of what is going on inside him, subconsciously this plays an all the more intensive part. Subconsciously, or semi-consciously, it makes the adolescent compare the world he has now entered with the world which he formerly had within himself. Previously, he had not experienced the spiritual world consciously but, nevertheless, he had found it possible to live in harmony with it. His inner being felt attuned to it and ready to cooperate freely with the soul and spiritual realm. But now, in these changed conditions, the external world no longer offers such possibilities to him. It presents all kinds of hindrances which, in themselves, create the wish to overcome them. This, in turn, gives rise to the tumultuous relationship between the adolescent and the surrounding world, lasting from the fourteenth or fifteenth year till the beginning of the twenties.

This inner upheaval is bound to come and it is well for the teacher to be aware of it already during the previous years. There may be people of an unduly sensitive nature who believe that it would be better to save teenagers from such inner turmoil, only to find that they have made themselves their greatest enemy. It would be quite wrong to try to spare them this tempestuous time of life. It is far better to plan ahead in one's educational aims so that what has been done with the pre-puberty child can now come to the help and support of the adolescent's soul and spiritual struggles.

The teacher must be clear that with the arrival of puberty an altogether different being emerges, born out of a new relationship with the world. It is no good appealing to the pupil's previous sense of authority, for now he demands to know reasons for whatever he is expected to do. The teacher must get into the habit of approaching the young man or woman rationally. For example, if the adolescent who has been led by the spiritual world into this earthly world, becomes rebellious because this new world is so different from what he had expected, the adult must try to show him —and this without any pedantry—that everything he meets in the world has had a prehistory. He must get the adolescent to see that present conditions are the consequences of

228

what had gone on before. One must act the part of the expert who really understands why things have come to be as they are. From now on, one will accomplish nothing by way of authority. Now one has to be able to convince the adolescent through the sheer weight of one's indisputable knowledge and expertise and by giving him waterproof reasons for everything one does or expects of him. If, at this stage, the pupil cannot see sound reasons in all the content given to him, if conditions in the world appear to make no sense to him, he will begin to doubt the rightness of his previous life. He will feel himself in opposition with what he had experienced during those years which, apparently, only led him into these present unacceptable outer conditions. And if, during his inner turmoil, he cannot find contact with people who are able to reassure him, at least to a certain extent, that there are good reasons for what is happening in the world, then the inner stress may become intolerable to the extent that the adolescent breaks down altogether. For this newly emerged astral body is not of this world. The young person has been cast out of the astral world and he is willing to place himself into this earthly world only if he feels convinced of its rightful existence.

You will completely misunderstand what I have been describing if you think that the adolescent is at all aware of what is thus going on within him. During his ordinary day-consciousness it rises up from the unconscious in dim feelings. It is surging up through blunted will impulses. It lives itself out in the disappointment of apparently unattainable ideals, in frustrated desires and perhaps also in a certain inner dullness towards what presents itself out there in the unreasonable happenings of the world.

If, during this stage, education is to be effective at all—and this indeed must be the case for any youngster willing to learn—then the teaching content must be transmitted in the appropriate form. It must also be a preparation for the years to come, up to the early twenties or even later in life. Having suffered the wounds inflicted by life and having paid back in his own coinage, the young person of fifteen to twenty-one or twenty-two eventually will have to find his way back again into the world from which he had been cast out during puberty. (The duration of this period varies, especially so during our chaotic times which tend to prolong it even further into adult life.) The young person must feel accepted again, he must be able to make a new contact with the spiritual world, for without it, life is not possible. However, should he feel any coercion coming from those in authority, this new link will lose all meaning and value for life.

If we are aware of these difficulties already well before the arrival of puberty, we will make good use of the child's inborn longing for authority in order to bring it to the stage when there is no longer any need for an authoritarian approach. And this stage should coincide with the coming of sexual maturity. But by then the educator must always be ready and able to give convincing reasons for everything he wishes his pupil to do.

Seen from a wider, spiritual perspective, we can thus observe the grandiose metamorphosis which is taking place in the human being during the period of sexual maturity.

It is of the greatest importance to realize that the whole question of sex becomes a reality only during puberty, when the adolescent enters the external world in the way I have described it. Naturally, since everything in life is relative, this, too, has to be taken as a relative truth. Nevertheless, one has to recognize that up to the stage of sexual maturity the child lives more as a general human being and that an experience of the world, differentiated according to whether one lives as a man or woman, only begins with the onset of puberty. This realization—which in our generally intellectual and naturalistic civilization cannot be taken for granted —will allow people who, without prejudice, are striving for

230

a knowledge of man, a real insight into the relationship between the sexes. It also helps them to understand the problem regarding the position of women in society, not only during our present times but also in the future.

Only if one can appreciate the tremendous metamorphosis which is taking place in the male organism during voice mutation—to mention just one example—will one be able to understand fully the statement that up to the age of sexual maturity the child retains a more general human character, as yet undivided into sexes. Other similar processes occur also in the female organism, only in a different area. The human voice with its ability to moderate and to form sounds and tones, is a manifestation of man's general human nature. It is born out of the soul and spiritual substance which is working upon the child up to puberty. Changes of pitch and register, on the other hand, occurring during mutation, are the result of external influences. They are forced upon the adolescent from outside, as it were. They are the means by which he places himself into the outer world with his innermost being. It is not only a case of the soft parts in the larynx relating themselves more strongly to the bones, but a slight ossification of the larynx itself takes place which, fundamentally, amounts to a withdrawal of the larynx from the purely human inner nature into a more earthly existence.

This stepping out into the world should really be seen in a much wider context than is usually the case. Usually, in people's minds, the capacity to love, which awakens at this time, is directly linked to sexual attraction. But this is by no means the whole story. The power to love, born during sexual maturity, embraces everything within the adolescent's entire compass. Love between the sexes is but one specific and limited aspect of love in the world. Only by seeing human love in this light can one understand it correctly, and then one also understands its task in the world.

We may well ask: What is really happening in a human being during the process of sexual maturity? Prior to this stage, as a child, his relationship to the world was one where he first imitated the surroundings and when, subsequently, he stood under the power of authority. Outer influences were working upon him for, at that time, his inner being mainly represented what he had brought down with him from pre-earthly life. Humanity as a whole had to work upon him from without, first through the principle of imitation and then through authority. But now, at puberty, having found his own way into humanity and no longer depending on its outer support to the same extent that a pre-puberty child does, there rises up in him a new feeling, and entirely new appraisal of mankind as a whole. It is this new experience of humankind which represents the spiritual counterpart to the physical faculty of reproduction. Physically, he becomes able to procreate. Spiritually, he becomes capable of experiencing mankind as a totality.

During this new stage, the polarity between man and woman becomes very marked. Only through a real understanding of the other sex by means of social intercourse, also in the realm of soul and spirit, is it possible for the human potential to come to some kind of realization on earth. Both man and woman fully represent humankind, but each in a differentiated way. The woman sees in humanity a gift of the metaphysical worlds. Fundamentally, she sees humanity as the result of a divine outpouring. Unconsciously and in the depths of her soul she bears a picture of mankind which acts as her standard of values, and she evaluates and assesses mankind according to this standard. If these remarks are not generally accepted today, it is due to the fact that our present civilization shows all the signs of a male-dominated society.

For a long period of time the most powerful influences in our civilization have displayed a decidedly masculine char-

232

acter. An example of this—however grotesque it may sound —can be found in freemasonry. It is symbolic of our times that men, if they wish to keep certain matters to themselves, separate themselves off into lodges of freemasonry. There are also lodges in which both men and women congregate but in these, freemasonry has already become blunted, they no longer bear its original stamp. The constitution of freemasonry is of course a specific example, but it is nevertheless indicative of the male-dominated character of our society. Women, too, have absorbed a great deal of the masculine element in our civilization and because of this they are actually preventing the specifically feminine element from coming into its own. This is the reason why one so often gains the impression that with regard to inner substance and outer form, there is hardly any difference between the ideals and programs of the various women's movements and those of men, even to the very tone of speeches in which they are delivered. Obviously these movements are different from each other inasfar as on the one side demands are made to safeguard women's interests, while on the other they are made on behalf on men, but with regard to inner substance, they are scarcely distinguishable from each other.

Man, in his innermost being, experiences humanity as something of an enigma. To him it appears as something unfathomable which poses endless questions, the solutions of which seem to lie beyond his powers. This typically masculine characteristic expresses itself in all the mysterious ceremonial with its dry and manly atmosphere which belongs to freemasonry. This same male tendency has permeated our culture to such an extent that, on the one hand, the women are suffering under it and, on the other, they are wanting to emulate it, wishing to make it part of their lives, too.

If you take a good look at modern medicine with all its materialistic features, if you see how it fails to comprehend human nature, especially with regard to its physical aspect,

233

so that it depends on experimentation—if you observe modern medicine, you will find there the product of a distinctly masculine attitude—however strange this may sound to you. In fact, one could hardly find a better illustration of male thinking than in what modern medicine so blatantly reveals to us.

If one expounds the truth today, people tend to think that one does so merely for the sake of putting paradoxical statements into the world. Yet the reality is often paradoxical. Therefore if one wishes to speak the truth, one has to put up with appearing paradoxical, however inconvenient this may be.

While womankind lives more in the image it creates of humanity, man's experiences of humanity are more of a wishful and enigmatic kind. In order to understand this situation, one needs to become clear about one other symptom of our times, which is of particular significance for the art of teaching: When people speak about love today, they do not generally differentiate between the various kinds of love. Of course, one can generalize the concept of love, just as one can speak about condiments in a general way. But if someone puts abstract speculations about certain matters into the world and then holds forth about them, it always strikes me as if he were talking about salt, sugar or pepper merely in terms of condiments. He only needs to apply such abstractions to practical life by putting salt into his coffee instead of sugar—because, after all, both are condiments— to realize his foolishness. Anyone who indulges in general speculations instead of entering the concrete realities of life, commits the same folly.

A woman's love is very different from that of a man. Her love originates in the imaginative realm and it is constantly engaged in making pictures. A woman does not love a man just as he is, standing there before her in ordinary humdrum life—forgive me for saying this but, after all, men are not exactly of the kind a healthy imagination could fall in love with—but she weaves into her love the ideal she has received as heaven's gift. Man's love, on the other hand, is tinged with desire; it is of a wishful nature. This differentiation needs to be made, no matter whether it shows itself more in an idealistic or a realistic sense. Ideal love may inspire longings of an ideal nature. The instinctive and sensuous kind may be a mere product of fancy. But this fundamental difference between love as it lives in a man or a woman is a reality. A woman's love is steeped in imagination. In man's love there is an element of desire. It is just because of this complementary character that the two kinds of love can become harmonized in life.

An educator should bear this in mind when confronted with pupils who have already passed through the stage of sexual maturity. He should realize that by that time it is no longer possible to bring to them certain things which belong to the pre-adolescent stage and that the opportunity for doing so has been missed. Therefore, in order to prevent a one-sided attitude in later life, one must endeavor to give to pre-puberty children enough of the right content to last them through the coming stages.

In our times when, fortunately, coeducation in both primary and secondary education is accepted more and more readily so that boys and girls work side by side in order to learn how to cooperate as men and women in social life later on, it is of special importance to pay heed to what has just been said. Through it, a contemporary phenomenon, such as the women's movements, will be placed upon a really sound and healthy basis.

If we now expand these considerations by taking a worldwide viewpoint, we are led to the fundamental differences which exist between East and West, between Asia on the one side and Europe and America on the other. This difference between East and West is far greater than any other differences we may find when comparing, let us say, Europe with America. Throughout Asia there still exist traces of ancient and wisdom-filled civilizations. Outwardly they show all the signs of decadence; outwardly they may have become completely decadent, but nevertheless, this wisdom lives on like a memory. It is revered as a sacred memory to such an extent that fundamentally speaking, an Asian cannot really understand a European and vice versa. Anyone who is under illusions about this fact will delude himself about the greatest historical world secret of our present times. It is a secret of special significance not only for our present times, but very much so for the future.

Despite its manifold complexities, life in the West bears a more uniform character than life in the East. The Western people's main concern is life in this earthly civilization, a civilization which draws its ideas, above all, from what happens between birth and death. The people of the East—at least as far as their inner religious lives are concerned—do not limit their outlook to their earthly time between birth and death, to life in the outer mechanical civilization. The man of the West, however, does live for this earthly time, also as far as his religious feelings are concerned. The man from the East asks himself searching questions, such as: Wherefore was I born into this world? Why did I enter this sense-perceptible world at all? The Westerner takes life in the physical world more or less for granted, even if he should end it by committing suicide. He takes earthly life for granted, and only because it would be a source of dissatisfaction and disappointment to him if this earthly existence were to be entirely wiped out through death has he developed an inner receptivity for a belief in life after death.

There is a fundamental difference between these two outlooks. But, again, we shall not get to the bottom of it merely by characterizing it abstractly instead of entering life in its fulness. The further we move from the East towards

236

the West, the more do we find that the Western woman, despite all her outward consciousness, cherishes a longing for the spirituality of the East. The man of the West, however, presents a totally different picture. He, too, has his secret longings, but not for something vague and misty. His longings spring from what he is inwardly experiencing. From cradle to grave he is enmeshed in the activities and pressures of his civilization. But something in him longs to get away from it all. This mood of soul we can perceive in all civilized countries around us, from the River Vistula in Eastern Europe through Germany, France, Britain, right across the American continent even to the shores of the Pacific Ocean. In all these lands do we find this common attribute. The educator who has to deal with adolescents experiences it, too, perhaps to his despair and without realizing the underlying causes. Only a teacher wearing blinkers could possible overlook it.

During our previous meetings I already mentioned that really one ought to throw away all school textbooks, because only the direct and personal relationship of teacher to pupil should work upon the child. But when it comes to teaching adolescents, all available textbooks and, for that matter, almost our entire outer civilization, become one great source of pain. I know that there are many people who are unaware of this, because they do not enter real life with sufficiently open eyes. But here, again, in this outer civilization we find a marked and one-sidedly masculine character. Any book on history, on the history of civilization or anthropology will confirm this trend. As representative of Western civilization, man longs to escape from the physical world in which he is caught up, but he lacks the courage to do so. He cannot find the bridge from the sense-perceptible world to the spiritual world. And so we find everywhere in our civilization a yearning to get away from it all and yet, at the same time, an inability to act accordingly.

237

It is hard enough to achieve the right outer conditions for teaching children of pre-puberty age. But anyone who has to teach adolescents could almost feel helpless because the means available for meeting their needs are so totally inadequate. This fact alone should kindle a real longing in their teachers for deeper insight into the human being. This longing may of course be there already in teachers of younger children but it is a prerequisite for anyone of sound pedagogical sense who is teaching adolescents.

A woman's nostalgia for the ways of the East and a man's wish to free himself from the bondage of Western life represent a fundamental feature of our times. This differentiation between the sexes is less apparent in pre-adolescent children who still bear more general human features. Yet as soon as we are confronted by adolescents, we meet the resulting difficulties quite concretely.

Let us assume, for example, that a teacher of German literature wanted to recommend a book about *Goethe*—as seen from a German point of view—to an adolescent pupil. He really would find himself in a quandary, for there simply are no suitable books on the market. If he chose one of the available ones, his scholar would not gain the right picture of *Goethe*. If he chose a biography of *Goethe* written by, let us say, *Lewes*, a German scholar would learn to know the more outward features of *Goethe* better than from any of the German books on the subject, but again he would not become acquainted with the specifically German characteristics of *Goethe*. This is the general situation today, for we simply do not have an adequate literature for teaching adolescents.

To remedy this situation, everything will depend on the women taking their proper place in our cultural life. They should be allowed to contribute their specifically feminine qualities but, at the same time, they must be careful not to introduce anything they have adopted from our male-orientated civilization.

During the nineties of the last century I once had a con-

238

versation with a German suffragette. She expressed her views in radical terms, but I could not help feeling that instead of enriching society with what only womanhood can give, she was trying to force her way into our one-sidedly masculine culture by employing similar masculine tactics. What is meant here must not be taken in a philistine or prejudiced way. I felt that I had to tell this free and uncompromising lady, "Your movement does not yet offer what the world really needs. The world does not need ladies who wear the trousers—forgive me, I believe that such a remark is unforgiveably rude in England—but that both masculine and feminine qualities make their specific contributions towards the general enhancement of our society."

Whenever we, as teachers, approach the growing human being, we must be aware of the striking contrast between pre-puberty and post-puberty years. Let us take a concrete example: There is Milton's *Paradise Lost*. It would be good to use it in our lessons. The question is, when? Those of you who have thought over what has been said so far and who have understood my remarks about the right time of introducing the narrative and descriptive element, will find that this work by Milton—as all epic poetry in general—would become suitable material after the tenth year. Also Homer will be appreciated best if taught between the tenth and the fourteenth year. On the other hand, it would be premature to use Shakespeare as study material already at this stage for, in order to be ready for dramatic poetry, the pupil must at least have entered puberty. To absorb the dramatic element at an earlier age would mean that the pupils concerned would have to drive something out of themselves prematurely, something which, later on, they would definitely miss.

What I tried to indicate just now can be experienced vividly if one has to give, for example, history lessons to boys and girls after their entry into puberty. Both masculine and feminine forces were at work during the actual historical happenings, though in a different form from that of today. Yet all historical accounts available for teaching adolescents bear a decidedly masculine quality, as if they had been compiled by Epimetheus.* Girls who have reached sexual maturity show little inclination towards such an approach. Boys may find it somewhat boring, but in their case it is not impossible to use this Epimethean way, which is one of judging, of holding on to what can be ascertained and established.

But there is also a Promethean way of looking at history which does not only record the events that actually occurred, but which shows their metamorphosis into ideas current at the present time. This latter approach to history shows how impulses which led the past have become current ideas of the present, and how impulses, in turn, continue to lead present times further. This Promethean way of looking at history appeals especially strongly to the feminine element.

However, it would be very one-sided to teach history in the Promethean style in a girls' school and in an Epimethean style in a boys' school. The minds of the young men would simply flow back into past times to become even more rigid than they are already. If only the Promethean way of teaching history were to be applied in a girls' school, the pupils would feel tempted to fly off into futuristic speculations. Everywhere they would feel attracted to those impulses for which they happened to have a natural liking. We will achieve a more balanced social life only if we add to the Epimethean way which up till now is practically the only one available—also a historical outlook bearing the prophetic marks of Prometheus. Then, if both attitudes are alive in our lessons, we shall at last achieve the right approach to history for pupils who have reached the age of sexual maturity.

---

*Prometheus ("Fore-thought") and Epimetheus ("After-thought") were brother Titans in Greek Mythology

240

LECTURE XIV
Dornach, 5th January 1922

The description of the human organization with its different bodies or members, which I have given to you, helps to gain knowledge of the entire human being. It is a picture which can be presented from many different viewpoints, and it is just these manifold aspects which enable us to fathom further what lies behind the constitution of man. I have spoken to you about man's astral body as being that member of the human being which, using both spatial and time relationships in its own sovereign way, breaks all bounds of space and time, as it were. I have tried to show you how we can experience something of this quality in our dreams which emanate to a large extent from the astral body and which weave together incidents of our lives, separated in time, into one continuous dream picture.

One can characterize the astral body from many different aspects, and one of them is based on what happens in the human being during the development of sexual maturity. If one observes the relevant phenomena and their underlying forces, one will arrive at a picture of the astral body because puberty is the time of its birth, the time when it can be freely used by the human being.

St. Augustine*, the medieval writer, tried to approach the human astral body in yet another way. Here I wish to point out that in his writings one finds a description of man's invisible members which is still in agreement with the

---

*St. Augustine, 354–430 A.D. "De quantitate animae"

241

one given in Anthroposophy. His findings, however, were the outcome of an instinctive clairvoyance, once the common heritage of all mankind, and not the result of a conscious investigation into the spiritual realm, as practiced in Anthroposophy. The way in which St. Augustine describes the astral body becoming independent at puberty is truly characteristic of human life. He says: It is due to the fundamental properties of the astral body that the human being is able to become acquainted with everything of a man-made origin which affects human life. If we build a house, make a plough or invent a spinning machine, we do so by making use of forces which are directly bound to the astral body. It is a fact that the human being learns with his astral body to know everything which is the product of human activities within his surroundings. It is therefore fully consistent with a true knowledge of man if we, as educators, introduce the adolescent to the practical sides of life which represent the results of human ingenuity. This, however, is a far more complicated process today than in St. Augustine's times, when life was altogether simpler. Only by applying what, during previous lectures, I called "soul-economy in teaching," can we hope to succeed in planning an education for pupils aged fifteen to twenty, or even older, which will gradually introduce them to the manifold contrivances surrounding them today. Just think for a moment of how much we fall short of this task in our present civilization. You only need to ask yourselves how many people there are who regularly use the telephone, the tramway or even a steamship without having the faintest idea of how they work. In our civilization people are almost engulfed by a technology which they do not understand. Those who believe that only our conscious experiences are of real importance, will dismiss these remarks as irrelevant. Certainly, it is easy enough to enjoy life consciously if one is satisfied with buying a tram ticket in order to be set down at the place of one's choice, or if one receives a telegram without having any idea of how the message ever reached the recipient, without having the slightest notion of what a Morse apparatus is like. The ordinary consciousness is unconcerned about whether it understands the processes or not, and from this point of view it is arguable enough whether these things matter or not. But if one looks at what is happening in the depths of the unconscious, the picture looks entirely different. Anyone who uses products of modern technology without having any knowledge of how they work or of how they were made, is like a person in a prison cell without a window through which he would at least be able to look out into nature, into freedom.

knowledge of modern technology

Educators ought to be fully aware of this fact. With the adolescent's experience of the differentiation between the sexes, the time is ripe for the understanding of yet other differentiations in modern life. The pupil now needs to be introduced to the practical aspects of life, and this is the reason why, with the approach of puberty, we include crafts, such as spinning and weaving, in our curriculum. Naturally, such a plan brings many difficulties in its wake, certainly from the timetable point of view. When planning our curriculum, we must also bear in mind the demands of other training centers, such as universities, technical colleges or other similar institutions, to which our pupils may wish to gain entry. This, in turn, makes it imperative for us to include some subject matter which, in our opinion, is of lesser value for life. It really causes us a great deal of trouble and pain to achieve a balanced curriculum which is entirely dependent on strict soul economy in teaching. It is a most difficult task, but not an impossible one. It can be achieved if the teacher develops a sense of what is of real importance for life and if he is capable of getting it across to his pupils in the most economical and in simplified ways, so that eventually they will learn to know what they are doing when using a telephone, a tram or any other modern invention. We must aim at making our pupils familiar with the ways of our present civilization, so that they can see sense in it.— Already before the age of puberty the teacher has to prepare his chemistry and physics lessons in such a way that, after the onset of puberty, he can build upon what was given and extend it to become the basis for an understanding of the practical spheres of life.

Here we must consider yet another point, namely that the pupils are now entering an age when, at least to a certain extent, they need to be grouped according to whether they will follow a more academic or a practical career later on. At the same time we must never forget that an education based on a true knowledge of man will always strive for balance in teaching, for teaching the whole man. What is needed here is the knowledge of how to achieve this in practice. Naturally, we must equip pupils of a more academic disposition with what they will need for their future schooling. At the same time, in order to retain a proper balance, any specialization—also during later ages—should be compensated by some widening out into otherwise neglected areas. If on the one hand we direct the pupils' will impulses more towards the academic side, we must give them also some concrete insights into practical life so that they will not lose sight of life as a totality. In this way we are actually fulfilling the demands of the human astral body which, when it guides conscious will impulses in a certain direction, at the same time feels the need for appropriate counter impulses.

To give a concrete example: It would be quite wrong—to quote an extreme case—if a statistician were to spend his time making statistics of the consumption of soap in certain districts without having the slightest notion of how soap is manufactured. No one can arrive at a proper understanding of such statistics unless he has at least some general knowledge of how soap is made in factories.

But life has become so complex that there seems no end to all the things to be considered. Hence the principles of soul economy in teaching has become more important than ever. In fact, it is the only way of dealing with this great educational problem. What makes it even more difficult is the fact that we ourselves are clogged up with clinkers of outworn forms of education administered to us during our own school days, clinkers resulting from educational traditions which are no longer justifiable in our modern times.

An ancient Greek would have pulled a long face if the young people of his time, before being sent out into life, had been introduced first to the ways of the Egyptians or Chaldeans, that is, to the ways of a previous civilization. Yet, this is what is being done, more or less, in our present-day Grammar Schools.* And yet, it is not possible to talk freely about these matters, because we have to consider how to fit our pupils into the existing forms of our society.

Those of our pupils who are likely to follow an academic career, should gain at least some experience of practical work involving manual skills. On the other hand, pupils who are likely to take on an apprenticeship for a trade should become acquainted also with the kind of background needed for the more academic types of professions. All this should be part of the general school curriculum. It is not right to send boys and girls straight into the factories to work there alongside grownup workers. Rather should the various crafts be introduced at school, so that the young people can use what they have learned there as a kind of model before they find their way into more professional skills. Nor do I see any reason why older pupils should not be given the task of manufacturing certain articles in school workshops to be sold on the open market.** This has

---

*In German: Gymnasien
**The Waldorf Toys originated in this manner (Translator's note)

245

already been achieved in some of our prisons, where prisoners' products are being sold outside.

A young person should remain within a school setting for as long as possible, provided that life at school is both constructive and healthy. For it is in keeping with the inner nature of the human being to enter life gradually and not to be flung into it too early and all of a sudden. It is just because the older generation has shown so little understanding of the needs of the younger generation, that there exists today such a strong international youth movement, the justification of which is understood least of all by the older people. There are deep reasons for the emergence of this movement which ought to be not only recognized, but also guided into the right channels. This, however, is only possible if the principles of education, too, are guided into the right channels.

One of the main objectives of Waldorf Education is to fit the students for life as far as this is possible, so that when a young person reaches the early twenties—when his ego enables him to take his full share in social life—he can develop the right relationship to the world at large. At that time, the young people should be able to feel a certain kinship with their elders for, after all, it was their generation which had provided the wherewithal used by the young generation. The young folk should feel appreciation of and understanding for the achievements of the older generation. Thus, when sitting in a chair, they should not only realize that the chair was made by someone belonging to the generation of their fathers, but they should also know something about how it was made.

Naturally, there exists today many a prejudice against the idea of introducing young people to practical life in the way indicated. But I speak about it here from an entirely practical point of view. For it is true to say that of all the past ages in mankind's development, our present materialistic age, in its own way, is the most spiritual one. Perhaps I

246

can explain myself better by telling you something about some theosophists whom I once met and who were striving towards a truly spiritual way of living. And yet, in actual fact, they were real materialists. They spoke of the physical body with its density. The etheric body they visualized as also having a certain density and corporeality, though of a far more rarefied kind. The astral body they described as being infinitely less dense than the etheric body, yet as still retaining a certain density. In this way they talked about all kinds of other mysterious things, believing that they were reaching ever higher and more spiritual spheres, until the substances they were imagining became so thin and attenuated that one didn't know any more what to make of it all. All their images bore the stamp of materialism and, consequently, never reached the spiritual world at all. Strange to say, the most materialistic outlook I have come across I witnessed among some members of the Theosophical Society. For instance, after having given a lecture to theosophists in Paris, I once asked a member of the audience what impression the lecture had made upon him. Then I had to put up with the answer that my lecture had left behind such good vibrations in the room. It really sounded as if it were possible to smell the impressions created by my talk! In this way, everything was gradually reduced to the level of a materialistic interpretation.

On the other hand, I like to tell those who are willing to listen to me, that I prefer a person holding a materialistic conception of the world but who, nevertheless, is capable of the spiritual activity of thinking, to a theosophist who, though striving towards the spiritual world, falls back on materialistic images. A materialist is in error, but what he thinks does contain spirit, real spirit. It is spirit in diluted form, it is abstract spirit, but spirit it is nevertheless; and his way of thinking compels him to enter into life's realities. Therefore I have found some materialists richer in spirit

247

than those who were anxious to overcome materialism, but who did so in an entirely materialistic manner. It is characteristic of our times that people absorb spirit in such diluted forms that they can no longer recognize it. But the most spiritual activity in our time can be found in technological endeavor. There everything proceeds out of the spirit, out of the human spirit.

It does not require great spiritual accomplishment to put a vase of beautiful flowers on a table, for nature has provided them. But to construct even a most simple machine does indeed require spiritual activity. The spirit plays its part, although it remains unnoticed because people do not observe themselves in the right way. The spirit remains in a person's subsconscious during such an activity and this, human nature finds difficult to bear unless a person has mastered the necessary objectivity. Only by finding our way into practical life do we gradually learn to bear the abstract spirit which we have poured out over our present civilization.

I can assure you that once the art of education, based on anthroposophical insight, has gained a firm foothold, it will put into the world people who are far more practical than those who have gone through our more materialistically inclined forms of education. Waldorf Education will be imbued with creative spirit, and not with the dreamed-up kind which tempts people to close their eyes to outer reality. To find the spirit without losing firm ground from under one's feet, this is what I should like to call true anthroposophical endeavor.

A teacher who wishes to introduce adolescents to the practical sides of life could easily despair over the lack of manual skill, symptomatic of our times. One really has to ask oneself: Is there a possibility at all of turning children between their second dentition and puberty into more practical and skilful people? And if, without theorizing, one looks at life as it really is—if one allows oneself to be guided by life itself and not by abstract ideas—then one is led to the answer which lies in bringing children, as much as possible, into close contact with beauty. The more they can be led to an appreciation of what is beautiful, the better will they be prepared, at the time of puberty, to tackle the practical tasks without being harmed for the rest of their lives. Only if at the right age the aesthetic appreciation of a painting or a sculpture has been cultivated, can a pupil, later on, safely gain an understanding of how a tram or a railway engine works. This is a fact a teacher should fully bear in mind. But beauty needs to be seen as being part of life and not as something separate, something that is complete in itself. In this respect our present civilization has yet to learn a great deal, especially so in the field of education.

A few examples of the simplest kind may give you a better idea of what is meant by cultivating in the pupils a sense of beauty which is not estranged from daily life. You may have been present when handwork was done, perhaps in the home of a family or at school in a classroom. You may have seen girls sewing patterns onto ribbons, perhaps of the following kind. (see diagram two)

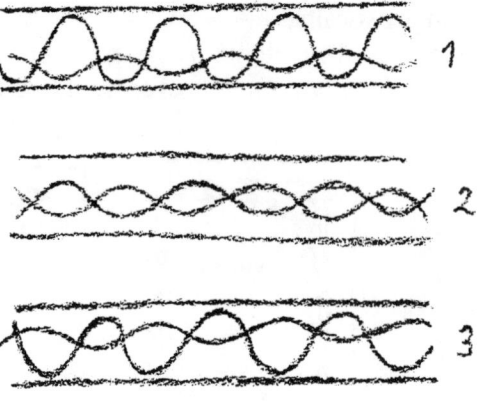

I will keep it as simple as possible and draw it merely for the sake of clarification. If then one asks a pupil, "What are you doing there?", the answer may well be, "We sew this pattern, first around the neck of the dress, then on the waistband and also round the hem of the dress." This kind of remark is enough to make one despair, for it shows a total disregard for beauty's fitness for purpose. If one is sensitive to these matters and sees a girl or young lady engaged in sewing the same pattern to the upper, middle and lower parts of a dress, one can't help feeling that anyone wearing such a dress would appear to have been compressed, or telescoped, from top to bottom! One must open the pupils' eyes to the necessity of adapting such a pattern according to whether it appears around the neck, the middle or round the hem. The uppermost ribbon could be varied somewhat like this (diagram 1), and the bottom one in this way (diagram 3). I keep the patterns as simple as possible, merely for the purpose of clarification. Now the pupil can safely sew the first pattern around the neck, for its form indicates that the head will tower above it. Pattern two can be sewn onto the belt and pattern three to the hem, showing that its right place is down below. For there is a difference between the above and the below in the human figure and this needs to be expressed artistically.

I once discovered that pillows had been embroidered in the following way (diagram 4). Whoever would wish to rest

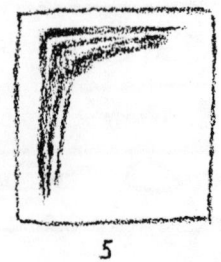

4

5

6

his head upon a pattern with a center that would scratch one's face? It certainly was not designed for putting one's head on it! This pattern does not express in the least the function of the pillow.

This is how it should be done (diagram 5). But now one can use it only if one's face is turned to the left! In order to solve the problem artistically, one needs the same arrangement also on the opposite side (diagram 5 and 6). This, however, is not the proper solution either. Fortunately, art enables us to create impressions of something which is not actually there. And so the pattern ought to create the feeling that the pillow allows the head to assume any position it may wish to choose.

These matters lead us right into what I should like to call the reality within the world of appearances, as expressed through the medium of art. Only by entering this reality will a faculty be developed which could be looked upon as the counter sense of what is merely practical. Only when one's sense of beauty enters the fulness of life, can one experience the practical realm in a right and balanced way.

Just now it has become fashionable to embellish Pompadours* with all kinds of ornamentation. When I see these knitting bags, I often wonder where to look for the opening. Surely the pattern on the bags ought to indicate their tops and bottoms and also where to put in the wool. Usually these things are ignored altogether, just as in the case of book covers where so often a design does not give any indication as to where the pages should be opened. Such designs are chosen at random, often encouraging the beholder to leave the book closed rather than to read it.

I gave these examples merely to indicate how a practical sense of beauty can be developed in the young. Only when

*Pompadours were small knitting bags for ladies. They were called after the Marquise de Pompadour, a lady at the Court of Louis XV.

this has been achieved can we proceed to the next step which is to fit the young people into the practicalities of life.

What is needed is a sense of reality in the child. Again I will choose only a very simple example to show what I mean. One could draw such a pattern (see diagram). The teacher has to be able to call forth a feeling in the child—and a little practice with pupils who react healthily will soon enable him to do so—that such a pattern is so intolerable because it does not represent a reality. This healthy feeling he should intensify—not by his own suggestions, but by drawing it out of the pupils—to the extent that they will feel: If I see such a pattern, it is as if I were seeing a person with only a left half of a face, or only one left arm or foot. Such a thing goes against the grain because it does not represent a reality. This is the kind of reaction the teacher should induce in the pupil, for it is all part of an aesthetic sense. In short, he should allow the pupils to feel that they cannot rest until they have completed the pattern by drawing the missing complementary part. In this way one cultivates in the children an immediate and living sense of beauty.

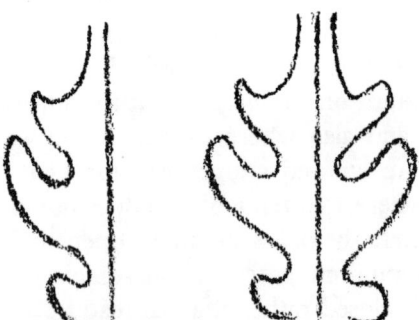

The word "schön" (beautiful) is related to the word "Schein" (shine, lustre, glory). Such an approach stimulates the child's astral body to become flexible and mobile and so to function well as a living member of the human being.

252

It is important for the teacher to cultivate an aesthetic sense also in himself. He will soon see how this enlivens his children. Then he will also nurture an artistic approach to the other activities which I have already mentioned during the course of these lectures. I then pointed out that everything a teacher brings to the child when it enters Class I should be permeated by an artistic element. Also when talking to the children about their surroundings, the teacher should do so with real artistry, as otherwise he might easily slip into what is called anthropomorphism, into restricting everything to narrow human interests. For instance, when clothing his content in fairy tales or legends, he may be misled into telling his class that certain kinds of trees spring up from the ground so that, from the bark, people can make corks with which to seal their bottles. The pictorial approach must never be coached in such terms. The pictures a teacher uses at this particular age must be created out of a sense of beauty. And beauty demands truth and clarity which directly speaks to human feeling. Beauty in nature does not need any anthropomorphism.

If we encourage a sense of beauty for everything the pre-puberty pupil meets, he will, from puberty onwards, bring human qualities also into the practical life he is now entering, harmonizing his way of looking at the world with the practical tasks awaiting him.

All this has an important bearing upon the social question which needs to be tackled from many different angles. Few people are aware of this today. It is absolutely possible that all the ugliness which surrounds us in practically every European city—and you can hardly deny that from an aesthetic point of view we find ourselves surrounded, at least to a large extent, by atrocities of all kinds in almost every large city—that all this ugliness would gradually be transmuted if we could cultivate for a few generations the sense of beauty which lives unspoiled in every child.

Today we look at man from the outside and we see his physical body. We observe also the inner man from the point of view of his personality, his ego. Between the ego and the physical body there live the astral and the etheric bodies. These latter two members are becoming more and more stunted in our times. On the whole they are developed properly only in oriental peoples. In the Western peoples they are atrophying. In the West they cannot develop properly. However, by awakening an all-comprehensive feeling for beauty, we can nurture their free development. And during the school years the growing human being is most receptive for the appreciation of what is beautiful. We ought, therefore, to do everything possible to awaken and cultivate the sense of beauty, especially during the time between the second dentition and the coming of puberty. In this way it will live on into later life.

This if of special importance also with regard to the element of speech. Languages are the outcome of a direct human response to inner experiences. If one is able to immerse oneself in the quality of spoken sounds, one can still hear in them the important part which such inner responses have played in the formation of certain words. But in our abstract life, when the logical content of language plays the leading part, this perception of the artistic element almost has been lost. True, there is an inherent logic in language, but this represents only its skeleton, something which is dead. There is much else besides logic in language. Its breath and pulse can be felt only by those who have been touched by the creative genius of language itself.

From this point of view try to feel how words want to project themselves into outer life. I will give a characteristic example, hoping that you will understand it although it is chosen from the German language. If you take the German word "Sucht" (sickness), you can detect in it the word "suchen" (to seek).* The body has a "Sucht," a sickness. It is seeking for something which, under normal conditions, it would not do. Certain additional words then point to what the body is seeking. For example, "Gelbsucht" (jaundice, yellow-sickness), or "Fallsucht" (epilepsy, falling-sickness). The word "Sucht" (sickness) enables the human soul to experience what the body is seeking through certain forms of sickness.

The further West we go, the more we find that people have lost this ability of appreciating the artistic element in language, which the Oriental is still able to experience. It is of great importance for us to regain at least some fundamental experience of the living genius of language. This will be of special benefit for greater international understanding within the social sphere.

You must forgive me if I choose another example, near and dear to me, in order to explain what I mean. But I must ask you to be very careful not to misunderstand what I am about to say. You see, on page 88 in the English translation of my book, *Die Kernpunkte der sozialen Frage*—translated as *The Threefold Commonwealth*** I find the following sentence: "The freedom of one cannot prosper without the freedom of all." This sentence, when weighed up by a deep-seated feeling for words, is nonsense. As mentioned just now, you must not misunderstand me, but this English sentence simply makes no sense, for it expresses something quite different from the original German words which read, "Die Freiheit des Einen kann nicht ohne die Freiheit des Anderen gedeihen." This sentence really wants to say something al-

---

*"sick" is a variant of "seek"—see: Chambers Twentieth Century Dictionary—(Translator's note)
**The current edition is called *Toward Social Renewal*. (Rudolf Steiner Press, 1977, London)

together different. In order to convey its meaning correctly, the translator would have to circumscribe it completely. The translation of any book ought to read as if it had been written directly out of the genius of the new language. Anything else is not really acceptable. I know for certain that *Bentham's** hair would stand on end, if in the astral world, he were to come across the sentence: "The freedom of one cannot prosper without the freedom of all." This sentence simply does not stand the test of clear thinking and this for a special reason.

If you came across such a sentence in a book, your immediate response would be, especially if you related it to education: Yes, there is such a thing as freedom. But the author talks about a situation which does not apply in England. In the original German language, however, this is not the case. There its content does make sense. But if translated in the way quoted, the real meaning conveyed by the original version cannot be understood. And what are the reasons?

I will show them by focusing on the significant word in the sentence. In English the word is "freedom." If one were to match the quality of this word with the corresponding German word, one would have to choose: "Freitum" (the ending (–dom) in English corresponds to the ending (–tum) in German). If such a word existed in the German language, one could use "freedom" with impunity. "Freitum" would then be translated with "freedom," and there would be no misunderstanding. But the word used in the original text is "Freiheit" (The ending (–heit) corresponds to the English ending (–hood)). In order to show you that the translation of "Freiheit" into "freedom" is not in harmony with the genius of language, I have to quote yet

---

*Jeremy Bentham, 1748–1832, Founder of the Philosophy of Utilitarianism

another German word, which is "Irrtum" (error). This word expresses a definite fact, something which happens once only. If one wanted to give this word the ending (–heit), one would have to form the word "Irreheit." Although you won't find this word in a German dictionary, you would not go against the genius of the language if you were to coin it. It would be quite possible to use it. "Irreheit" immediately leads us into the inner being of man. It expresses a quality of man's inner nature. There are no words in the German language ending with (–heit) which do not point to something which is mobile within a person. Such words carry their meaning towards a person. Actually, it is a pity that we do not use the word "Freitum" in German, for if it existed, we could directly express the meaning of the English word "freedom" without having to circumscribe it.

This kind of thing leads us right into the depths of language itself. It makes one aware of the genius of language. Therefore, when I write a book in German, I try to choose words which can be translated correctly into other languages. (My German readers promptly call it a bad style!) But this is not always possible. If, for instance, a book is addressed to the cultural life in Germany, it may be necessary at times to consider the German situation first of all. And this is why I have repeatedly used the word "Freiheit" which, however, should never be translated as "freedom." My book *Die Philosophie der Freiheit* should never bear the English title *The Philosophy of Freedom*. The right title for this book in English has yet to be found.

It is quite interesting to look at these things also from a statistical point of view. In doing so, I am neither being pedantic nor unscrupulous, but my findings are the result of deliberate investigation. If I were to write a book about education in German, the word "Freiheit" would appear time and time again in certain of its chapters. To find out whether the corresponding word "freedom" would be used also in an English book on education, I carefully looked through the likely chapters of such a book and lo and behold! the word freedom did not appear at all, not even a single time! This is the sort of thing for which one ought to develop a fine perception, for it is the very stuff we need for greater international understanding. It ought to be taken into account already during the school years. I am certainly keenly aware of it when writing books, as already mentioned. Consequently I am very cautious in the choice of certain words. If, for example, I use the German word "Natur" in one or another of my sentences, I can be quite sure that it will be rendered as "nature" in an English translation. There is no doubt at all that "Natur" would be translated as "nature." And yet, the English word "nature" would awaken quite a different conception from that of the German word "Natur." This is the reason why, in anticipation of future translations, I have paraphrased certain words in some of my writings. I have done so in order to avoid a wrong interpretation of what I wished to say. There are of course many occasions when I did use the word "Natur," but when it was important to match the German concept with a foreign one, I paraphrased "Natur" with "the world of sense" (die sinnliche Welt), especially if the book was likely to be translated into Western languages. To me, "the world of sense" seems to match, more or less, the concept of "Natur," as used in the German language. Obviously, I expected "sinnliche Welt" to be rendered as "nature" in an English translation, only to find that, once again, it had been translated literally into "the world of sense!" It really is of great importance to become aware of the living genius of language, especially where an artistic treatment of language is concerned.

Apart from the fact that in the translation of the sentence quoted the genius of language had not been recognized—I

258

only mention this in passing—you also find there the following wording: "The freedom of one cannot prosper without the freedom *of all*." This again makes no sense in German. It was neither written nor implied. What the original sentence says is: "The freedom of one cannot prosper without the freedom *of the other*" (of his brother, or of his neighbor). And this is the real point.

I must ask you again not to misunderstand my intentions. I choose this example, near and dear to me, to show how we have reached a stage in human development where, instead of experiencing the realities of life, we tend to skim them over, and language offered a particularly striking example for showing it. Gradually, our civilization has made us rather slovenly. We must make the effort to live ourselves into the language again, to live again with its words. Only then will we be able to bring to fruition the request I have made earlier on, that the child, having been introduced first to grammar, then to the rhetorical aspect of language, that is, to its beauty, should eventually also be brought to an appreciation of the artistic element of language. We must open the pupils' eyes and hearts to the artistic element living in language. This is important also in fostering a greater feeling of brotherhood with other nations. And it is equally important to recognize that what is generally referred to as the social question, often has to be looked upon from quite new and different angles.

LECTURE XV

Dornach, 6th January 1922

What I have to tell you today mainly concerns the child's physical education. It is in the nature of this subject that I can talk about it only aphoristically, chiefly because, in these matters, people tend to have already formed their own opinions. When it comes to talking about physical development, everybody seems to have definite preferences or dislikes which all too often strongly color people's theories about this subject. But everything issuing from personal sympathies or antipathies easily leads to fanaticism which is something far removed from the real aims and workings of Anthroposophy. Any form of fanaticism or agitation for this or that particular cause is entirely alien to the nature of the Anthroposophical Movement. All it wishes to do is to draw attention to the effects of various attitudes and deeds in life, and then to leave everyone free to relate personal sympathies and antipathies to the case in question.

Only consider with what fanaticism the case for and against vegetarianism is being argued today, each under the umbrella of unassailable scientific proofs. And yet, one cannot help noticing that never before has dilettantism been flourishing quite as much as in the defense of this and other similar movements. It really is so that Anthroposophy does not have the slightest leaning towards any form of fanaticism. It cannot be a party to those who, as ardent vegetarians, would wish to enforce their views upon people of a different attitude and who, in their fanaticism, even go as far as to deny non-vegetarians a fully human status in society. If, occasionally, fanaticism does creep into the Anthroposophical

Movement, it does not reflect the true nature of Anthroposophy at all.

Now, there is one more aspect which we have to consider within the context of these lectures. You will have noticed that the main emphasis with regard to the educational principles presented so far has always been that we must take appropriate measures in the child's soul-spiritual realm, so that the physical development will have the best possibilities of unfolding naturally and healthily. One could say: We are studying an educational system which, provided it is put into practice correctly and effectively, offers the best means towards a healthy physical development. Hence, the fundamentals of a sound physical education have already been given. Nevertheless it is good to review and summarize them once more, even though this can be done only aphoristically because of shortage of time. To do proper justice to this subject would mean my having to devote a whole lecture cycle to it.

Our theme naturally falls into three main parts which are: The way we feed the child, the way we relate the child to conditions of warmth or cold, and our approach to gymnastics. Fundamentally, these three categories comprise all that is of importance for the child's physical education.

Present-day means of knowledge, based as they are on an intellectualistic approach, do not offer us the possibility of coming to terms with the complex nature of the human organism. What is needed—despite the scientific attitude of which the present-day public is so proud—is that we acquire a certain instinctive knowledge of what is healthy or damaging to health, a knowledge which covers all the many grades lying betweeen these two poles. A healthy instinct for these matters is really of immense importance. For is it not true to say that our general natural science is gradually becoming dyed more and more in the color of materialism? Just consider how many secrets have been wrested from nature through research under the microscope or through dissecting certain lower animals so that the functioning of their parts could be investigated. How many conclusions have been drawn with respect to human behavior by observing animal behavior, without taking into consideration the fact that the human organization, as far as its most important characteristic is concerned, is radically different from that of all the animal species. At least, not enough emphasis has been laid upon this significant difference, mainly because today's science depends on investigating every detail separately, thus obtaining only a partial view of life.

Let me try to illustrate this situation by a comparison: Imagine that I meet two persons at nine o'clock one morning. They are sitting on a bench and I stop for a while to talk to them about various things, thus gaining a general impression of their characters. Then I go on my way again. At three o'clock in the afternoon I see them still sitting on that same bench. Now, there are various possibilities of what may have happened in the meantime. It may be that these two persons have been sitting there on that bench the whole time, talking together. Or, according to the different ways in which people belonging to different races or nationalities behave, quite other things may have happened. Perhaps they have been sitting together in silence. Or again, unknown to me, one of them may have gone away soon after I had left, while the other remained sitting on the bench. The former may have returned just before my reappearance, and so on. Outwardly nothing appears to have changed between 9 a.m. and 3 p.m., despite the fact that the two persons were very different in temperament and life-style.

Life will never reveal its secrets if one observes outer appearances only. And yet, with our present-day scientific methods, this happens far more frequently than is generally realized, as anyone can find out for himself. Present-day scientific attitudes can lead to a situation, such as I witnessed not long ago. In my young days I once had a friend whom I knew to be living a normal and healthy life. Subsequently we went our different ways and did not meet for many years. Then, one day, I visited him again. When he sat down to his midday meal, the food was not served in the usual way, but a pair of scales was put on the table. With these he weighed the meat and the vegetables, for he had begun to eat scientifically. He had complete faith in science which prescribed the correct amounts of the various foods to be consumed if one wished to be a healthy human being. Needless to say, such a method may be perfectly justified under certain conditions, but nevertheless it will thoroughly undermine any *healthy* instincts. Yet these instincts for what is wholesome or damaging to health are a most essential attribute of any teacher and educator worthy of his calling. He or she will surely know how to elaborate and make use of all that has already been given in the previous lectures, also with regard to the physical education of the child.

We have seen, for instance, how before the change of teeth the child lives entirely in its physical organism. This applies especially to the baby stage, and particularly so with regard to nourishment. As you know, when a baby begins to take in food, it is completely satisfied with a totally uniform diet. If an adult were to have to live, day in, day out, on exactly the same kind of food for breakfast, lunch, or any other meal, he would find it quite intolerable both physically and mentally. The adult likes to vary his food, he likes a mixed diet. The baby, on the other hand, does not get any change of food at all. And yet, only very few people realize the bliss with which a baby receives such a "monotonous" diet, for its whole body becomes saturated with intense sweetness from the mother's milk. A grownup has the possibility of tasting food only with his taste buds and their adjacent organs. He is unfortunate in that all his sensations of taste are confined to the head and thereby he is so very different from the baby whose entire body is one great sense organ of taste. At the end of the baby stage this way of tasting with the whole body ceases, soon to be forgotten for the rest of life. People who live with ordinary degrees of consciousness, are completely unaware of how different their sensations of tasting food were during their babyhood. And, true enough, later life does its best to wipe out this memory. To give you an example: I once took part in a conversation between an abstainer and another person of the opposite view. The abstainer who, like so many like-minded people, was also inclined to be fanatical, tried to convert the gourmand who replied—I won't tell you the whole story, for it would take us too far from our theme—"But I have been totally abstemious for two full years!" Greatly surprised the abstainer asked him when. The answer came pat, "During the first two years of my life." In this humorous, though rather frivolous manner important facts of life were talked about. Only very few people have a deeper and proper knowledge of them.

A baby is related to its physical body in such a way that it can only eat with its entire physical organization, deriving the utmost benefit and pleasure from this condition. The gradual transition to the next stage consists in the fact that forces begin to concentrate in the head region, finally bringing about the change of teeth. These forces are so powerful that they can push out the milk teeth and push the second teeth through. This is a slow and gradual process which takes place between birth and second dentition, affecting various other regions. After the stage of babyhood the sense of taste withdraws into the head. The child no longer eats with its physical organization only, but soul forces, too, are involved in the act of eating. The child learns to discriminate, also by means of its souls forces, between the various tastes.

At this stage it is important to watch with understanding

264

the child's reactions to different foods. Its likes and dislikes in themselves are a valuable indication for healthy or unhealthy inner conditions. But in order to be able to judge such questions, we need to have acquired at least an elementary knowledge of nutrition.

When talking about this subject today, people generally think of the weight aspect. This, however, is not the essential point. What really matters is the fact that each kind of food contains a certain amount of forces. Each item of food holds a definite total of forces by means of which it has become adapted to conditions of the outer world. What goes on inside the human organism, on the other hand, is something entirely different. The human organism must completely transmute the food it has taken in. It has to transform the processes undergone by the various foods during their growth into those which are to be active within the human organization itself. What goes on there is a continual conflict during which the dynamic forces contained in the food are metamorphosed into something entirely different. It is this inner reaction to substances eaten which we experience as stimulating and as something that sustains life. This is the reason why it is not good enough merely to ask: How much in weight of this or that food must we eat? But rather: How does our organism react to even the smallest amounts of certain food substances? For the human organism needs these forces which generate resistance against outer natural processes.

Processes going on in certain areas of the human organism —roughly speaking between the mouth and the stomach— though somewhat modified, can still be compared with forces occurring in the external world. However, those taking place in the stomach and in the subsequent stages of digestion, already are very different from what can be found outside the human being. But when it comes to what is happening in the head region, one finds there exactly the opposite processes from those occurring in outer nature. This shows how the human organism in its totality has to be stimulated in the right way through the food taken in.

As I have to be brief, there is no time to go into the terminology representing the deeper aspects of this subject. However, for our present needs a less specialized and more popular terminology will suffice. As you know, there are foods which in ordinary life are called rich in nutritive value, and others which are called poor nutriments. It is possible to live on food of only poor nutritive value. Just think of how many people are fed mainly on bread and potatoes, both of which definitely have a low nutritive value. On the other hand, you have to remember how, in cases of ill health, great care has to be taken not to burden a patient's digestion by feeding him on foods containing little nourishment. Bread and potatoes make very great demands upon the digestive system with the effect that only little will be left over for the remaining functions. Therefore a diet of bread and potatoes is hardly likely to promote physical growth. Other foods are looked for, foods which do not put an undue strain upon the digestive system, foods which make the digestive system work but little. However, if these things are taken to extremes, an abnormal activity is set up in the brain. This in turn will set into motion other processes which have no resemblance whatever to those going on in external nature. These again affect the remaining human organism and in consequence the digestive system will relax. It will become too slack. All this is extremely complicated and it is extraordinarily difficult to penetrate all the ramifications of what is happening there. It is one of the most difficult tasks of a thorough scientific investigation— not the kind so common today—to really know what is happening when, for instance, a potato or a piece of roast beef is put into a human mouth. Each of these two processes is very complex, and each is very different from the other. In order to investigate the subsequent stages of digestion with scientific precision, a great deal of specialized knowledge is necessary.

A mere indication of what is happening there must suffice. Imagine that a child eats a potato. First the potato is tasted in the head, the seat of the organs of taste, and the sensation of taste then induces further reactions. Though the sense of taste no longer permeates the child's entire organism, it nevertheless has certain effects upon it. Now, a potato does not have a particularly stimulating taste and, consequently, it leaves the organism somewhat indifferent and inactive. The organs are not particularly interested in what is happening there with the potato in the child's mouth. The potato is then passed on into the stomach in the ways known to you. The stomach, however, does not receive it with alacrity either, because it has not been previously stimulated by the sensation of its taste. Taste always provokes the stomach to take in food with either more or less sympathy. In this case the stomach will not exert itself in order to incorporate the potato with its dynamic forces. Yet, this must happen, for the potato cannot be left lying there in the stomach. If the stomach has the necessary strength, it will absorb the dynamic forces of the potato, working on them with a certain distaste. It allows the potato to enter without developing a marked reaction to it because it does not feel stimulated by it. This process continues in the remaining digestive tract where, what is left of the potato, again is worked upon with a certain reluctance. Only very little of what once was the potato ever reaches the head organization. These few indications, which ought to be deepened considerably for any proper understanding, are to give you a mere impression of the complex nature of the processes going on in the human organism. Nevertheless, an educator ought to acquire a working knowledge of these things, and in order to do so, I believe it to be necessary for him or her to go into the why and wherefore. I could imagine that some of the listeners might think it good enough simply to be told what to give to children to eat and which kinds of food to avoid. But this won't do, for in order to act rightly—especially when matters of a physical nature are involved—the educator needs to have sufficient insight into the problems. There are so many possibilities of dealing with them that one needs to be guided along the right path in order to recognize what needs to be done in each particular case. And for this the teacher needs at least a simplified picture of how a child should be fed.

Perhaps in no other realm does one notice quite as much how far educational principles have deviated from prevailing social conditions as in the case of physical education. Unless pupils happen to live in boarding schools where one is able to put into practice what I have been indicating, one will find it necessary to win the cooperation of parents or others in charge of children and this, as we all know, can cause considerable difficulties. Only after overcoming great obstacles may it be possible to implement measures which one deems right and beneficial for a pupil. Let me give you an example:

Imagine you have a pupil of an excessively melancholic disposition in your class. Extreme symptoms of this kind always indicate an abnormality in the physical organization. Abnormalities in the soul region always have their basis with physical abnormalities of one kind or another, and physical symptoms are a manifestation of the soul and spiritual life. So let us imagine that there is such a child in a day school. (In a boarding school one would of course deal with such a problem in cooperation with the dormitory.) What would I have to do? First I must try to establish a contact with the child's parents and—if I am absolutely sure about the real causes of the problem—I may have to ask them to increase the child's sugar consumption by at least 150% and in certain cases even by 200% compared with what is given to a child who behaves normally. I must advise the parents not to withhold this additional amount of sugar which could be given, for instance, in form of sweets.

Why am I doing this? Perhaps it will become clearer to you if I take the opposite case as an example: let us imagine that I have to deal with a pathologically sanguine child. If what I am saying is to make sense, we must take an abnormally sanguine case; we must imagine an excessively sanguine child. Again its symptoms betray an abnormality within the physical organization and in this case I should have to ask the parents to decrease the sugar content given to the child. I must ask them to reduce greatly the amount of sweetness given to the child.

What are my reasons? One can find out to what extent one has to increase or decrease sugar content only if one is aware of the following facts: Mother's milk in particular, but all milk and milk products, spread their effect uniformly throughout the entire human organism in such a way that each organ receives what it needs in a harmonious manner. The other foods, on the other hand, exercise their influence more upon one particular organic system. (Please note, I am not saying that the other foods exercise an exclusive influence, but a predominant one upon the various organs.) The way in which a child, or an adult, responds to a specific taste or to certain kinds of foods depends on the general condition of a particular organic system. In this respect certain luxury foods play as important a part as do ordinary foods.

Milk affects the entire human being, whereas other nutriments affect one particular organic system. With regard to sugar we must turn our attention to the activity of the liver. So, what am I doing if I give an abnormally melancholic child plenty of sugar? I diminish the activity of the liver because sugar, in a certain sense, takes over the activity of the liver. The liver activity is now directed more towards something extraneous and, consequently, the liver's activity is reduced. In this way it is possible, purely by dietary means, to lesson a super-melancholic tendency in a child—which can also appear as a tendency towards anemia—for under certain circumstances, pronounced melancholic symptoms can be the consequence of a child's liver activity.—And what am I doing if, in the case of a super-sanguine child, I recommend a reduction of sugar intake? Here I try to lessen the activating effect of sugar in order to induce the liver to become a little more active by itself. In this way I stimulate the child's ego forces, thus helping him or her to overcome the physical symptoms of a super-sanguine temperament.

This example illustrates that it is possible to counteract certain abnormalities if one observes the human physical organization as an entity. Consequently the why and wherefore is of importance. Naturally, there are always countless details to contend with but it is quite possible to relate these to the wider aspects which generally lead to polarities. A really good teacher—an even better one than those who exist already—through close contact with his pupils, would know prophetically and instinctively what to do with a child under given circumstances. In any case, it is of utmost importance for the teacher to perceive any deviations from a child's normal and healthy behavior, so that he can take appropriate action.

If one practices such close attention for a longer time, one generally learns to find out what preventative measures need to be taken. As a rule, this faculty is developed only if an alert and dedicated teacher has made it his second nature to spot even slightly-unusual symptoms in his pupils. (Obviously, one must never allow abnormal features to deteriorate to an extreme degree before taking action.) In order to achieve this ability, a teacher must be willing to deepen his understanding all the time and also to overcome many personal hindrances. Otherwise, I am afraid that teachers will attain the necessary thoroughness only by the time they reach their retirement!

What one has to watch very closely is, on the one hand, the interest which the child, as a being of body, soul and spirit, shows not only for him or herself, but also for the environment. One has to develop an instinctive awareness for the child's interest, or for the lack of it. This represents the one pole. The other consists in the teacher being aware of the first signs of fatigue in the pupils.

Where does each child's characteristic interest come from? It has its seat in the metabolic and limb system, but mainly in the metabolism. If I see that a child loses interest, let us say in matters involving mental activities—and this is the most obvious case—or if it shows little interest for outer activities, if it no longer wishes to take part in games or similar pursuits, or if I see that it even loses interest in its food—the worst sign of all, for children by nature are interested in the tastes of different foods and they should learn to distinguish between the various tastes—if a child suffers from lack of appetite (for lack of appetite is lack of interest in food), then I know: The cause lies in a wrong diet. The food given to such a child makes too great a demand upon its digestive system. I must find out what kind of food, containing relatively little nutritive value, is being given to this child—food that overloads and burdens its digestive system. Just as I can deduce the weather from reading the barometer, so can I deduce a wrong diet by noticing a marked lack of interest in a child. Interest or apathy are most important pointers with regard to the right diet for the child.

Now let us look at the opposite pole: If I notice that a child tires too quickly through either mental or physical activities, again I can trace back the cause to physical conditions. In this case the child may eat with a normal appetite, but after taking in food it may sink into a state of drowsiness, not unlike that of a snake after feeding. If, after a meal

271

a child has an abnormal desire to curl up on the sofa, it is a sign that it cannot cope with its digestion properly, that it becomes exhausted by the activity of digestion. It is a sign that it has been given too much food of the kind which does not stimulate the digestion sufficiently, with the effect that the unfulfilled demands of its digestive system now enter the child's head region, thus causing fatigue.

If a child shows a marked lack of interest, I must give it food of concentrated nutritive value. There is no need to wax fanatical about these things. Fanatical vegetarians will say: This child shows lack of interest and it has been fed on meat. You must get it used to a diet of raw fruits and it will recover its interest again. This may be the case. On the other hand, those who believe in giving meat to children, will maintain: If a child tires too easily, one must stimulate it with a meat diet.—These things should not provoke too much argument, simply because it is quite possible to balance different kinds of foods through appropriate combinations which, in this case, might well take the place of meat. Nor is it essential to turn children into vegetarians. What matters is that one recognizes that lack of interest in a child can be overcome by an improved diet, namely by feeding it on specially nutritious foods and that, on the other hand, a tendency towards fatigue can be overcome by working in the opposite direction. This is one way of simplifying a highly complicated subject for easier understanding. If, for instance, I find that a child tires too easily, I must realize that its digestion is not sufficiently engaged. Hence I must alter the diet accordingly.

We must learn to develop a kind of human symptomatology which will help us forward in a concrete and practical way. It is not always necessary to go into all the details. If, in matters of nutrition, one interprets certain symptoms correctly, one will learn to see through a given situation and know what steps to take.

Closely related to all this, and yet in a certain sense its very opposite, is the whole question of warmth in childhood. Here external phenomena offer an even clearer guideline than in the case of nutrition; we only need to interpret them correctly. On the other hand, they easily lead to exaggerations and then they can become harmful. Well, the catchword I am referring to is: "hardening," "toughening-up." Under certain circumstances this can be a good thing and much has been done in its favor. And yet, if one stands on firm ground with regard to knowledge of man, one can't help feeling thoroughly alarmed at seeing adults who, in their childhood, were systematically hardened and who are now unable to cross a hot and sunlit square without feeling oppressed by the heat. This can reach such proportions that their psychological as well as their physical makeup actually stops them from ever venturing across a sunny, open square. Surely, hardening can be right only if it enables a person to put up with physical hardships of any kind.

When considering the question of warmth or cold, two facts need to be borne in mind. First, that nature has given us a clear directive in that we feel well only so long as we are unaware of the temperature surrounding us. If we are exposed to too much heat or cold, we very quickly lose our sense of well-being. Obviously, we need to be able to perceive outer temperatures with our senses, but this must not have an adverse effect on our entire organism. To protect ourselves from heat and cold, we neutralize their effects by the kind of clothing we wear. If a human being is exposed to too much cold, he or she becomes incapable of keeping certain inner organs functioning normally. If, on the other hand, outer temperatures are too high, the body will react by an excessive functioning of these organs. So that one can say: If a person is exposed to abnormally low temperatures, his inner organs develop the tendency of coating themselves with a layer of mucus, thus giving rise to the type of illnesses which, coining a popular expression, I should like to call "internal mucositis." Organs are being lined with metabolic excrescences, and this process results in a hypersecretion of mucus.—If, on the other hand, a person is exposed to too much heat, these organs will react by drying up. A tendency of forming crusts develops, while the organs themselves ossify and become anemic to a high degree.

This way of looking at the human organism will give us the right indications of how to proceed in educational matters. Every symptom, every phenomenon can teach us something. For instance, as human beings we can safely expose our faces to much colder temperatures than other parts of our body. By being exposed to greater degrees of cold, the face actually prevents the other organs from drying up. It stimulates these organs and there is a continuous interplay going on between the face which readily accepts certain degrees of coldness and the other members of man's physical organization. However, we must not mix up the position of our face with that of a very different part of our anatomy. Forgive me for putting it so crudely, but we must not confuse a person's face with his or her calves! This is the kind of mischief one comes across so frequently today, for in cold weather children are allowed to walk about with bare legs up to their knees and sometimes even higher up. This, in fact, is a real mixing-up of the two ends of the human physical body. If people were aware of the hidden interconnections between such things, they would realize how many cases of appendicitis, developing in later years, are linked to this confusion between the two human extremities.

On the other hand, it also needs to be said that one should not be oversensitive to minor changes of temperature, and that children should be brought up to bear them with equanimity. If a child overreacts to slight changes of temperature, we must know that, once again, we can help by making corresponding changes in its diet. These are the things which show us that warmth and nutrition have to work together, for eating and keeping warm are complementary to each other. If someone is oversensitive to changes of temperature, he or she should be given food of high calorie content which will generate inner strength to withstand outer changes of temperature.

Again you can see how a real knowledge of man can help also in such a situation and how, fundamentally, everything within the human organism not only must work together harmoniously but, above all, how those entrusted with the task of educating the young must be able to recognize this cooperation among the various organs.

The third major aspect regarding physical education concerns the various forms of movement given to pupils. The human being is constituted in such a way that he has to be active not only within his own bodily functions, but he must also partake in the happenings of the external world. He must be able to experience himself as a link with the outer world. It is true to say that no separate organ of the human being can be understood properly if it is considered merely in a state of rest. Only if we relate it to the activities and movement inherent in its functioning, are we able to understand it also in its state of rest. This is the case, no matter whether it be an outer organ, the form of which—even in its resting position—already indicates the type of movement it has to perform, or an inner organ whose shape and configuration in themselves are expressive of its function and mobility, thus making it part of the overall processes of the human organism. All this is taken into account if we introduce the various forms of movement to the child in the appropriate way. Again, we must bear in mind the wholeness, the totality, of the human being and we must aim at giving proper due to his physical, soul and spiritual being. In the case of the child this will happen only if we allow it to perform movements of the right kind and of a style

275

which will give satisfaction because they are in harmony with the child's innate intentions. Consequently these movements will always be accompanied by a feeling of well-being.

The first step in this direction in an education based on knowledge of man, is to learn to understand the particular ways in which children want to move if given free rein. The kind of stereotyped games with their inhibiting rules are really quite alien to the young child's nature, for they suppress what should be left freely mobile within the child. Through such organized games the child's own inner activity is gradually being dulled down, and as an activity is being imposed upon the child from without, it loses interest in such movements. This one can see quite clearly if one observes what happens when the free movements of a child at play are channelled too much into fixed gymnastic exercises. As I said before, I do not wish to condemn gymnastic lessons out of hand but, in general, one can surely say that when a young pupil is doing gym exercises, his or her movements are called forth from without. Anyone working out of a real knowledge of man would much rather see young children play freely on parallel bars, on the horizontal bar or on rope ladders, instead of their having to follow the exact commands of a gym instructor shouting: "One, two, three," while they have to put their feet on the first, second or third rung of the rope ladder, or perform precise movements on the gym apparatus, movements which tend to impose stereotyped forms upon their bodies.

I know that these remarks go a little beyond the general trend of modern gymnastics whose advocates often are tinged with fanaticism. One easily rouses antipathy if one throws light on the kind of gymnastic exercises which are imposed from outside, and compares them with the child's natural movements arising out of its own involvement in free play.

Yet it is precisely this free play which ought to be observed and studied. One must get to know the child intimately, and then one will know what to do in order to stimulate the right kind of free play in which, of course, both boys and girls should take part together. In this way, through the inner mobility which accompanies the children's outer movements, their organic functions will act together harmoniously. This method will also open one's eyes to what lies behind certain symptoms, such as those indicating anemia in young girls. In most cases these symptoms are simply the result of the young girls having been artificially separated from the boys because it was considered unseemly for them to romp about with the boys during free play. Girls, as well as boys, should be allowed to be boisterous in their free play, though the girls perhaps in slightly modified ways. The conventional ideas of what is ladylike, which so often are held up to young girls, are frequently contributary causes of anemia, occurring in later life. (I must ask you not to take this remark as a personal criticism of an established way of life, but rather as an objective observation.) We can obviate a tendency towards anemia simply by allowing young girls, too, to engage in the right kind of free play. In this way we safeguard their inner functions from becoming sluggish to the extent that they are no longer able to form the right kind of blood out of the digestive activity.

In our times it has been difficult to win full understanding for these matters, simply because the kind of knowledge fostered today is not the outcome of observing the inner nature of man, but rather that of collecting detailed data. By the so-called method of induction these facts are then made into some kind of hotchpotch of general knowledge. Admittedly, by following this method it is possible to discover all kinds of interesting facts. But what really matters is to observe what is of significance for life itself. Otherwise it might easily happen that an ardent admirer of modern science objects by saying, "You have told us that anemia can be caused by young girls having been denied the possibility of free play; yet I have come across several cases of anemia in a village where the young girls had by no means been restrained in their free play.'' In this case one would have to investigate the causes of anemia in this particular situation. It might have happened that as a child, a girl once nibbled an autumn crocus (Colchicum autumnale), thus inducing a tendency to anemia which developed in later life.

Another important aspect of our theme concerns the consequences of mental strain in children. If we overburden their mental powers, we definitely exert a harmful influence upon their general condition of health. If we prevent the child from finding a natural relationship towards movement and play, its metabolic organization does not receive the necessary stimuli. By burdening the child with too much knowledge of the world, we artificially increase a metabolic activity in the head. Although man is a threefold being, all activities dominating one of the three spheres are, to a certain extent, also present in the other two systems. And if we overload a pupil, not with spiritual content, but with what the external world offers in the material realm, we divert some of the normal activity of digestion from the metabolic sphere to the head region, in this way calling forth a kind of abnormal activity of the entire metabolism.

This, too, can lead to conditions of anemia during puberty. Again someone might object by pointing out that in a certain village, where pupils were not at all subjected to intellectual pressure, such cases of anemia had occurred. Again one would have to investigate the particular situation involved. For instance, it might then be discovered that one of the houses in this village was covered in Virginia Creeper and that a child whose curiosity had been roused by its black and glistening berries had eaten a few overripe ones, in this way increasing an already innate tendency towards anemia.

In conclusion I should like to say: To collect separate

data and then extract from them general knowledge can be a perfectly correct method of procedure. But if one aims at the kind of knowledge which is closely allied to practical life, one has to observe the actual life situations carefully in order to find out where and how one should tackle the problems as they present themselves. Only a real knowledge of man will offer the educator this kind of insight into the human being, and it will enable him to fulfil his task by leading the child into the right forms of movement and by being on his guard against subjecting the children entrusted to his care to too much mental strain. The realization of these possibilities is our first and foremost task.

Of course we cannot always prevent a child from sucking an autumn crocus or from eating the black berries of the Virginia Creeper. But what we can do is to infuse intuitions into the child—and this at the right time—which will enable it to develop physical powers in an all-round way and to cultivate greater flexibility.

LECTURE XVI

Dornach, 7th January 1922

In this final lecture of our conference about an education based on Anthroposophy, based upon anthroposophical insight into the human being, I should like to speak about the moral and religious aspect in teaching, two kindred subjects which naturally belong together. Once again, there is only time for a few characteristic observations.

There is hardly any other subject where one feels equally strongly how important it is that an all-embracing and unifying spirit, born out of a real knowledge of man, should pervade all aspects and all branches of education. Yesterday I spoke to you about physical education. Today's theme can only be considered to be a truly spiritual one, and this very much so when we look at it from the spirit of our time. Right from the beginning I wish to emphasize that these two subjects—physical and spiritual in nature—will have to flow together to form a unity in the kind of education we are considering here, although they tend to be treated as two rather separate branches in traditional education. For this to happen in general may well take its time. But in our Waldorf School we have tried to make a small beginning of this intimate flowing together of spiritual and physical activities by introducing eurythmy, which is an obligatory subject in all its classes and which could be looked upon as a kind of soul and spiritual form of gymnastics. This eurythmy uses the human physical body as a medium in order to express everything it has to bring. Yet, at the same time, right down to the smallest detail, every movement is meaningfully permeated by what is of a soul and spiritual nature. Eurythmy

280

depends on the physical organs in a similar way in which speech depends on the human speech organs, without which there could be no oral communications. These physical speech organs are the carriers of soul and spiritual content.

Just as the spiritual element in language can lead one directly into the moral and even religious sphere if one is only perceptive enough—for it is not without reason that the Gospel of St. John begins with: "In the beginning was the Word"—so one can say: This flowing together of body, soul and spirit, though in a lesser known subject and in an as yet more instinctive way, is being cultivated by the teaching of eurythmy in every class of the Waldorf School. Although directly linked to physical movements, eurythmy is one of the subjects which can show perhaps more clearly than any other, how this unification of body, soul and spirit can be methodically practiced in actual class lessons. In future times many other activities will have to stand side by side with eurythmy, offering possibilities as yet undreamed of by present-day mankind, and working even more directly into the soul and spiritual realm. Such possibilities are inherent in what has already been given, waiting to be realized. The way is there. Even if our first efforts in eurythmy are far from perfect and limited in scope, all one-sidedness in gymnastics, resulting from the materialistic influences of our times, will eventually be overcome through the principles of eurythmy.

One really feels an inner urge to speak about the ethical and religious aspects of education, even if this can be done only aphoristically. On the one hand one wishes to appeal most strongly to what all human beings share as a common bond beyond the confines of race and nationality. On the other, one cannot help realizing that it is almost impossible to speak about matters so intimately connected with people's inner lives in a way which will be both understood and accepted by members of all nations. One example may suffice to show how very different people's moral and religious attitudes are in different regions of the earth and how one therefore feels inhibited when trying to reach them on this particular level. In reality, such intimate questions of morality and religion can be approached only through the national and religious background of the people concerned.

In all previous considerations of our conference theme I could speak in far more general terms about human affairs than is possible for me today. But the anthroposophical way of looking at the world engenders a strong desire to build bridges across all divisions into nationalities, races, and so on. In its inmost being Anthroposophy feels impelled to speak with a supranational, with an international voice. Nevertheless one is acutely aware of the difficulties involved when speaking with the voice of universal humanity about such intimate matters of human life, especially in the contemporary scene which, after all, is the reality confronting us. Therefore I must beg you to take what I am going to say with the attitude mentioned just now. It is given as an example to illustrate the deep gulfs dividing mankind.

During the course of these lectures I have already referred to *Herbert Spencer*★ who, whatever one's personal opinion of his philosophy may be, nevertheless has to be regarded as an exponent of Western civilization. I have also indicated that this *Herbert Spencer* has put into the world definite educational principles, one of which could be summarized in the following way: It is man's aim on earth to reproduce his kind and, consequently, it is in his moral interests to bring up and to educate his offspring accordingly. He must therefore endeavor to provide suitable parents and educators. Such, approximately, are *Herbert Spencer's* views which begin with, and aim at, a physical picture of man. He follows the development of the human race with an eye on its

---

*Herbert Spencer, 1820–1903, see his work "Education" (1861)

282

reproduction and adapts his educational aims accordingly.

Now let us look at another personality who, though living a little later, nevertheless can be regarded as a representative of the Eastern world outlook. Let us consider the philosophy of *Vladimir Solovieff*.* Though expressing himself in Western terminology, a truly Russian folk soul speaks through his works. And so we find that the ethical and religious aims of *Vladimir Solovieff* have a very different message for mankind, one which is permeated by the spirit of the East. He says: On the one hand man must strive for perfection with regard to truth and, on the other, he must partake of immortality. Here *Solovieff* does not imply the earthly kind of immortality resulting from fame or glory, but he speaks of the real immortality of the soul which rightly belongs to every human soul. He goes on to say: Without this striving towards perfection in truth, in other words, without the attainment of real knowledge, human existence would be worthless. Only if one is able to perfect oneself more and more, will human life gain in value. However, if the human soul were denied immortality, then all perfection, all ability to strive towards perfection, would be nothing but a monstrous cosmic deception, for then all human achievements in the search for truth would sink under, and humankind would be cheated of its most precious aspirations by the very cosmic foundations themselves. However, so claims *Solovieff*, this would be the case if in its earthly development mankind were to look upon the reproduction of the human species as the final and most important aim. For then mankind's special task in the world would be shunted from one generation to the next and man's course would be like the rolling of an unchanging wheel, at least with regard to his moral values of existence.

---

*Vladimir Solovieff, 1853–1900. (See the introduction to his work "The Spiritual Foundations of Life"–Vol. I)

In short, out of the Eastern spirit, *Solovieff* rejects in the clearest and strongest terms the Western ideals of Herbert Spencer.

This twofold way of experiencing and judging mankind's task on earth colors all the many divisions with regard to moral and religious issues. If one wishes to gain an understanding of mankind's ethical and moral aims, one must first of all free oneself from any prejudice, and then one needs to make an honest effort to comprehend the various diverging philosophies of life. The opposite views of the two representative thinkers quoted above can serve as an indication of how differently mankind is constituted with regard to the intimate subject under discussion today. It is the very aim of the anthroposophical world outlook to help people wherever they may live on earth towards an understanding beyond the barriers of race or national language. Consequently Anthroposophy endeavors to speak in a supranational language—this, of course, not in any physical sense—but in a language which can be understood throughout our present civilization. Today these aims can be realized only to a limited extent. But even the first steps will enable us to appreciate also wider issues. For as soon as we become clearer about what has just been said, we will realize how little we can achieve in the moral and religious field of education, if we introduce religious dogmas or fixed moral concepts to children. At best we could teach them to become Christians, Jews, Roman Catholics or Protestants according to our own religious beliefs. However, any attempt to indoctrinate the young in our own particular ideology must be eradicated from the true art of education.

One specific problem in education may help to clarify and illustrate this point. It is something which will make us pay due respect to matters pertaining to human freedom, also in the case of a child. And that we must have respect for the inherent freedom of the child, we shall soon realize if we say to ourselves: a feeble-minded pupil ought to be treated with the same care as a bright one, or even as a budding genius. What would happen if teachers adopted the principle that pupils ought to absorb only what was near to their own souls? Through his corporality a person of subnormal intelligence is born with a heavy burden. A genius is born with wings to his soul. We must confess to ourselves that we are called upon to carry our share of the burden of the imbecile. But we must also admit that as teachers we may not be able to follow the flight of a young genius. Otherwise every school would have to be staffed with geniuses of the highest order, and this is hardly possible. Nevertheless, our ways of teaching must ensure that we do not impede the progress of an inherent genius. Never must we clip the wings of a genius's spirit. This we can achieve only by developing an art of education which does not interfere with the spiritual forces that must be allowed to work freely in the growing human being.

Towards this end all previous considerations of this conference have been directed and if you examine them at greater depth, you will find it so. You will also find that the principles of Waldorf Education can be implemented in practical life in such a way that the teacher needs to deal only with what can be developed in the child by him, even if the pupil will eventually grow into a genius. Just as a dwarfed teacher cannot prevent his pupil from growing into a physical giant —just as he cannot intervene in the free unfolding of the pupil's physical growth—so his own spiritual limitations need not hamper his pupils' innate possibilities of spiritual growth. Their later lives will remain unimpeded by a teacher's inevitable shortcomings, if he takes his stand on a knowledge of man which emanates from the complete human being in the same way in which the powers of physical growth do.

I therefore welcome the fact that something has emerged

in the Waldorf School at Stuttgart, which may easily escape the notice of a passing visitor, but which nevertheless is a concrete reality: It is the spirit of the Waldorf School which has its own independent existence, irrespective of the personal situation of the individual staff members, whose soul and spiritual lives thrive on the communal efforts to cultivate it. It is this spirit which will encourage the teachers more and more to educate children even if it means having to bear their heavy yoke of subnormality. The teachers' joint study of the human being will help them to carry this burden, but at the same time, they will also make every effort to avoid the educational sin of hampering the free unfolding of a highly gifted pupil. This is our ideal. It is an ideal of which it need not be said that it exists only in cloud-cuckoo-land, for every day concerted efforts are being made to bring it down into daily life at the Waldorf School.

When dealing with moral and religious aspects of education, we cannot draw our content from existing ideologies, confessional religions or established ethical impulses. Our task will be so to reach the pupils' inner being that, in accordance with their destinies, they will be able to find their way in freedom towards working together with their fellow men in the social sphere. Consequently, in our teaching we do not begin by appealing to their conceptual faculties, for knowledge, though providing content, does not offer the possibility to live oneself into the intimate regions of the soul. When imparting knowledge, and this we are bound to do in our school, when addressing ourselves to the faculty of thinking as one of the three soul faculties, we must realize that this thinking, too, will have to be channelled towards ethical aims. However, when we are dealing with the moral and religious aspects of education, we must appeal, first and foremost, to the pupils' life of feeling. Neither can we address ourselves directly to the will sphere because a person's activities immediately link him or her to the social scene, and what has to be performed there is largely determined by the prevailing conditions and contemporary demands within the social sphere.

And so we cannot turn directly to thinking which always wants to go in a certain direction, nor to willing which is bound to take its impulses from prevailing social conditions, but we can always appeal to feeling which, to a certain extent, is the private domain of each individual. And if we appeal to this element in our teaching, we shall meet with those forces in the human soul which are of a moral and religious order. Yet we must go further than cultivating the pupils' thinking, feeling and willing as if each faculty were a separate entity. We must endeavor to train all soul forces simultaneously. Obviously it would be wrong to concentrate on the training of thinking in a one-sided way, nor would it be right to concentrate on the will alone. What we have to do is to let the element of feeling flow into both the sphere of thinking and of willing.

With regard to thinking, only knowledge of the world and of man which rests on an anthroposophical foundation can be of real help to us, for it allows us to build upon a physical and material basis. With this kind of knowledge we can safely turn to subjects such as physics and chemistry without falling into the danger of being unable to rise to a metaphysical, to a spiritual level. But if we reach the supersensible world along such a path, then not only our thinking, but also our feeling life will become engaged. For at the moment in which we raise knowledge of the world to a supersensible level, we begin to gain a moral relationship with the world foundations, with the supersensible beings themselves.

This element of feeling is the first one of the three soul faculties to which we have to turn in our moral and religious education. If fostered in the right way, it will become transmuted into a feeling of gratitude. This mood of gratitude, something in which today's educational practice plays only a comparatively minor and less conscious role, is what we must develop in the child quite systematically, right from the very beginning of school life. With each concrete example which we take from life itself, we must try to engender this mood of gratitude for everything the child receives.

And if this feeling is rightly developed, it is capable of rising to the highest realms of cosmic laws which can be reached through cognition. At such a moment a human being feels how nature is surrounding him. He learns to know nature's laws, sees himself within nature. He learns to know that what he can discover by means of his senses alone, will never make him into a full human being. Gradually he finds the way to a knowledge of man which points to what goes beyond the bounds of the sense-perceptible world but which, nevertheless, can be reached by scientific methods. He then experiences in himself not only the working of universal cosmic laws, but he divines the existence of spiritual beings. Such awareness changes his knowledge into a deep feeling of gratitude towards the supersensible beings who have placed him into the world, towards the supersensible beings themselves. Knowledge broadens into gratitude towards divine beings. No knowledge of the world is rightly imparted to the young, unless it eventually wells up into a feeling of gratitude towards the supersensible world.

And so the first quality within the three human soul faculties which will lead into the moral and religious sphere and which we must cultivate in the young is a feeling of gratitude. Gratitude in itself includes a certain cognitional quality, for we must know why we are grateful. It is characteristic of such a feeling that it is closely allied to our powers of comprehension. In the Waldorf School we do not appeal to a faith handed down by tradition. That is left to our visiting religion teachers who, after the ground has thus been prepared by the regular Waldorf teachers, are invited to relate what they have to give to life in general. With regard to the pupils' faculty of thinking, we first of all try to create a mood of gratitude. And when we turn to the life of feeling, we find there something which takes us out of ourselves, which leads us out into the surrounding world. When experiencing gratitude, we find ourselves confronting other beings. But if we can identify ourselves with other beings to the extent of experiencing them as ourselves, then something begins to develop in our feeling life which we call love in the true sense of the word. Love is the second mood of soul which needs to be nurtured with regard to the ethical and religious life. It is the kind of love which we can foster at school by doing everything we can so that the pupils will love each other. It is the kind of love to which we can give a firm grounding by aiding the children's gradual transition from the stage of imitation and that of authority between their ninth and tenth year to a genuine feeling of love for their teachers, whose bearing and general behavior at school naturally must warrant it.

In this way we lay the foundations of a twofold human quality: On the one hand we implant what is contained in the ancient call "Love thy neighbor as thyself." And as at the same time we are also developing a feeling of gratitude which points more to a comprehension of the world, "Love thy neighbor as thyself" is complemented by the words, "Love the Divine Being above all things."

Such words of truth have a familiar ring to most people today, for they have been sounding across the ages. However, to know them in theory and to repeat them is not the point. What matters is that in our immediate present, and every age sees a renewal of mankind, we find ways and means of putting them into practice. Nowadays one hears all too often, "Love thy neighbor as thyself and God above all things." Yet one sees little evidence of it. Life at school should help to bring about that such things are not merely talked about, but that they become infused with new life.

There is only one way which will offer a firm foundation for a mature capacity to love, and that is the natural transformation of the childhood stages of imitation and authority to that of love. And if we work in harmony with the child's natural development towards the attainment of love, the quality of which should be self-evident when seen in this context, we no longer need to invent long-winded theories of the kind that are fabricated by materialistic thinkers with the intention of guiding the newly sexually mature adolescent in his first experiences of love. A whole literature has been written on this subject, all of which suffers from the simple fact that one no longer knows what to do with youngsters when they reach sexual maturity. And the reason for this failure lies in the children not having been prepared adequately for this event, because one did not know how to handle the previous stages of childhood. If adolescents have been guided rightly up to this incisive time in their lives, one does not have the same difficulties with them.

Also in the case of the child's life of will, we must guide his developing soul in such a way that his feelings freely flow into his willing, and this in the right way. The child naturally must express manifold will impulses outwardly. But what is it that now asserts itself? We could not be human in the physical sense if, at the moment we express our will impulses, and particularly so when our deeds are seen in the light of morality and religion, we were unable to make use of our physical powers. In engendering love, we pour ourselves out into the world, as it were. In willing we draw back again into ourselves, and since willing is an essential part of our lives, we now enter the domain of our instincts, drives and emotions. At the moment when we are seeking the path to morality and religion, we must become conscious that into our instincts and desires there must flow that which makes us truly human. It will reveal itself to us when we knowingly contemplate the universe and find the human being there.

It is what was put into words by an old tradition in the saying, "Man is the image of the Godhead." Only if we can carry such an experience into our willing, only if even in the impulses of our instincts we can still find the image of God, will the kind of willing come into being which bears an ethical and also a religious character. Then we know that also in the domain of our willing we remain truly human. If a person lets his will impulses enter the world in such a way that, right down to the level of his instincts, people still recognize in him a true human being, what is he doing then? By developing a feeling for his own humanness which he pours into his activities, into his will impulses, he reveals the third of the three soul moods. And for this third element there exists no word in the German language! Therefore, to make my meaning clear, I have to borrow a word from the English language. It is the word "duty".* There is no German word for duty. Those who can experience how words reveal the genius of language, in the sense spoken of during a previous meeting, will be able to feel what I mean. True enough, anyone who, without further ado, translates simply according to what he finds in a dictionary, would translate the word "duty" with the German word "Pflicht." But "Pflicht" does not meet the case at all. As a noun, formed from the verb "pflegen,"** it comes from quite a different region of the soul. One would have to approach this whole line of thinking quite differently, if one were to base it on the word "Pflicht."

In this difficulty to find the right word you have another example of how differently people are constituted in different parts of the earth. If one aims to be conscientious and

---

*duty = that which is due. Latin origin: debere = to owe
**The verb "pflegen" has a double meaning: a. to nurture or to nurse; and b. to be accustomed to, to be in the habit of (eg: Er pflegte spazieren zu gehen = he used to go for a walk)

correct in one's use of language, one cannot translate "duty" with "Pflicht" in order to express the third mood of soul, for this would be an untruth. It would be a lie, even if only a technical one.

1) Gratitude
2) Love
3) Duty

And again it is characteristic that one can use the German words for gratitude (Dankbarkeit) and love (Liebe), but that there is no German word for expressing the third mood of soul. It is characteristic because as soon as we step out of the sphere of cognition which links us to humanity, for thought can be shared by all thinking people, and as soon as we leave the realm of love which can unite people everywhere, and enter the sphere of individual willing, we find ourselves placed into a definite geographical locality. There we are called upon to form our lives and to become conscious of the individuality which is being developed in us through our having been placed into a definite location on earth.

However, if we approach our pupils through their life of feeling, when, between the ninth and tenth year, the children's previous powers of imitation and their inborn sense of authority have gradually changed into new faculties, our teaching, by its very nature, will lead to a moral and religious experience on their part. And when a human being is permeated by the feeling that he wants to be truly human, that he must conduct his life in such a way that, right down to the level of his instincts, his fellow men will recognize in him a true human being, and when he himself can recognize his own humanity, at this moment he becomes a messenger, an angelos of the divine world. Then his moral life will become pervaded by a religious mood.

If a pupil has been rightly guided up to the twelfth year, new subjects introduced at that time will lead him out into what lies outside the human realm. This will make him acutely conscious that by observing outer nature he is entering another world, sense bound and obeying the laws of the lifeless, the inorganic world. (We have characterized this point of time and also indicated what form the right pedagogical approach should take.) But at that moment, deep down, the child will feel that he wants to be truly human also at the level of man's lower nature, at the level of his instincts and drives. And then the third mood of soul will arise: The feeling of a sense of duty. In this way, through our education and in conformity with the child's own nature, we have guided the pupil to an experience of the three moods of soul. Naturally the ground had to be prepared already during the previous school years.

At the stage of development which occurs towards the twelfth year, a certain loss of inner harmony will make itself felt in the pupil's religious experiences. By this I mean that in his religious life a most important moment has come. Naturally the pupil must have been prepared for this turning point so that he can pass through it in the right way. What must not happen is that the educator simply accepts the fact that certain conflicts, brought about by our present civilization, are inevitable.

In our times people have their moral and ethical views which are deeply rooted in the human soul and without which they cannot imagine human dignity and human values. On the other hand they find themselves surrounded by the effects of natural laws which, in themselves, are completely amoral, laws which affect human lives irrespective of any moral issues and which can be dealt with only if questions of morality are left entirely out of consideration.

Today there is a widespread trend in educational circles, conveniently to bypass this problem in the case of children who have reached this critical point in their lives. But in our present civilization this conflict in the soul of man is a deep

293

and a tragic one. Unless it is resolved in some way or another before adulthood is reached, unless pupils are able to reconcile the moral with the natural order of the world so that these two worlds can be seen as part of one overall unity, they could well fall victim to an inner conflict strong enough to tear their lives apart. Today such a conflict exists in the lives of nearly all thinking people, only they remain unconscious of it. They prefer to fall back on traditional religious creeds, in this way trying to bridge what remains an unbridgeable gap unless one is able to rise from the sense-perceptible world to the spiritual world, as Anthroposophy endeavors to do.

For the adult, such a conflict is a tragic one indeed. Should it ever arise in childhood before the eleventh year, the disturbances it brings in its wake are serious enough to ruin the soul life of the child. It should never happen that a child says to himself: "I learn zoology and there I find nothing about God. I learn religion and I am told of a God, it is true, but this does not help me to explain zoology." To allow a child to be caught in this dilemma would be a dreadful thing, for this kind of questioning could completely throw it off its proper course of life. Needless to say, the kind of education we have been considering during the last few days would never allow such a schism to appear in the soul of a child, for it fully takes into account the importance of the eleventh to twelfth year and of all that follows after. Only then, but not before, is the right time for the pupil to become aware of the disharmony between life looked at from the natural, and life looked at from the moral point of view. For we should not overprotect the child by glossing over certain facts of life, such as that, apart from an experience of gratitude, love and duty, there also exists a split in the world, when seen through human eyes. However, if education is founded upon the principles elaborated here, pupils will be able to resolve this apparent disharmony in the world, especially at this particular age. These are problems which will deepen and enrich the pupils' religious lives far more than if they were to be fed merely on the traditional types of religious instruction which have to be accepted on faith. Such real content will give pupils the assurance that a bridge can be built across the abyss which they have experienced for the first time because it is a reality.

Our present civilization demands that we should let our ethical and religious views play their proper part in life as it is. And in our religious teaching we must take our cue from the critical moments of the pupils' developing life of feeling. The difficulties of finding the kind of bridge which I have spoken of, are highlighted by a book which was published in London* towards the end of the eighties. It is called "Lux Mundi" and among its contributors are several authors representing the official point of view of the High Church of England. In this book an attempt was made to integrate what has become crystallized within the Church more into social life. Here, even members of the High Church are at pains to build such a bridge, needless to say, from their point of view. You can find people everywhere discussing this subject, which could well become the real content of our religious life.

However, are we really able to offer the growing child something that carries weight in a subject which is being debated so much today? Are we in a position to lead young people into Christianity while theologians are arguing more and more about the real being of the Christ? Should it not be our task to find ways of helping each individual to relate him or herself to Christianity in freedom? We must not impart accepted dogmas or fixed formulae in our ethical and religious instruction, but we must learn to nurture the

---

*"Lux Mundi" – A Series of Studies in the Religion of the Incarnation, edited by Charles Gore, London 1889, reprinted in 1913

divine and spiritual element that lives in the human soul. Only then shall we guide the child rightly and without impinging on his inner freedom towards his eventual choice of his own religious denomination. Only then will pupils be saved from inner uncertainties on discovering that one grownup is a member of the High Church while another may be a Puritan. We must succeed in enabling our pupils to get hold of the real essence of religion. Likewise, through the cultivation of the three moods of soul we must succeed in allowing morality to develop freely in the child's soul instead of trying to inculcate it by means of set moral precepts. This problem lies at the very bottom of the social question and all talking about it or working in the social field will depend on our being able to provide the right basis for the moral education of the young. A significant part of the whole social question is simply a question of education.

It was only possible to present a few rough outlines of the moral and religious aspect of Waldorf Education which we have been studying during the last few days. If our educational aims are rooted in a true knowledge of man, and as long as we realize that we must refrain from introducing dogmas, theories, or moral obligations into our teaching, we shall finally succeed in laying the right foundations for the moral and religious life of our pupils.

And so we must continue to work towards a true art of education, in conformity with the needs of our times. Perhaps I may hope that what I had to tell you during the last few days will have shown that I was not at all prompted by any opposition against the achievements of general education up to date. Broadly speaking, our present civilization is not lacking in good educational aims and principles. These have been proclaimed in abstract terms by the great educationalists of the nineteenth century in various countries of the earth. Waldorf Education has no intention of opposing or belittling their findings, but it believes it knows that these ideas can become implemented only through the appropriate measures, and that such measures can grow only out of a real and deep experience of man and the world. Fundamentally speaking, Waldorf Education is trying to bring about what most people are looking for, though their aims may be somewhat abstract or ill-defined. If among those who have shown genuine interest in an anthroposophically founded education as practiced in the Waldorf School, a feeling has arisen that here ways and means are being sought in order to achieve what in reality everyone wants to see in education, then the right kind of response will have been evoked.

That I was permitted to speak to you out of this spirit, ladies and gentlemen, has meant a great deal to me. For it is more important to me that you should appreciate the spirit out of which I have spoken than that you should listen to the details of what I had to bring. Details may well have to be modified or adapted in one way or another. What matters are not the details but the spirit underlying them. And if I should have succeeded in calling forth at least some experience of that tolerant and humane, yet *active* spirit out of which anthroposophically-based education wishes to speak, then perhaps just a little of what I wished to bring in these lectures may have been achieved.

In conclusion, I wish to emphasize once more my firm conviction that it is of utmost importance to speak out of this spirit during our present times. I should like to thank you for the interest you have shown in these lectures. I should also like to thank you for spending your time at this conference, especially so during this festive season, and I hope that, as you go away again, you may feel at least some justification for having made your journey to Dornach.

If this should be the case, I should like to give you my heartiest farewell greetings in the hope that we may meet again, in the sense in which I spoke to you at the opening of this lecture course.

ANSWERS TO QUESTIONS

From the Discussion held on 1st January 1922

Rudolf Steiner: As a number of questions* have been handed in, perhaps it would be best if I began this meeting by trying to answer some of them. If there should be other matters you wish to be discussed, we could meet at another time during this conference.

Regarding the First Question:

It is certainly possible to believe that spreading one main-lesson subject over a longer period of time** could have its drawbacks. Neither can one deny that it is difficult to engage the attention of children on one and the same subject for a longer time. Other opinions, representing official contemporary educational theory, also seem to speak against such an extension of one subject into block periods. Nevertheless it was decided to introduce this method in the Waldorf School. The point is that the results of recent experimentally-based, psychological research, which is chiefly responsible for the disapproval of our methods, do not represent the real nature of the human being. These methods do not penetrate the deeper layers of the human being.

Why are psychological experiments carried out at all? I

---

*The questions were not taken down in shorthand
**In Waldorf Schools, a main-lesson period—or block period—of one single subject lasts approximately four weeks

do not object to them, inasmuch as they are justified in their proper sphere. Within certain limits I am quite willing to recognize their justification. Nevertheless the question remains: Why are experiments made with the human psyche in our present times?

The answer is that we experiment with the human soul because during the course of human evolution we have reached a point where we are no longer able to build a bridge, spontaneously and naturally, from one soul to another. We no longer have a natural feeling for the various needs of the child, of how or when it feels fatigued, and so on. This is the reason why we try to acquire by external means the kind of knowledge which human beings once possessed in their full presence of mind, linking one soul to the other. We ask: In what way does a child feel fatigued after having occupied him or herself with one or another subject for a certain length of time? We compile statistics, and so on. As I said, in a way we have invented these procedures in order to find out in a roundabout way what we no longer can recognize directly in a human being.

But for those who wish to establish a close rapport between the soul of a teacher and that of a child, something else is of far greater importance than questions such as whether too much claim is made upon the pupils' powers of concentration if one teaches the same subject for a longer period of time. If I understand the question rightly, it seems to imply that if one were to introduce a greater variety into the lesson* by changing the subject after a comparatively short time, that then something valuable would be gained. Well, something would be gained, certainly. One cannot deny that. But these things affect the pupils' whole lives and they should not be calculated mathematically. One ought to

---

*Rudolf Steiner here refers to the main-lesson which lasted two hours.

be able to decide intuitively whether what has been gained in this way, is of greater value when seen against the whole life development of an individual, or whether something has been lost in the long run. It is an entirely different matter whether one teaches the same subject for two hours (as in a main-lesson) or whether one teaches one subject for an hour and then another subject for the second hour, or even to change subjects after shorter periods of time. Although pupils will tire to a certain extent—a factor for which the teacher has to make due allowance—it is better for their overall development if one proceeds in this concentrated way than if one artificially limits the lesson time in order to fill the pupils' souls with new and different content in a following lesson.

What we consider to be of utmost importance in the Waldorf School is that the teachers make use of their available lesson time in the most economical way, that they apply "soul-economy" with regard to their pupils' potential. If one builds up the lessons along major lines of content which pupils are able to follow without becoming tired, or at least without feeling overcome by tiredness, and if one can work against any oncoming tiredness by introducing variations of the main theme, one can achieve more than by following other methods for the sake of advantages these may possibly bring.

In theory it is always possible to argue for and against such things, but it is not a question of preference for one or the other of them. The only thing that matters is the question: What is best for the overall development of the child, as seen from a long-term viewpoint?

There is one further point to be considered: It is quite correct to say that a child will tire if made to listen to the same subject too long. But nowadays there is so little insight into what is healthy or unhealthy for a child, that one looks upon the child becoming tired merely as something nega-

300

tive, something to be corrected. In itself, to become tired is as healthy as feeling refreshed. Life has its rhythms. It is not a question of holding the pupils' attention for half an hour and then to give them some five minutes' break to recover from the strain—which in any case would not balance out their fatigue—before cramming something different into their heads. It is an illusion to think that such a method would solve the problem. In reality one has not tackled it at all. One has simply poured something different into the child's soul instead of allowing the consequences of the organically-based causes of tiredness to fade away.

In short, one has to probe into the deeper layers of the human soul in order to realize that a longer concentration upon the same subject is of great value for the overall development of a child.

As I said, it is easily possible to reach the opinion that quicker changes of subjects offer an advantage, but one must also realize that a perfect solution will never be found in life as it is. The real question is: What is, relatively speaking, the best solution of a problem? And then one will find that short lessons of different subjects do not offer the possibility of giving the children content which will unite deeply enough with their spiritual, their soul and their physical organizations.

Perhaps I should add that if a school, founded on the principles I have been describing, were ever condemned to put up with boring teachers, one would certainly be forced to cut down the length of the lesson time. I have to admit that if teachers were to give boring and monotonous lessons, it would be better to reduce the length of each lesson. But if teachers are able to stimulate their pupils' interest, the longer main-lesson is definitely the better one.

For me, the essential point is never to become fixed or fanatical in any way, but always to consider the circum-

301

stances. Certainly, if one expects interesting lessons to be given at school, one must not engage boring teachers on the staff!

Question Two:

There may be justifiable reasons for looking upon eurythmy as a conversion of one art form into another, rather than considering it as a new form of art. But whenever one deals with an artistic medium or with the artistic side of life, it is not the "what" that matters, but the "how." In my opinion, there is no real meaning in the statement that sculpture, music, speech, rhythm and so on, are only the means of expression, while the underlying ideas are the real substance. There seems little point in making such abstract discriminations when one is dealing with life itself. Naturally, if one is keen on finding unifying ideas in the abstract, one can also find different media through which these are expressed. But in real life, these modes or media do represent something new, something different. To give an example: According to *Goethe's* theory of plant metamorphosis, a colored flower petal, when seen in the abstract, is inherently the same as a green plant leaf. *Goethe* sees in the flower petal a metamorphosed green leaf. And yet, from a practical point of view, a petal is something altogether different from a leaf. Whether eurythmy is a new form of expression or a conversion of one art form into another, is not the point at all. What matters is this: During the course of human evolution, speech and also singing—though the latter is less noticeable—sound, speech and singing, have become more and more a means of expressing what works through the human head. (Again, this is putting it rather radically but, from a certain point of view, it does represent the truth.) Today, human language, human speech, is no longer expressive of the whole human being. Speech has become thought-oriented. Among modern nations it has become closely linked to the life of thought and through this development, speech reveals what springs from man's egoism. Eurythmy, on the other hand, goes back again to man's will nature and, by doing so, it engages the whole human being. Through eurythmy man is revealed as standing within the entire macrocosm. And while, for example, during certain primeval times, gesture and miming always accompanied the spoken word, especially during artistic activities, so that word and gesture combined into a single form of expression and the two became inseparable, today word and gesture have fallen far apart. Therefore a need is felt to engage the whole human being again by calling into play also what belongs more to his will sphere and in this way to relate him again to the macrocosm.

Altogether, there seems to be too much theorizing going on these days, whereas it is so important to consider the practical aspects of life, especially in our present time.

Anyone observing life from this point of view without prejudice, knows that for every "Yes," there is a "No," and that everything can be proved both right and wrong. Yet the ultimate value does not lie in proving something right or in refuting it, in finding definitions and in making distinctions, but in what leads to new impulses and to new life in the world. You may well have your own thoughts when hearing all this, ladies and gentlemen, but anthroposophical research does give insight into the development of mankind, and mankind today has a leaning towards overcoming the intellectualistic element, to feel drawn more to what belongs to the soul of man and to life which produces creative activities rather than definitions.

And so, it does not really matter whether one looks upon eurythmy as a conversion of one art form into another, or whether one calls it a new art. A little anecdote may illustrate what I mean: When I studied at Vienna University, some of the professors there had been given a much-coveted title of distinction, they were called "Privy Councillors" (*Hofrat*). In Germany I found that such professors received the title of "Confidential Councillors" (*Geheimrat*). In certain quarters the distinction between these two titles seemed to be of importance. As for me, what mattered was the personality behind the title rather than the title itself. This seems similar—forgive me, for I really do not wish to offend anybody—to the situation where people engage in philosophical arguments in order to define the difference or to discriminate between transferring one art form into a different medium or, for want of a better word, to call it a new dimension in the realm of art.

To Question Three:

I am not quite clear what this question is meant to convey, but to me it seems to express a somewhat evangelical attitude of mind. At best, discipline, as I have already said, can become a natural by-product of the ordinary life in the classroom. I have also told you how during the last two years of the existence of the Waldorf School discipline has improved in quite a remarkable way, and I have quoted substantiating symptoms. With regard to this "sense of sin,"* it would appear that, because of one's own moral attitude, one believed in awakening such a feeling in the child for its own benefit. But, please let us look at this point free from any religious prejudice, an awakening of such an awareness of sin would pour something into the soul of the child which would remain there in the form of a certain insecurity for the rest of its life. Putting it into psycho-analytical terminology one could say that such a method could create a kind of vacuum, an inner emptiness, within the soul of the child which, in later life, could degenerate into a weakness as compared with a more active and energetic response to life

---

*Here Rudolf Steiner used these English words

in general. If I have understood the question rightly, this is all I can say in answering it.

Question Four:

In my opinion this question has already been answered by what I said during the first part of my lecture this morning. Generally speaking, one cannot say that at this particular age boys have to go through yet another crisis, apart from the one described this morning. There would be too many different grades of development, if one were to speak of an emerging turbulence affecting all boys of this age. Perhaps some people are under delusions in this respect. For if the inner change of which I spoke this morning, is not guided in the right way by the teachers and educators, then children, and not only the boys, but also the girls, can become very turbulent. They become restless and inwardly unwilling, so that it becomes really difficult to cope with them.

What happens at this age can vary a great deal according to the temperament of the adolescent, a factor which needs to be taken into account. If this were done, one would not make a generalization of the kind which appears here in the first sentence. It would be more correct to state that, unless children are guided in their development, unless the teacher knows how to handle this marked change between the ninth and tenth year, they will become unwilling, unstable and so on. And only then the situation will arise which has been mentioned in the question. It is essential for the teacher and educator to give full consideration to this turning point in the development of the child.

To Question Five:

What has been written here is perfectly correct and I believe that no more need be said about it than: "Yes." Of course one will need a certain tact when talking to pupils between the age of ten and twelve about the human being. If a teacher is heedful of how much he can tell his pupils about the nature of the human being, then I certainly agree that one has to enter into the individual life of the personality concerned.

Question Six:

With regard to this question I should like to say that one must reckon with the possibility of an ever-increasing interest in the development of new methods for penetrating the secrets of human nature, for spiritual research into the human being is a more penetrating one than that of natural science. Of course, the possibilities of this study will not be available in every field, but where they do exist, they should be made use of. It is of benefit not only for teachers and educators to learn how to observe the human being beyond what the outer appearances can tell us, but also, for example, for doctors. I think that one could safely say without causing any misunderstandings, that only prejudice will stand in the way of such methods and that their development is desirable. It really is so that much more could be achieved in this direction, if old or intellect-bound prejudices would not bar the way to higher knowledge. These paths, in their initial stages only, have been described in my book *Knowledge of the Higher Worlds and Its Attainment.*

To Question Seven:

In the Waldorf School mathematics definitely belongs to the main-lesson subjects and as such it plays its proper part according to the pupils' various ages and stages. In no way is this subject relegated to lessons outside the main-lesson. This question rests on a misunderstanding.

From the Discussion of 3rd January 1922

Rudolf Steiner: A wish has been expressed that, because of the impending departure of various conference members, the practical application of Waldorf principles should be discussed first. In this case it is surely appropriate for me to speak about the Waldorf School. Nevertheless, I wish to broaden the subject, because I believe that a great deal of strength and real enthusiasm in face of the present world situation are necessary before our educational aims can be put into practice.

It seems to me that, only if one can recognize the necessity to move towards the educational impulses described here, will it be possible to achieve anything in the nature of a breakthrough in education.

I am convinced that anyone willing to observe, without prejudice, the recent development of mankind, cannot but realize that we are living in the midst of a cultural decline and that all objections against such a judgment are based on illusions.

Of course it is not very pleasant and looks pessimistic, though in reality it is meant to be optimistic, if one speaks in the way I am doing now. But there are so many symptoms of a declining culture in evidence today, that the situation is really quite clear. And only if this is fully recognized, does the whole question of education rise up in heart and soul in the right way. In view of this, I can look upon the founding of the Waldorf School only as a first example of the practical application of the education we have been talking about.

How did the Waldorf School come about? It owes its existence, and that much can surely be said, to the realization of educational principles based on true knowledge of man. But what made it happen? The Waldorf School is the indirect result of a total collapse of society which occurred all

307

over Middle Europe in the year 1919. This general collapse embraced all spheres of society, the economical, the social-political and the spiritual life of all people. Perhaps one could also call it a collapse of the economical and political life and complete bankruptcy of the spiritual life. In 1919 the stark realities of the situation made the entire public only too aware of this fact. Roughly speaking, halfway through the year 1919 there existed a general and complete consciousness of it.

Today there is a lot of talking going on, also in Middle Europe, about how mankind will recover again, of how eventually it will pull itself out of the trough again, and so on. Such talk is the figment of an all too comfortable way of thinking and in reality such thoughts are nothing but empty phrases. The truth is that the decline is bound to accelerate. Today, the situation in Middle Europe is not unlike that of a person who has known better days in which he bought himself plenty of good clothes. He has these clothes now and wears them out to their last shred. The fact that he cannot buy any more new ones is patently clear. Although he knows that he is unable to replenish his stock, he lives under the illusion that all is well and that he is adequately provided for. In a similar way the world at large fails to realize that it is no longer possible to obtain "new clothes" out of its cultural past.

During the first half of 1919, the people in Germany were ready for a serious reassessment of the general situation. This, however, was not yet the time of the founding of the Waldorf School, but it was the time when I gave social-pedagogical lectures* which contained, though only in sketchy

---

*See Rudolf Steiner's lectures given in Stuttgart on 11th and 18th May and 1st June 1919 (G.A. Nr. 192)

outline, what I have been telling you during this conference. Some people saw sense in it and this is what led to the founding of the Waldorf School.

I emphasize this point because the precondition for a renewal of education is an inner readiness and openness to size up the real situation which, in itself, will indicate clearly what needs to be done. At the founding of the Waldorf School I said: It is good to have such a school to serve as a model, but in itself it is not enough, for as the only school of its kind it cannot solve the educational problems of our times. Only if during the next three months at least a dozen Waldorf Schools will have been founded, will the first steps have been taken towards a solution in this field. However, since this did not happen, we can hardly look upon what has been achieved in Stuttgart as representing a success. We have but a model, and even this model is not yet representative of what one would wish to see. I will give you an example: Apart from our eurythmy room which at long last we managed to get, we also badly need a gym hall. We still are without one and therefore anyone who visits the Waldorf School must not look at it in its present state as the realization of our aims. Above all the other problems, the school has always been short of money. Financially it stands on extremely weak and shaky legs!

Now, in my opinion two things need to be done: First, the principles of this education, based as they are on a true picture of the human being, should be made widely known and the underlying ideas need to be thoroughly taken hold of. Everything possible should be done in this direction.

You see, throwing sand into one's eyes leads nowhere in dealing with such serious matters. Therefore I must ask you to allow me to speak freely and frankly. Often I am told when talking about these things, and also when my views on money are being discussed, "Well, in England one would have to proceed in quite a different way, or one would merely put people off."

If we were to leave it at that, there would be little progress. Unless we decide to overcome certain objections, we shan't be able to go forward at all. For instance, people say, "In England practical results have to be seen." This is precisely what the civilized world has been saying during the last five to six hundred years! Only what people could see with their own eyes was considered to be of real value. This is what drags us down. And if we insist on this stance, we shall never be able to pull ourselves out of this chaos.

We are not talking here about small and insignificant matters. What is really necessary is that we take our courage in hand in order to give a new impulse. So often well-meaning people believe that I do not appreciate what they are saying when they point out to me, "In England one would have to do things quite differently." I understand this only too well, but this does not get to the root of the matter at all. If the catastrophical conditions in 1919 had not hit the people of Central Europe so hard, though this ill fortune was really a stroke of good luck as far as the founding of the Waldorf School is concerned, if the terrible situation had not opened their eyes, there would be no Waldorf School in Central Europe, even to this day. For in Central Europe, and especially so in Germany, there is every need for a new impulse because of an innate lack of the ability to organize, because there is so little sense for a structured social organization. If people outside Middle Europe talk so much about German organization, they talk about something which does not reflect the actual facts. There is no outspoken talent for organization in Germany. Above all, there exists no articulated social organism. Instead, the real living culture is carried by single individuals, and not by the general public. Look, for instance, at the German universities. These are not in the least representative of the real character of the German people. They are quite abstract formations, and not at all an expression of what is truly German. The real German spirit lives only in single individualities. This is of course only a hint, but at the same time it also goes to show what is likely to happen if one appeals to a national mood in Germany: One meets a nothingness, one meets only a lack of understanding for the things we have been talking about here. With other words, the Waldorf School owes its existence to an "unlucky stroke of luck."

And now, with regard to the second point, what matters most, apart from the necessity to build further upon what was spoken of here, is that something like a Waldorf School should be founded also in countries where the population was not jolted into action by abysmal and cataclysmic conditions, such as were experienced in Germany in 1919. If, for instance, a kind of Waldorf School could be opened in England, this would mark a mighty step forward. Naturally, such a school would have to be adapted to the conditions and cultural background of that country.

When I realized that the Waldorf School Movement was not going to spread its wings because the original Waldorf School had in fact remained the only one of its kind, I tried to initiate a worldwide movement for Waldorf Schools, a "Waldorf School Movement." I did so because during the preceding years there had been a very great expansion of the Anthroposophical Movement, at least in Middle Europe. Today the Anthroposophical Movement is a factor to be reckoned with in Middle Europe. As a spiritual movement it has made its mark. But there is no organization to direct and guide this movement. The Anthroposophical Society, this needs to be said, for it is right if this is generally known, the Anthroposophical Society is not in the position to carry the Anthroposophical Movement. For the Anthroposophical Society is so riddled with the tendency towards sectarianism,

311

that it is not capable of carrying the Anthroposophical Movement as it is today and as it has developed. All the same, I wanted to make one last appeal to the stronger elements within the Anthroposophical Society because I was hoping that some individuals might respond by making a final effort to bring about a "Waldorf School Movement." Well, it did not happen. The World School Movement is dead and buried, for it is not good enough merely to talk about such a thing; it needs to be carried out in a down-to-earth and practical way. To implement such a plan, a larger body of people is needed.

The Waldorf School in Stuttgart is one of the results of the German revolution. Itself it is not a revolutionary school, but the revolution was its matrix, as it were. If something like a Waldorf School could be founded also in another country, say in England, because the general world situation was clearly recognized, this would mean a big step forward.

Perhaps later, when time has been given to the discussion, a little more could be said about it.

Millicent MacKenzie (Professor at University College, Cardiff; a shortened translation by George Kaufmann-Adams): Professor MacKenzie wishes to say to this point that among the members of this conference there are several personalities from England present who, recognizing the needs of mankind, would be in a position to work in this direction and who could exert considerable influence in an effort to bring about the realization of this educational impulse. As a first step they would like to invite Dr. Steiner to England some time during this year, and they are eager to create the right mood and setting for this visit during which they hope a number of prominent personalities and educators would also be present to welcome Dr. Steiner.

Rudolf Steiner: I wish to add that such a step must be taken only in a practical sense and that it would be harmful if one were to talk too much about it. Those among you, who are in a position to take a step forward in this direction, would have to prepare the ground so that, when the right time has come, one is able to take appropriate action.

I am sure that *Mrs. MacKenzie* and her friends will agree if now other conference members who have come from different countries and who may also have ideas upon this subject, will come forward and voice their suggestions.

Mrs. K. Haag: Today we have heard a great deal about England. We are pleased about this and have found it useful. But there are various other matters which we, who have come from our little Holland, have on our heart. Actually, we have come with a very guilty conscience because the idea of a World School Movement was discussed for the first time in Holland! Somehow we did not do what we might have done about it, partly because of misunderstandings and partly because of lack of strength. But we have not been quite as inactive as people might think and I can assure you that we are more than ready to make good our failure, as far as this is possible. Despite our shortcoming I should like to ask Dr. Steiner to tell us whether the plan he outlined for England could also be implemented in Holland. And since Dr. Steiner has promised to visit us in April, I should like to ask him whether he might be willing to discuss this matter with a larger circle of persons who have a particular interest in education.

Rudolf Steiner: There already exists a plan for Holland which, as far as I know, is being worked out. From the 5th to the 12th of April of this year an Academic Course is to be held there which, similar to other such courses given elsewhere, has the task, first and foremost, of introducing Anthroposophy at depth.

It has been a somewhat depressing experience to witness how, after the need to work for Anthroposophy in Holland had been pointed out again and again, and after February and the beginning of March of last year lectures and performances had been given, there was a notable falling off, not with regard to the understanding of Anthroposophy, but definitely as far as the inner life of the Anthroposophical Society in Holland was concerned. It therefore seems to me very necessary that, especially in Holland, the Anthroposophical Movement should make a new and vigorous start. From which angle this should be done will depend on prevailing circumstances, but the educational movement could well be the prime mover.—Another question has been handed to me which has a direct bearing on this point:

X: According to Dutch law it is possible to found a free school, if the government is satisfied of the serious and genuine intentions behind such an impulse. If we in Holland were unable to raise the necessary capital for founding a Waldorf School, would it be right for us to accept state subsidies, as long as we were allowed to arrange our curriculum and our lessons according to Waldorf principles?

Rudolf Steiner: There is one part of the question I do not understand, and another which fills me with doubts. What I cannot understand is that in Holland it should not be possible to get enough money together for a really free school. Forgive me if I am naive, but I do not understand it. For I believe that, if there is enough enthusiasm, it should at least be possible to start such a school. After all, not so very much money is needed to start a school.

The other point which seems dubious to me is that it

should be possible to run a school with the aid of state subsidies. For I very much doubt whether the government, if it pays out money for such a school, would not insist on the right to inspect it. Therefore I cannot believe that a free school could be founded with state subsidies which in themselves imply supervision by inspectors of the education authorities.

It was yet another stroke of good luck for the Waldorf School in Stuttgart that it was founded just before the new Republican National Assembly had passed a law forbidding the opening of independent schools. For, is it not true to say that with an increasing liberalization we are actually losing our liberty more and more? So that now, when in Germany we are living in a time of progress, most likely it would no longer be possible to found a Waldorf School in Stuttgart. But it was founded just in time. Now the eyes of the world are on the Waldorf School. It will be allowed to exist until those circles which have been instrumental in instituting the so-called elementary schools,* will become so powerful that, out of mistaken fanaticism they will do away with the first four classes of the Waldorf School. I hope that this can be prevented, but also in this respect we are facing menacing times. This is the reason why I keep on emphasizing the importance of putting into deeds, as soon as possible, what needs to be done. For a wave is spreading all over the world which is fast moving towards state dictatorship. It is a fact that Western civilization is exposing itself to the dangers of one day becoming flooded over by a culture of some kind of Asiatic character, which will have a spirituality of its own. People are closing their eyes to it, but nevertheless it will happen.—To return to our point: I think that more or less it amounts to a delaying of the issue, if one believes that one

---

*German: Grundschule

should first claim state help before starting a school. Somehow this does not look promising to me at all. But perhaps other people have different views upon the subject. I ask everyone present to voice their opinion freely.

X: He states that at the present time it is not possible to found a school in Holland without interference by the state, which would demand, for instance, that a certain set curriculum would be achieved, and so on.

Rudolf Steiner: If these things were not as they are, I should never have decided at that time to form a World School Movement, for as an idea it borders on the theoretical. But since the situation is as you described it, I thought that such a movement would have its practical uses. The matter is like this: Let us take as an example the little school which we used to have here in Dornach. For the reason already mentioned several times, we only managed to have a very small school because of our everlasting "superabundance of lack of funds." Children aged below and above ten came together in this school. Now, in the local state of Solothurn, in Switzerland such a state is called a Canton, there exists a very strict law in education which, in actual fact, is not so much different from similar laws all over Switzerland. This law is so fixed that when the local education authorities found out that we were actually teaching children under the age of fourteen, they declared such a school to be totally unacceptable. Such a thing was simply unheard of! Whatever we would have done to come to some agreement, we should never have been given permission to apply Waldorf methods in teaching children under fourteen. Hindrances of this kind will of course be placed in our way all over the continent. How this would work in England, I dare not say at the moment. However, if it should be possible to found a totally

316

free school there, it would really mean a stupendous step forward. But because one meets resistance practically everywhere whenever one tries to put Waldorf Education into practice, I thought that a worldwide movement for the renewal of education might possibly be of some practical value. I hoped that it might make an impact on people interested in education, thus creating possibilities for founding new Waldorf Schools. For I consider it of utmost importance to bring about a countermovement against present-day currents which have reached their culmination in Bolshevism in Russia. These currents find their fulfillment in absolute state dictatorship in education. One can see it looming everywhere but people won't realize that *Lunatscharski** is only the ultimate consequence of what lies thus latent all over Europe. As long as it does not interfere with people's private lives, the existence of such currents of thought is conveniently ignored. Well, in my opinion, one should react by generating a countermovement working against *Lunatscharski's* principle: "The state is to be made into a giant machine and each citizen is to be a cog within this machine." The countermovement should have as its aim to *educate* each person. It is this, which is so necessary.

In this respect one can make most painful experiences even in the Anthroposophical Movement. Today it would be possible to call into life from out of the grounds of the Anthroposophical Movement also a real medical movement. All the antecedents are there. But what would be needed is a movement capable of putting this impulse before the eyes of the world. Yet everywhere one finds a tendency of calling those who are able to represent a truly human medicine "quacks," thus putting them outside the law. As an exam-

---

*Anatol Wassiljewitsch Lunatscharski, 1875–1933, political author; Commissionary for the Enlightenment of the People from 1917–1929

ple, which is entirely unconnected with the anthroposophical medical movement, I should like to tell you of what happened in the case of a minister in the German government who rigorously upheld a strict law against the freedom of the healing profession, a law which is still operative today. However, when members of his own family fell ill, he surreptitiously called for help on unqualified healers, thus showing that where his own family was concerned, he did not believe in the official medical science, but only in what the law condemned as "quackery."

This is symptomatic of the root causes of sectarianism. A movement can free itself from them, if it will stand up to the world, fully within the laws of the land, so that there can be no confusion with regard to the legal aspects. And this is what I had in mind with regard to the World School Movement. I wished to create the right mood for the introduction of laws which would grant freedom to found schools entirely out of the needs for educational renewal. Schools can never be rightly founded out of majority decisions. This is why they cannot be run by the state.

So much about the planned World School Movement, an idea which in itself does not at all appeal to me. I am not in sympathy with it because it would have led to the founding of an international association, a "world-club," and to the creation of a platform for the purpose of making propaganda. My way is to work directly where the needs of the times present themselves. All propaganda-making, all agitating is alien to me. I abhor these things. But if one's hands are tied and if there is no possibility to found free schools, one first has to create the right climate for ideas which may eventually lead to freedom in education. Compromises may well be justified in various instances, but we are living in times in which each compromise is likely to pull us still further into difficulties.

Question: How can we best work in political life?

Rudolf Steiner: I believe that if we were to look at the deep and significant questions which we are to discuss here, from a political angle, we should digress too much from our main theme. Unless present-day politics undergo a regeneration, at least in the various countries known to me on the physical plane, they hold but little promise for me. I am of the opinion that just in this area such definite symptoms of decadence are clearly noticeable, that one would expect society to realize the need for renewal, e.g. the threefold social order. Such a movement would then be running side by side with the Anthroposophical Movement.

Where has the old social order landed us? I will indicate this only very briefly, thereby possibly causing misunderstandings. Where has the old social order, which did not recognize its own threefold nature, landed us? It has led to a situation in which the destinies of whole populations were determined by political parties whose ideological backgrounds consisted of nothing but phrases. None can maintain that the phrases used nowadays by the various political parties contain anything of real substance.

A few days ago* I drew attention to *Bismarck***, who in his later life became a rigid monarchist although in his younger years he had been something of a bashful and masked republican. This is how he spoke of himself. This same *Bismarck* made certain utterances which expressed the same opinions as those made by *Robespierre*. Anyone can make all kinds of statements. What matters in the end is

---

*See lecture of 1st January 1922 "Old and New Methods of Initiation," G.A. 210

**Fürst Otto von Bismarck, 1815–1898 and Maximilian Marie Isidor Robespierre, 1758–1794

what comes to light when the real ideology of a party reveals itself.

For some years I was a teacher at the Berlin Center for the Education of the Working Classes,* which was a purely social-democratic institution. I always availed myself of any opportunity to spread the truth wherever people were willing to listen, no matter what the political color or program was of the organizers of such institutions. And so, among people who by their political outlook were rigid Marxists, I taught a purely anthroposophical approach to life, both in courses on natural science and on history. Even when giving speech exercises to the workers, I was able to express my deepest inner convictions. The numbers of my students grew larger and larger and, lo and behold, the social-democratic party leaders soon began to take notice. It came to a decisive meeting, attended not only by party leaders, but also by all my adult students, who were unanimous in their wish to continue with their courses. But three to four party leaders stolidly declared that this kind of teaching had no place in their establishment because it was undermining the character of the social-democratic party. In my reply I declared that surely the social-democratic party wanted to build for the future and that, since mankind inevitably was moving towards greater freedom, a future school or educational institution would have to respect man's freedom. Then a typical party member rose and said, "Freedom in education we do not know. What we know is a reasonable form of compulsion." This was the decisive turning point which finally led to the closing down of my courses.

Although it may appear rather silly and big-headed for me to say so, I feel convinced that, had the fast-growing movement among the students of the courses I gave there at the end of the nineteenth and the beginning of the twentieth

---

*From 1899–1904; see Rudolf Steiner's autobiography, G.A. Nr. 28

century been allowed to live and expand unchecked, conditions in Middle Europe would have been different during the nineteen-twenties.

And so you can see that I do not have much trust in working with political parties. Especially with socialist parties you will least succeed in bringing freedom into education. They, above all, will strive in most incredible ways for the abolition of freedom in education. As for the Christian parties, they are bound to clamor for independent schools, simply because of the constitution of the present German government. But if they were placed at the helm, they would immediately claim this freedom in education only to suit themselves. It is a simple fact that we shall not be able to make progress in public life unless we first create the necessary foundations for a threefold social order in which the democratic element prevails exclusively in the middle sphere, namely in the sphere of rights. This in itself would safeguard the possibility of freedom in education. We shall never achieve it through electioneering.

Z: If children of the present generation were educated according to the principles of anthroposophical knowledge, would this in itself be sufficient to stem the tide of decadence and decay, or would it not be necessary for them to be sent out into the world with the declared intent to change present society in order to bring about a new social organism?

Rudolf Steiner: The ideas which I tried to express in my book *Toward Social Renewal* (1919) are hardly understood completely. The reasons which led me to write this book are decades old . . . Mankind has reached a stage when someone who might turn up with the best and most promising ideas about improving social life and people's social attitudes, would not be able to bring them to fruition simply because of the lack of practical possibilities available for such purposes. The first step would be to create the right conditions for people to be able to implement their opinions and their insights into social life.

I therefore do not believe it helpful to ask whether, if a generation were to be educated in the way we have been describing, then the desired social conditions would automatically follow, or whether a change of the social order in one or another direction would still be necessary. I should like to say: We must be clear that the best we could achieve in practical life would be for us to help as many members of one generation as possible to make progress through an education based on knowledge of man. This in itself would obviate the second question, for the thoughts and ideas needed to change society would be the very ones such a generation would develop. Since their human conditions would be different from those of the general public today, they would have quite different possibilities for implementing their aims.

The point is that if we wish to be practical, we have to think in practical and not in theoretical terms. And to think practically means to do what lies in the realm of possibilities and not to attempt to realize an ideal. Our most promising aim would be to give to as many members of one generation as possible an education which springs from knowledge of man and then to trust that these former pupils in their adult lives would also be able to bring about a desirable social order. The second question can be answered only through the deeds of those who, through their education, have been prepared for the task which you outlined. It cannot be answered theoretically.

Question: How can one make use of what we have heard in this course of lectures for the education of seriously mentally-retarded children?

Rudolf Steiner: In answer to this question I should like to give you an actual and practical example. When I was twenty-three or twenty-four, I was called to work as a tutor in a family of four boys.* Three of the boys presented no educational problems, but one of them who, at that time, was eleven years old, had the following pre-history: At the age of seven, a private tutor had tried in vain to teach him according to the accepted methods of an elementary school. You must remember that this happened in Austria where it was possible for anyone to teach children quite freely, because the only thing that mattered was that they should pass an examination at the end of each year. Pupils were allowed to sit for these exams at any of the state schools. No one bothered about whether they had been taught by angels or by devils, as long as they passed their exam which was looked upon as proof of their proper education.

Well, among those four boys there was the one who had some four to nearly five years of such private coaching behind him. His latest drawing book was presented to me—he was then eleven years old—which he had brought home from his last annual exam. In all other subjects he had either remained completely silent or talked sheer nonsense, but he had not put anything down on paper. His drawing book was the only document he had handed in during his exam, and all it could boast of was a big hole in the paper of the first page. For all he had done was to scribble something down only to rub it out immediately afterwards until only one big hole was left as evidence of his efforts. It was the only tangible result of his exam. In other respects it proved to be im-

---

*At the recommendation of *Karl Julius Schröer*, Rudolf Steiner was engaged as a teacher of the four sons of *Ladislaus Specht*, a cotton dealer in Vienna, from 10th of July 1884 to 29th September 1890. See Rudolf Steiner's autobiography, chapter VI

possible, sometimes for several weeks on end, to get him to talk or even to say one single word to anyone. For a time he also refused to eat at table. Instead he went into the kitchen where he ate out of the garbage can. He ate refuse but not proper food.

I am describing these symptoms in fair detail so that you can see that here one had to deal with a child who certainly belonged to the category of the "seriously mentally handicapped."

And now I was told: With that child nothing much can be done, for everything has been tried already. Even the family doctor who, by the way, was one of the leading medical practitioners of Vienna and a greatly respected authority, had given up the boy, and the entire family was very unhappy. One just did not know what to do with that boy.

I requested that the education of this child, as also that of the other three brothers, was to be left entirely in my hands and that I should be given complete freedom in how to deal with the boy. All members of the family refused to grant me this freedom, all except the boy's mother. Out of certain unconscious depths, mothers sometimes do have the right feeling for such things. The boy was given into my care. When preparing my lessons, above all else, I followed the principle of approaching such a child, who would be commonly called feeble-minded, entirely from the point of view of his physical development. This meant that everything that was to be done had to be based on the same principles which I have already elaborated to you for the healthy child. What matters in such a case is that one gains the possibility of looking into the inner being of such a child. He was a marked hydrocephalus. This meant that it was very difficult to treat this boy. And so my first principle had to be: Here education meant healing. It had to be placed upon a medical basis.

After two-and-a-half years the boy had made enough

progress to be able to work at the curriculum of a Grammar School,* for I had succeeded in teaching him with the strictest economy. At times I limited his academic work to only a quarter or, at most, to half an hour per day. In order to be able to concentrate the right content into such a short time, I sometimes needed some four hours' preparation for a lesson lasting about half an hour. To me, the most important thing was that he should not be under any strain whatsoever. I did exactly as I thought fit, for I had reserved the right to do so. Much time was spent on music lessons, for these seemed to help the boy. From week to week this musical activity was increased and I could observe how gradually his physical condition was changing. Admittedly, I did not allow any interference from anybody. The rest of the family, with the exception of the boy's mother, registered their objections when they noticed that time and again the boy looked pale. I insisted on my rights and told them that now it was up to me whether I made him look pale, or very pale. I told them that he would look ruddy again when the right time came.

My guiding line was to base the entire education of this child upon insight into his physical condition and to arrange all soul and spiritual measures accordingly. I believe that the details will always vary in each individual case. One has to know the human being thoroughly and intimately, and therefore I must point out time and again that everything depends on a real knowledge of man. When I asked myself the question, "What is the boy's actual age and how do I have to treat him?"—I realized that he had remained a young child of two-and-a-quarter years and that I should have to treat him as such, despite the fact that according to his birth certificate he had completed his eleventh year. I had to teach him according to his actual mental age. Always

---

*In German: Gymnasium

keeping my eyes on the boy's condition of health and applying strictest soul economy, at first I based my teaching
entirely on the principle of imitation, which meant that
everything had to be systematically built upon his powers of
imitation. I then went on to what today I called "further
structuring"* of lessons. Within two-and-a-half years the
boy had made sufficient progress for him to be able to study
the curriculum of a Grammar School (Germ. Gymnasium).
I continued helping him, also during the time when he was a
pupil at the Grammar School. He was finally weaned of any
extra help. In fact he was able to go through the last two
classes of his school entirely independently. Afterwards he
became a medical doctor who held his practice for many
years, to die, approximately at the age of forty, from an in-
fection which he had contracted in Poland during the World
War (I).

This is just one example, I could quote many another
one, to show that especially in the case of feeble-minded
children one needs to apply the same principles which I
have elaborated here for healthy children. In the Waldorf
School there are quite a number of slightly and also "seriously mentally-retarded children"—to quote the phraseol-
ogy of the question. Naturally, the more serious cases would
disturb their classmates and therefore we have opened a special remedial class for feeble-minded children of mixed ages
whose members are drawn from all our present classes. This
group is under the guidance of *Dr. Schubert.*** But whenever one has to decide whether to send a child into this
remedial class, I have the joy, if I may express it so, of having to fight with the class teacher concerned. None of our
class teachers wants to let a member of his class go. Every

---

*Germ. Gestaltung
**Dr. Karl Schubert, 1881–1949, Waldorf teacher in charge of the reme-
   dial class.

one of them will put up a fight to keep such a child, doing his or her utmost to carry it within the class, often successfully. Although our classes are by no means small, by giving individual attention it is possible to keep such children in their classes. The more serious cases, however, have to be put into our remedial group, where it is absolutely essential to give them individual treatment. *Dr. Schubert*, who is freed from having to follow any set curriculum, lets himself be guided entirely by the individual needs of each child. Consequently he may be doing things with his children which are completely different from what is usually done in a classroom. The main thing is to find the specific treatment from which each child will benefit.

For instance, there may be some very dull-witted children in such a group and once one has developed the necessary sense for these things, one may realize that their faculty of making mental pictures is so slow that they lose the images during the process of making them. They lose mental images, they never achieve making them. This is only one type of retardation. One can help such children if, instead of giving them the ordinary kind of school work, one calls out unexpected commands, if they are capable of grasping their meaning. We have also children who are unable to follow such instructions and then one has to think of something different. For instance, one may suddenly call out to them, "Quickly hold your left earlobe between your right thumb and second finger. Quickly grip your right arm with your left hand!" If in this way one lets them orientate themselves first by their own body geography and then by objects belonging to the world outside, one may be able to make real headway with such children. Another way would be to try to get them to recognize quickly what one has drawn on the blackboard. (Here Rudolf Steiner drew an ear on the board). It is not at all so easy to get such a child to respond by saying "ear." But it is this flash of recognition which matters. One has to think up the most varied things in order to wake up such children. It is this awakening, this becoming active which can lead to progress, though, naturally, not in the case of children who fly into uncontrollable tempers. They have to be dealt with differently. But these examples may at least indicate the direction in which one has to move. What matters is the individual treatment and this must spring from a real knowledge of the human being.

From the Discussion of 5th January 1922, held in the evening

Rudolf Steiner: Several questions have been handed in and I will try to answer them as far as this is possible within the short time available.

Regarding the first question:

The answer to the question about the relationship between sensory and motor nerves is, to begin with, a matter of interpretation. As long as one considers it from a physical point of view alone, one can hardly reach a conclusion which differs from the customary one. According to the usual interpretation, one is dealing with the central organ. Let me take a simple case of nerve conduction. In this case the sensation would be transmitted from the periphery to the central organ from which the motor impulse would be passed on to the appropriate organ. Now, as long as one considers the physical aspect only, as I have already said, it is perfectly possible to be satisfied with this explanation. Neither do I believe that any other interpretation would be acceptable, unless one is willing to consider facts which result from supersensible observations, that is, from fully comprehensive and real observations. As already said when I was dealing with this question during the last few days, from an anatomical and physiological point of view the difference between the sensory and motor nerves is not a very significant one. I did not say that there was no difference, but I did say that the difference was not very marked. The actual anatomical difference does not contradict the interpretation given by me. Let me repeat it: We are dealing here with only *one* type of nerves. The so-called sensory and motor nerves are of one and the same kind and therefore it does not really matter whether one chooses the term sensory or motor nerve. Such a distinction is irrelevant because the soul experiences of which these nerves are the physical tools, if one wishes to use such a metaphor, are not strictly differentiated from each other. For in every thought process there also lives a will process and, vice versa, in every predominant will process there is also an element of thought or a residue of sense perception, even though these processes remain mainly in the unconscious.

And now, every will impulse, be it a direct one or the result of a thought, always has its beginning within the upper reaches of man's members, namely in the mutual working together of the ego and the astral body. If we now follow through a will impulse with all its accompanying processes, we are not led to the nerves at all, for every will impulse directly intervenes in the human metabolism. The difference between the interpretation which must be given on the basis of anthroposophical research and that given by ordinary science consists in the latter's claim that a will impulse is first transmitted to the nerves before the relevant organs are induced to perform the various movements.

In reality this is not so, because a soul impulse directly initiates metabolic processes in the organism. Let us take as example a sensation, that is, something revealed by a physical sense, say in the human eye. (In this case the whole process would have to be drawn in greater detail). First a process would be going on in the eye, to be subsequently transmitted to the optic nerve which, according to ordinary science, is classed as a sensory nerve. This optic nerve is the physical mediator of seeing.

If we really want to get at the truth of the matter, I have to make a correction regarding what I said just now. I spoke a little hesitantly about the nerves being the physical tools or instruments of human soul experiences, because such a comparison does not really convey the correct meaning of physical organs and organic systems in the human being. One has to think of it in the following way: Let us assume that here, there is soft ground on a pathway (Rudolf Steiner began to draw), and that a cart was being driven over this soft ground. It would leave tracks behind from which I could tell exactly where the wheels had been. Now imagine that someone would come along to explain the existence of these tracks by saying, "Here, in these places, the earth must have developed various kinds of forces which have pressed in the soft ground." Such an interpretation would be completely illusionary, for it was not at all the earth which had been active. On the contrary, something was done to the earth: The cart wheels had gone over it and the cause of the tracks had nothing to do whatever with an activity of the earth.

Something similar is happening in the nervous system of our brain. What is active there are soul and spiritual processes, with other words: the cart. What is left behind are the tracks, the imprints. These can be found. But whatever is perceived in the brain, whatever is retained anatomically and physiologically, has nothing to do with the brain as such, for it has been pressed in, or molded, sculpted, by the activities of soul and spirit. It is therefore not surprising that one finds in the brain everything that corresponds to the happenings within the soul and spiritual sphere. But in reality this has nothing to do with the brain itself. The metaphor of physical tools or instruments is therefore not a correct one. Rather should one look upon the whole process in a similar way in which I can look upon my walking. My walking is in no way initiated by the ground on which I walk. The earth is not my tool. But if it were not there, I could not walk. That's how it is. My thinking as such, that is, the content of my soul and spiritual life, in itself has nothing to do with my brain. But the brain is the ground by means of which this soul content is retained. It is through this process of retention that man becomes conscious of his soul content.

So you see that the real situation is quite different from what one usually imagines. There has to be such a resistance wherever there is a sensation, whenever a sense perception takes place.

Just in the same way in which a process is going on, say in the eye, which can be perceived with the help of the so-called sensory nerve, so in the will impulses taking place, for example, in the leg, a process is going on and it is this process which is being perceived with the help of the nerve. The so-called sensory nerves are organs of perception which spread outwardly into the senses.

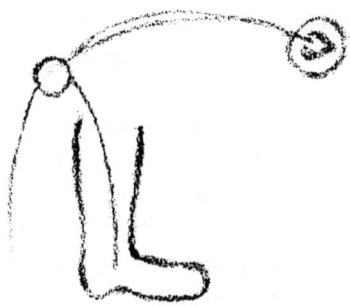

The so-called motor nerves are nerves which spread inward in order to convey the perceptions of what the will

331

forces are doing, thus making us aware of what the will is doing while it is working directly through the metabolism. Both sensory and motor nerves transmit sensations, the former ones spreading in an outward direction while the latter ones are working inwards. There is no significant difference between the two kinds of nerves. The function of the first kind is to communicate an awareness of processes going on in the sense organs in form of thought processes, while the other, the "motor" nerve, communicates processes taking place in the interior physical body, also in form of thought processes.

If one makes the well-known and usual experiments of cutting the spinal marrow in a tabes dorsalis case, or if one interprets this disorder realistically and without the usual prejudice of materialistic physiology, this illness can be explained particularly clearly. For in the case of tabes dorsalis, the appropriate nerve, I now will call it a sensory nerve, which, under normal circumstances, would make a movement sense-perceptible, is defunct and consequently the actual movement cannot be made, for only when such a process is consciously perceived, can movement take place. It is like this: Imagine a piece of chalk with which I want to do something. But unless I can perceive it with my senses, I cannot carry out my intention. In a similar way, in the case of tabes dorsalis the mediating nerve cannot function because it is injured and consequently there is no transmission of sensation. The patient loses the possibility of using it. In the same way I would be unable to use a piece of chalk if it were lying somewhere in a dark room where I cannot find it. Tabes dorsalis is due to the patient's inability to find the appropriate organs with the help of the sensory nerves which enter the spinal marrow.

This is rather a rough-and-ready explanation, but it certainly would be possible to explain it also in greater detail. In each single case, the cutting of the nerves is an absolute proof for this interpretation, if one looks upon them in the right way. This particular interpretation is the outcome of anthroposophical research. By this I mean that it rests on direct observation. What matters is that one is able to use outer phenomena to substantiate one's interpretation. To give another example: A so-called motor nerve may be cut or damaged. If one joins it to a sensory nerve and allows it to heal, it will function again. With other words, it is possible to join together the appropriate ends of a so-called sensory nerve with a so-called motor nerve and, after healing, the result will be a uniform functioning. If the two kinds of nerves were radically different from each other, such a process would be impossible.

There is yet another possibility. Let us take it in its simplest form. (Here Rudolf Steiner made a drawing) We here have a so-called sensory nerve which goes to the spinal cord and a so-called motor nerve which leaves the spinal cord, in fact also a sensory nerve. This would be a case of uniform conduction. In actual fact, all this represents a uniform conduction. And if we take, for example, a simple reflex movement, a uniform process is taking place. Imagine a simple reflex motion: a fly settles on my eyelid. I chase it away through a reflex motion. The whole process is a uniform one. What is happening is merely an interpretation here. (see drawing) One could compare it with an electric switch, with a lead towards it and one lead away from it. The process is really a uniform one, only it is interrupted here (drawing), just as if I had an electric current where, when I interrupt the current, an electric spark flashes across. When the switch is closed, there is no spark. When it is open, there is a spark as a sign of a break in the circuit. Such uniform conductions are also present in the brain. They act as links in a similar way in which, if I interrupt an electric current passing through a wire, there will be an electric spark. If I see a spark, I have a

break in the nerve current (drawing). It is as if the nerve fluid were jumping across like an electric spark, if I may use such a coarse expression. It is this which gives the soul the possibility of experiencing this process consciously. If it were a case of a uniform nerve current passing through without a break in the circuit, it would simply pass through the body without the soul being able to experience anything.— This is what I can say about it for the moment.

These theories are generally accepted in all countries of the world and if I am asked where one can find more detailed knowledge, I even quote *Huxley's* book on physiology* as a basic standard work upon the subject.

There is one more point I wish to make. This whole question is really a subtle one and the usual interpretations certainly appear convincing. To prove their correctness, the so-called sensory parts of a nerve are cut and then the motor parts of a nerve are cut, with the aim of showing that what is interpreted as sensation or as movement, no longer can take place. But if you take what I have said in its entirety, especially with regard to the interruptor switch, you will be able to understand all the various experiments made with cutting nerves.

Question: How can the educator best meet requests for various activities coming from children aged between five-and-a-half and seven?

Rudolf Steiner: At this age, a feeling for authority already begins to make itself felt, as I tried to indicate in the lectures here. Yet, chiefly predominant is a longing for imitation and this gives us a clue for what to do with such children. The movable picture books which I have mentioned are particu-

---

*See Thomas H. Huxley "Fundamentals of Physiology"

larly suitable for them, for they stimulate the children's awakening powers of fantasy.

If they ask to do something—and as soon as we have the opportunity of opening a kindergarten in Stuttgart, we shall try to put this into practice—if the children want to be engaged in some activity, we shall paint or model with them in the simplest way, first by doing it in front of them while they are watching. If children have already shed their teeth, one does not paint for them first, but encourages them to paint their own pictures. Only when the teacher wants to lead over to writing via drawing or painting, will he or she again appeal to the children's powers of imitation. But generally speaking, in a kindergarten for children aged between five-and-a-half and seven, one would first do the various activities in front of them and then let the children repeat them in their own way, thus gradually leading over from the principle of imitation to that of authority.

Naturally, this can be done in different ways. It is quite possible to get children to work on their own. For instance, one could first do something with them, such as modeling or drawing, which then they are asked to repeat on their own. One has to invent various possibilities of letting them supplement and complete what the teacher has already started. One can show them that such a piece of work is complete only when the child has made five or ten more such parts which together must form an entity. In this way one can combine the principle of imitation with that of authority. It will become a really stimulating task for us to develop such ideas in practice when we have a kindergarten in the Waldorf School. Of course it would be perfectly right for you to develop these ideas yourself. It would take up too much of our time if I were to go into greater details now.

Question: Will it be possible to have this course of lectures published in English?

Rudolf Steiner: Such things are always a question of time, but I myself would like to have the shorthand version of this course written out in full as soon as possible and when this is done, one can take the necessary steps to have it published also in English.

Question: Should children be taught to play musical instruments and if so, which ones?

Rudolf Steiner: In the Waldorf School I have definitely advocated the principle that, apart from introducing children to music in a more general way, at least those children who show some special gifts, should also learn to play a musical instrument according to technical possibilities. The choice of the instrument should not be made beforehand, but only in consultation with the music teacher. A really good music teacher will soon find out whether a child, on entering school, shows any specific gifts which, in themselves, may indicate a leaning towards one or another instrument. This is a case where one should definitely try to treat each child individually. Naturally, in the Waldorf School all these things are still in the beginning stage, but in spite of this, we have managed to get together quite acceptable small orchestras and quartets.

Question: Do you think that composing in the Greek modes which were discovered by *Miss Schlesinger,** would mean a real step forward with regard to the future of music? Would it be advisable to have instruments, such as the piano, tuned in such modes? Would it be a good thing for us to get accustomed to these modes?

---

*See Kathleen Schlesinger's "The Greek Aulos," 1939

Rudolf Steiner: For several reasons I am of the opinion that music will make progress in its development if, what I should like to call "the intensive melody"* will gradually play a more and more important role. This intensive melody would consist in one's becoming used to experiencing the sound of *one single note* already as a kind of melody. One will become accustomed to a greater complexity of the tones, of each single sound. This will eventually happen. When this stage is reached it also will lead to a certain modification of our scales, simply because the intervals will be "filled out" in a different way from what one is used to. They will be filled out more concretely and this in itself will lead to a greater appreciation of certain elements found in what I should like to call "archetypal music" (*Urmusik*), elements inherent also in *Miss Schlesinger's* discoveries, in which significant and important features can be recognized. I do believe that these will open a way towards enriching the experience of music and towards overcoming certain limitations imposed by our more or less fortuitous scales with all they have brought with them. So I agree that a fostering of this particular discovery does offer prospects for progress in musical development.

Question: Will it also be possible to give eurythmy to physically handicapped children or, possibly, curative eurythmy to fit each individual child?

Rudolf Steiner: Yes, certainly. One only has to find the way to use eurythmy in such different situations. First one has to look at the already existing general forms of eurythmy and

---

*See: Answers to questions, given on 29th September 1920, in "The Nature of Music and Man's Experience of Tone," G.A. 283; also "Eurythmy as Visible Song," G.A. 278, the lecture given on 21st February 1924

then one must consider whether a deformed child would be able to make the movements involved, or whether one may have to modify them. This can be done in any case. The way forward would be to use the existing artistic eurythmy for such children, and this will be of special benefit for the very young and also for young children. Quite surprising progress in the healing processes of such children may result from working with ordinary eurythmy.

Curative eurythmy* was systematically worked out, first by myself during a supplementary course given here in Dornach in 1921, immediately after the last course given to medical doctors. Its immediate task is to serve the various healing processes. This curative eurythmy is definitely suitable also for children suffering from malformations. For lighter cases, the already existing forms of curative eurythmy will suffice. In more severe cases, these forms may have to be intensified or modified. However, any such modifications will have to be made with great caution.

Artistic eurythmy will not harm anybody; it can be only beneficial. Harmful consequences will accrue only through excessive or exaggerated eurythmy practice, as would happen in any other field of movement. Naturally, just as one can make onself ill by excessive efforts in mountaineering or if, for example, one uses one's arms too much, so can an excess of eurythmy practice lead to all kinds of exhaustion, to general asthenia. However, here the cause does not lie in eurythmy, but in its wrong application. Any wholesome activities can lead to illnesses if they are grossly exaggerated.

---

*During the second course given to doctors and medical students from 11th–18th April 1921, Dr. Steiner developed a *therapeutic eurythmy*, now practiced by specially trained curative eurythmists in cooperation with qualified doctors. See "Curative Eurythmy," a course of eight lectures given in Dornach from 12th–18th April, 1921, and also in Stuttgart on 28th October 1922, G.A. 315

In the case of ordinary eurythmy it is unthinkable that it could have a harmful effect upon anyone. However, when one is dealing with curative eurythmy, one must be heedful of the general rule I gave during the curative eurythmy course. It is that curative eurythmy exercises should be planned only under the guidance and supervision of a doctor and jointly by the doctor and curative eurythmist, and this only after a proper medical diagnosis has been made.

If curative exercises have to be intensified, it is absolutely essential that one proceeds on a strictly medical and surgical basis and that only a specialist of pathological conditions, of pathological peculiarities, is capable of deciding what measures need to be taken. Just as it would be irresponsible to allow unqualified persons to deal with the dispensing of dangerous drugs and poisons, so it would be equally irresponsible to allow just anyone to meddle with curative eurythmy. If injury does result from such bungling, one really cannot lay the blame upon curative eurythmy.

Question: In yesterday's lecture we heard about abnormal consequences resulting from a shift of what was right for one period of life into later periods, and of the subsequent emergence of a super-phlegmatic and a super-sanguine temperament. The first question is: How does a pronouncedly choleric temperament come into existence? And secondly: How can one perceive whether a young child has an inclination towards an unbalanced melancholic or any one of the other three temperaments? Thirdly: Is it possible to counteract such imbalances already before the change of teeth?

Rudolf Steiner: The choleric temperament comes into being mainly through a person's ego working particularly strongly during one of the nodal points of life which occur around the second year and again during the ninth and tenth year. There are also other nodal points later in life, but the first two are of main interest to us here. It is not the case that the ego begins to exist only in the twenty-first year, but that it becomes free at a certain age. It is always there in every human being, from the moment of birth or, rather, from the third week after conception. This ego can reach too great an intensity and then it works particularly strongly during these special times. What is the meaning and the nature of such a nodal point?

Between the ninth and tenth year the ego works with great intensity, manifesting itself in that the child learns to differentiate him or herself from the surroundings. In order to retain normal conditions, a stability of equilibrium is needed especially at this stage. For it can happen that this state of equilibrium undergoes a shift in an outward direction and this can become one of the many causes of the sanguine temperament. When I spoke about the temperaments yesterday, I made a special point in saying that different contributory factors were working together and that I was going to single out those which were of importance from a certain point of view.

Now, it is also possible that the center of gravity shifts inward. This can happen already while the child is learning to speak or even when it learns to hold itself in an upright position, when it begins to pull itself up. At such moments, there is always an opportunity for the ego to work too strongly. One has to pay attention to this and must try not to do anything wrong at this point of life. This one would do if, for example, one forced a child to stand upright unsupported too early. It should do so only when it has developed the necessary faculty to imitate the vertical position of the adult.

One can appreciate the importance of this, if one pays heed to what man's upright position really means. In general, the animal is constituted in such a way that its spinal column is more or less parallel to the surface of the earth. There are, of course, exceptions, but these can also be explained just on the basis of their difference. Man, on the other hand, is constituted in such a way that, in his normal position, his spine extends in the same direction as the earth's radius. This is the radical difference between man and animal. And in this radical difference there lies one's reply to purely Darwinistic materialists—I am not saying Darwinians, but to Darwinistic materialists—when they deny that there exists a characteristic difference between a human skeleton and that of a higher animal because both have the same number of bones, and so on. Admittedly, this is correct, but the animal's skeleton has a horizontal spine and man's spine is vertical. In this vertical position of the human spine is manifested a relationship to the entire cosmos and the meaning of this relationship is that man becomes the bearer of an ego. When we talk about the animal, we only speak of three members, namely of the physical body, of the ether body or body of formative forces, and the astral body. An ego can incarnate only if a being is organized in line with the vertical.

I once spoke about this during one of my lectures and afterwards someone came to me and said, "But what about the human being when he sleeps? Surely, then his spine lies horizontally?"

So often people fail to grasp the point of what I say. Here the point is not merely that the human spine is constituted for the vertical position only when a person is standing, but that one has to look at the entire build of man, at the mutual relationships and positions of the bones which result in his walking with a vertical spinal column whereas in the case of the animal, the spine remains in the horizontal. The point is that the vertical position of the human spine is the characteristic distinguishing mark for the fact that man is the bearer of an ego.

And now observe how the physiognomical character of a person is expressed particularly strongly through the vertical. You may have noticed, if only the appropriate means of observation were used, that there are people who show certain anomalies in their physical growth; that, for instance, according to their organic nature, they were meant to reach a certain height, but that through the agency of another organic system, working in the opposite direction, the human form became compressed. It is absolutely possible that because of certain antecedents the physical structure of a person which was meant to be larger, was pressed together by an organic system working in the opposite direction. This was the case with *Fichte*, for example. I could quote many others, such as *Napoleon*, to mention only one of them. In accordance with certain parts of his organic systems, *Fichte's* stature could have been taller than it actually was. Yet he remained stunted in his physical growth. This meant that his ego had to put up with having to exist in such a compressed body, and the choleric temperament is a direct expression of the ego. The choleric temperament can definitely be caused by such an abnormality of growth. Regarding the question: How can one perceive whether a young child has an inclination towards the melancholic or any of the other temperaments?—Well, I believe that anyone who has frequently been in the company of children will hardly need special indications, for these symptoms almost force themselves upon one. Even with quite naive and untrained observation one will be able to discriminate between a choleric and a melancholic child, just as one can clearly distinguish between a child who "just sits," or another who appears morose and miserable and again between one who romps about wildly. In the classroom it is very easy to spot a child who, after having paid momentary attention to what was on the blackboard, suddenly turns to his neighbor to find something of interest there before looking out of the window again. This is what a sanguine is like. These are the things which can easily be observed on even quite a naive level.

If, next, the question is asked whether one can work towards balancing these traits already before the change of teeth, the answer must be: Yes, and fundamentally so by the same methods to be applied at a later age, methods which have already been described. Only, at such an early age, these methods need to be couched in terms of imitation.

Let us imagine a child who easily flies into tempers. If, at the right age, the adult simulates similar tantrums, he may succeed in making such a child tired of its behavior. It is quite possible to achieve something that way.

However, before the change of teeth, it is not at all necessary to try to counteract these temperamental inclinations because in most cases it is good if these things are allowed to die a natural death. Of course, this can be rather uncomfortable for the grownup. But here we have something about which one ought to think differently from the way this is usually done. I should like to clarify this point by a comparison. You probably know that there exists a type of lay-healer who does not possess a thorough knowledge of the human organism, but who nevertheless is able to judge abnormalities, symptoms of illnesses, up to a certain degree. It may happen that such a healer recognizes an anomaly in the movements of his patient's heart. When asked what should be done about it, it really can happen that the answer is, "Leave the heart alone, for if one were to bring it back to its normal activity, the patient would not be able to stand it. This heart irregularity is just what he needs." In a similar way it is often necessary to know how long a certain condition has to be left alone and in the case of a choleric child, how much time it must be given to get over its tantrums simply by exhausting itself. This is what needs to be borne in mind.

343

Question: How can a student of Anthroposophy avoid losing the capacity to love and the faculty of remembering, when crossing the boundary of sense-perceptible knowledge?

Rudolf Steiner: This question appears to rest on the assumption that during the ordinary state of consciousness love and the faculty of remembering are both necessary for life. In ordinary life one could not exist without the faculty of remembering. Without this spring of memory leading each individual back to a certain point in early childhood, the continuity of the ego could not exist. Enough cases are known where this continuity has been destroyed, where definite gaps appear in the faculty of remembering. This is a pathological condition. In like manner, ordinary life cannot unfold without love.

But now it needs to be said that, when a state of higher consciousness is reached, this higher consciousness has a different content from that of the ordinary kind. The question seems to imply that because of crossing the limits of ordinary knowledge, there is no unfolding of love and memory beyond the boundaries of knowledge. This is quite correct. But, at the same time, it has always been emphasized that the right kind of schooling consists in one's retaining qualities which one has developed for the ordinary consciousness, keeping them alive side-by-side with the newly-won qualities. It is even requested, as you can find out in my book *Knowledge of the Higher Worlds and Its Attainment*, that these qualities, developed in ordinary life, should become enhanced and strengthened when one is entering a state of higher consciousness. This means that nothing is taken away as regards inner faculties developed during ordinary consciousness and that what is required for higher consciousness is in addition to what was attained previously. To clarify this point, I should like to make use of a somewhat trivial comparison, even if it does not fully accord with the situation.

As you know, if I wish to move myself by walking on the earth, I must not lose my sense of balance. Other things are needed as well in order to walk properly, that is, without swaying or falling. Well, if anyone learns to walk on a tight-rope, he will lose nothing of the faculties which serve him in walking on the ordinary ground of the earth. If one learns how to walk on a tightrope, one meets completely different conditions, and yet a question such as: Can tightrope walking prevent one from being able to walk properly on an ordinary surface?—would be quite irrelevant. In a similar way the attainment of a different consciousness will not prevent one from retaining the faculties belonging to ordinary consciousness, whereby I do not imply in any way that I wish to compare the attainment of higher consciousness with a kind of spiritual tightrope walking! Yet it is so that the faculties and qualities gained in the ordinary consciousness are to be fully preserved when one rises to a state of enhanced consciousness.

And now, because of the lateness of the hour, I should like to settle the remaining questions as quickly as possible in order to end our meeting by telling you a little story.

Question: What should our attitude be towards the ever-increasing use of documentary films in schools and how can we best explain to those defending their use that their harmful effects are not balanced by their potential educational value?

Rudolf Steiner: I have tried to get behind the secrets of the film, and whether my findings will make people angry or not is not the point, for I am giving you the facts. I was forced to acknowledge that the film productions exert an ex-

345

tremely harmful effect upon what in my lectures here I have called the etheric or life body, and this especially with regard to the human sense organization. It is a fact that through watching film productions, the entire human soul-spiritual constitution becomes mechanized. Films are outer means of turning people into materialists. I have tested these effects, especially during the war years, when film propaganda was made for all kinds of things. One could witness how the audiences avidly took in what was shown. I was not particularly interested in watching the films, but I did want to observe their effects on the audiences. And there one could see how the film is simply an intrinsic part of the plan for the materialization of mankind, already on account of its weaving materialism into the perceptual habits of those who are watching. Naturally, this could be taken very much further but, because of the lateness of the hour, there is only time for these brief indications.

Question: How should one treat a child who, according to the parents, sang well in tune at the age of three and who now, at the age of seven, sings badly out of tune?

Rudolf Steiner: First one would have to examine whether, through some occurrence or other, the musical ear of the child has not become masked for the time being. But if that child really sang well at the age of three, if this is a correct statement, one should be able, with the appropriate pedagogical treatment, to help the child to sing in tune again. This could be done by studying the child's habits at the time when it had sung well. Find out how it occupied itself, what kinds of things it had done, and so on. Then, obviously with the necessary modifications regarding age, place it again into the entire setting of those early years and approach the child with singing again. Try quite methodically to call forth again the entire situation of the child's early

346

life. Possibly some other faculty may also have submerged, a faculty that might be recovered more easily.

Question: What is Anthroposophy's attitude towards the *Montessori* system of education and what would the consequences of this system be?

Rudolf Steiner: I am not really in sympathy with having to answer questions about contemporary methods which generally are backed with a certain amount of fanaticism. Not that I dislike answering questions, but I have to admit that I do not like answering questions such as: What is Anthroposophy's attitude towards this or that contemporary movement? There is no need for me to do so, for I consider it my task to represent before the world only what can be gained from anthroposophical research. I do not think that it is my task to throw light upon other matters from an anthroposophical point of view.

Therefore, all I wish to say is that when aims and aspirations tend towards a certain artificiality, such as bringing to the very young child what does not form part of its natural surroundings but what has been artificially invented and turned into a system, they cannot really be of benefit for the child's healthy development. A great number of new methods are being invented these days, but they all have in common that they do not rest upon a real and thorough knowledge of man.

Of course one can find a great deal of what is right in such a system, but in each instance it is necessary to reduce also the positive aspects to what accords with a real knowledge of man.

And now, ladies and gentlemen, with regard to the time left over after the translation of this last part has been made, I should like to drop a hint: I do not wish to be so discourteous as to say in so many words that every hour has to come to an end. But since I can see that many of our honored guests sitting here are feeling as I do, I wish to be polite enough to meet their wishes by telling a little story, a very short story: There once lived a Hungarian couple who always had guests in the evening—in Hungary people were very hospitable before the times came when everything went topsy-turvy—and when the clock struck ten, the husband used to say to his wife, "Wife, we must be polite to our guests. We must retire now because our guests surely will want to go home!"

Publishers' Notes

Before the beginning of this conference Rudolf Steiner addressed the participants who were gathered together in "the White Hall" of the first Goetheanum with the following words:

Ladies and Gentlemen,

Before beginning this lecture course, allow me to bring before you an administrative matter:

Originally, this course was intended for an intimate circle only, but it has evoked such a response that it is obvious that we cannot share it in this tightly-packed hall. It would be quite impossible. You would soon realize it, if you would have to be present not only during the lectures, but also during their translations. It is for this reason that I had to decide to give the lectures twice-running, the first time every day at ten a.m. and then again, especially for those members who wish to hear it in the English translation, at eleven o'clock. For technical reasons this is the only way. Therefore I shall begin each first lecture punctually at ten and the repeat lecture at eleven o'clock. I should like to ask those of you present who have come from England, Holland and Scandinavia, to attend the repeat lectures and the others to go to the first one."

Only the repeat lectures were taken down in shorthand. Each lecture was given in two or three parts, after each of which there followed the English translation given by *George Kaufman* (G. Adams)*

---

*It has not been possible to trace any of these translations.

The text of this edition—apart from a few slight alterations—follows the version given by *Marie Steiner* for the first publication.

The subtitles of the various lectures have been taken from the official program.

FOR FURTHER READING

WALDORF EDUCATION

The WALDORF or STEINER SCHOOL movement is one of the largest private school systems in the world. There are numerous Steiner schools in the United States with programs from kindergarten through high school. The Anthroposophic Press offers the following titles on this important approach to education:

INTRODUCTION TO WALDORF EDUCATION by Rudolf Steiner. A short essay going to the heart of the Waldorf approach. Steiner explains the important changes occurring in the child at the 9th and 12th years and the way the curriculum meets these changes. It is probably the best short introduction to the developmental philosophy of Waldorf Education available. (This essay is contained in the forthcoming book *Renewal of the Social Organism.*)

(10 pp.)   0-88010-137-7   Booklet, $2.50 #1006

THE EDUCATION OF THE CHILD by Rudolf Steiner. This is perhaps the best short introduction to Waldorf education available. It is suitable both for the prospective parent and teacher. The text is an essay revised by Steiner from a lecture of the same title in 1909.

(50 pp.)   Paper, $5.95 #44

THE RECOVERY OF MAN IN CHILDHOOD by A.C. Harwood. Piaget and other modern child development researchers attempt to study the emergence of adult capacities in the child. But, as A.C. Harwood points out in this absorbing study of Rudolf Steiner's educational work, childhood is a time of *losing,* as well as gaining, capacities. Is there a connection between the loss of a childish faculty and the acquisition of an adult one? Yes, answers Harwood—in fact, a threefold connection.

There follows an insightful survey of the three seven-year stages of child development as depicted by Steiner. This is presented in connection with numerous examples and anecdotes on Waldorf education's use of curriculum subjects to support and assist this developmental child-man exchange. Other chapters take up specific facets of Waldorf education, such as foreign languages, eurythmy and music, and the temperaments. These lucid and literate explanations qualify this book as the most intelligent and stimulating introductory work on that unique approach to educating known often as "education as an art."

(211 pp)   Paper, $7.95 #411